App Kid

App Kid

How a Child of Immigrants Grabbed
a Piece of the American Dream

Michael Sayman

ALFRED A. KNOPF
New York
2021

THIS IS A BORZOI BOOK
PUBLISHED BY ALFRED A. KNOPF

www.aaknopf.com

Knopf, Borzoi Books, and the colophon are registered
trademarks of Penguin Random House LLC.

Library of Congress Cataloging-in-Publication Data
Names: Sayman, Michael, [date] author.
Title: App kid : how a child of immigrants grabbed a
piece of the American dream / Michael Sayman.
Description: New York : Alfred A. Knopf, 2021.
Identifiers: LCCN 2020044835 (print) |
LCCN 2020044836 (ebook) |
ISBN 9780525656197 (hardcover) |
ISBN 9780525656203 (ebook)
Subjects: LCSH: Sayman, Michael, 1996– |
Computer programmers—United States—
Biography. | Hispanic Americans—Biography. |
Smartphones—Programming—Anecdotes.
Classification: LCC QA76.2.S385 A3 2021 (print) |
LCC QA76.2.S385 (ebook) | DDC 005.13092 [B]—dc23
LC record available at https://lccn.loc.gov/2020044835
LC ebook record available at https://lccn.loc.gov/2020044836

Jacket design by Tyler Comrie

Manufactured in the United States of America
First Edition

Contents

App Kid

Introduction

I WAS SIXTEEN, IN Bolivia to give a talk to fifteen hundred cheering students. Event organizers were attempting to clear a path to the stage. Hands pulled at my clothes and people stood up and began applauding my entrance as I muscled my way to the stage, wishing I were back in my hotel room, coding. In my peripheral vision, I could see reporters from local and international stations, filming. I tried to block out the thoughts that were crowding my head, one most of all: that I was not made for this. These people were looking for someone who could give them insight and guidance, and I wasn't sure if I was that person.

When I was thirteen, I'd launched my first app for the iPhone and quickly started earning $10,000 a month from downloads—enough to support my family when our middle-class house of cards (plastic ones provided by Mastercard and Visa) was flattened by the Great Recession. And for that, the Latin American press had dubbed me the Boy Genius of Apple. I was regularly featured in the news and had a huge social media following there. But I was afraid the news was celebrating me prematurely. My once moderately successful app was already declining in sales, and my next step wasn't clear to me. But that wasn't what all these kids had come to hear. They'd come to find out how I'd made something out of nothing, with only a computer. I owed it to them to try to explain: I wasn't a genius;

it wasn't magic. As long as they could get their hands on a computer with Internet access, they could make something from nothing, too.

On the stage, I launched into a rambling talk about growing up in Miami as the son of Bolivian and Peruvian immigrants. About how I got into coding. I told them how I'd taught myself using YouTube videos and how, since the recession, my apps had been helping my family pay the bills. I assured them that I wasn't on that stage because I'd changed the world with my products. I was standing up there because, despite all my insecurities and shortcomings, I'd never let my failures stop me from building things that changed *my* world. Whenever my lack of knowledge or ability brought me to a standstill, I explained, I wouldn't let myself stay stuck for long. I'd take a breath, then Google my way out of whatever hole I'd dug myself into. "If you want to be a coder," I told the room, "the Internet will be your best friend, your guide, and your inspiration."

As soon as I finished my spiel, the students started peppering me with questions about how to code. "Google Xcode or Eclipse and watch instructional YouTube videos about Java or Objective-C," I repeated, over and over. And this is just as true today. Coding changes so fast, there are no static resources that can keep up. If you want to learn to code, let the Internet be your guide.

Eventually, someone from the school called an end to the Q&A, and I was led out of the auditorium. Every few feet, I had to stop to take a selfie. Someone was yelling, "Make a line!" but no one was listening. People pushed and pulled and grabbed at me, and I glanced at my mom, who had accompanied me, helplessly. Back in our hired car, we crawled through traffic as some students followed in cars, rolling down their windows and snapping photos. At the hotel, my mom and I collapsed onto our beds.

The next day, I returned to the reality of my life in the United States. No one gave me a second glance at Miami International Airport. I was unsure whether all of it had been a dream. When I thought about my lineage, where my parents came from, and their parents before them, the last few days in Bolivia seemed even more improbable, if not impossible.

It wasn't until a number of years after I was born that my parents received their American citizenship. Although this book, including the stories of my family life, is written in English, my parents have only ever spoken to me in Spanish. When my parents immigrated to America, they learned just enough English to hold a basic conversation; to this day, they sometimes struggle to communicate effectively. I still don't know half the sayings that are common to people who grew up speaking English, because I never heard them at home. There are certain words, like "sequester," that I only knew how to say in Spanish until recently. And when I stub my toe, the curses come out in Spanish.

My mother, Maria Cristina Gálvez, was meant to be born in Arequipa, a region of Peru that is mostly dry and mountainous, but my grandmother wanted to have the support of her mother and family when she gave birth, so she flew to Lima, the capital, to be with family. My mother's father was a general in the Peruvian army, and during that time, a war was raging. As a little girl, my mom and her four brothers would often hear bombs from their bedroom windows, and sometimes my mom had to hide under tables and study by candlelight because the electrical towers had been hit. In spite of the war, my mother remembers her childhood as loving, sheltered, and secure.

My father grew up in a different world. He was born in La Paz, the capital of Bolivia, to a Jewish family. His parents moved the family to Lima when he was three years old; later they separated. His older brother died when he was twenty-one, a tragedy that rocked the family and set the tone for his future life. Having fled Europe during World War II, my dad's grandparents, both Jewish, had big dreams for their grandson, sending him to Israel to study systems and applied mathematics. But my father rebelled against the discipline demanded by the program. His grandparents threatened to stop supporting him financially if he dropped out, but he did anyway, moving to Los Angeles to pursue a career in video editing. He lived in an apartment with several roommates and studied at a trade school. A few years later, he moved to Miami and landed a job at Telemundo's headquarters doing production work. My father's father had rarely been a presence in his life, and his mother, still living in Peru, suffered from depression, so my father—cut off financially by his grandparents—was on his own, living paycheck to paycheck on a temporary work visa.

Miami was a hub for Latinos visiting the United States, and my mother traveled there when she was twenty with a group of girlfriends. At a party, my father spotted her from across the room. And that was the beginning of our family.

My mom returned to Peru and dated my father long-distance for the next three years. She dreamed of being a professional psychologist, but her mother suggested that she get a career or degree in something less demanding. My mom was in love with my dad, so she listened to my grandmother's advice and got herself a secretarial certificate. But my grandmother did not simply allow my twenty-three-year-old mother to move in with my father. She let my mother know that in order to do so and leave her parents' home in Peru, she had to get married. So my mom and dad got married. They certainly would have preferred to live together a few years first, but they didn't have a choice. My parents had a wedding ceremony and settled in Miami. Three years later, on August 24, 1996, I was born. My sister, Mariana, arrived a year after that.

Spanish wasn't the predominant language just in my household. It was what most everyone spoke in Miami, where 70 percent of the population is Latin American. There is no native-born dominant majority in Miami. Restaurant menus and some road signs are written in Spanish; if someone approaches to ask for directions, they'll immediately start speaking in Spanish; and in many parts of Miami, a visit to the doctor will automatically begin with questions in Spanish. In Miami, 70 percent Latin American means class and ethnic divides exist among the Latino population. Anyone can tell where you're from—Peru, Colombia, Bolivia, Chile, Mexico, Cuba—by the kind of Spanish accent you have. The majority of Latinos in Miami are Cuban-American. They began migrating to Miami and building businesses in the sixties, after Fidel Castro came to power in their country. Cubans in Miami tend to have more connections than most non-Cuban families, who tend to be more recent immigrants. If you're not Cuban in Miami, you're going to have a tougher time fitting in.

At the small Catholic school I attended from third to fifth grade, all the Cuban parents already knew each other. My parents felt like outsiders around that group. Based on her appearance, my mom could have passed for Cuban, but the moment the other moms heard her speak, they knew the truth. So my parents naturally gravitated toward couples from Colombia, Venezuela, and other South American countries. My sister and I both started speaking fluent English in kindergarten, but we still faced some of the same social barriers as our parents because of our South American background.

My entire life, I've felt pulled between identities. Am I Jewish or Catholic? My father is a Jew, my mother Catholic, but she converted to Judaism to marry my dad. My mom told me that for years, they debated over which religion we should observe, finally settling on both: my dad got to decide on a Jewish preschool for us, and my mom got to pick our Catholic elementary school.

Am I Peruvian or Bolivian? When I started to become well known, both countries tried to claim me as their own, though I never felt like I fully identified with just one or the other.

Am I a real American? My parents aren't from here, my teachers were Latin American, and my city predominantly spoke
Spanish; we were nothing like the typical Americans I grew
up watching on TV. Am I a kid or a grown-up? My childhood
mostly disappeared when I started supporting my parents as
a thirteen-year-old. But now that I'm in my twenties, I can't
exactly say I'm all that good at what they call "adulting," either.

I blame those famous Silicon Valley perks. In 2014, at the
age of seventeen, I traded my mother's cooking and laundry
services for those offered at Facebook, three thousand miles
away from home. I'd landed an internship, which turned into
a six-figure full-time job. After that, instead of going off to
college with my peers, I took a full-time job as the company's
youngest-ever engineer.

Today, at twenty-three, I don't have to worry about over-
draft fees or credit card debt or whether I'll be able to support
my parents if things fall apart for them again. I'm living every
tech geek's fantasy: at Facebook and Google, I've led projects
for apps used by billions of people, and I'm financially successful beyond my wildest dreams. But that doesn't stop me from
questioning myself, every day.

Will I one day feel like I made it here on my own merit, or
am I just an imposter, getting by in Silicon Valley because I'm
good at working the system? At times, the question of who
I am and where I fit in is still so overwhelming, I just wish I
could disappear. But I've come too far to allow that to happen.

I didn't get here on hard work and determination alone, of
course. For the first decade of my life, my family lived well—if
well beyond our means. I had the security and time and space
to play and fantasize about the future. I had family members
with the means to help me buy my first iPhone, which became
my door to that future. A lot of kids around the world never
have that kind of room to dream, let alone access to the technology that will help them build on those dreams. In Bolivia
today, only four out of every one hundred people have a home

Internet subscription, and only about 40 percent of the population accesses the Internet at all. Grown-ups love to ask kids, "What do you want to be when you grow up?" But if those kids aren't getting their immediate needs met—if they're hungry or stressed about where they'll sleep at night—that's a preposterous question. Who has time to think about what they want to be when they grow up when they're just trying to survive?

So that's why I didn't tell those Bolivian kids to "dream big" or "reach for the stars." I told them that if they wanted to code, there was a free education waiting for them on the Internet. Coding is an in-demand skill right now, with some of the most competitive salaries you'll find. But these aren't good enough reasons to become a programmer. You have to love this work to be good at it. They say it takes ten thousand hours of practice to master a calling. Since middle school, I've probably spent forty hours a week building websites and making apps—roughly thirty thousand hours—and I still don't consider myself an expert, let alone a master. I'll always be learning, and that's what I love about my job. I code because I lose track of time when I'm doing it—I'm never bored. If I were, a lifetime of hours could never make me great.

How do you start? No joke, just as I told those kids, you start by Googling what you want to know; everything you need to know about building an app or coding is available 100 percent for free on the Internet. While that may sound overly simplistic, I've found that it truly is the best way to learn. Any coding book you buy will be outdated by the time you finish it. And while coding boot camps and classes are absolutely great ways to jump-start your skills, they, too, can only teach you the most current coding languages in this ever-changing universe. I'm not exaggerating when I say that as fast as a programmer can learn to code, the coding language is being reinvented. As any engineer will tell you, it's gotten to the point where we have to leave a Google tab open at all times in order to keep up.

Which is why I think it's best to learn how to use Google to teach yourself from the very beginning.

Coding isn't a quick way to get rich, but it can be a way to get your start outside of the college-to-workplace pipeline—an alternative path to success beyond your wildest dreams.

Chapter 1

The American Dream

It had always been my parents' dream to own their own restaurant, so when I was three, they went for it. El Pollon Grill was one of the first Peruvian rotisserie chicken places in Miami, *pollo a la brasa,* as we called it. It didn't look like anything special from the outside—just a small building with a neon sign in the middle of a strip mall—but people couldn't get enough of my mom's chicken.

Other than arguing with my mom about the fact that the only thing I wanted to eat was chicken and French fries—she always offered me chicken and rice, chicken empanadas, *ají de gallina, pollo a la plancha, arroz con pollo*—I didn't have much to complain about. We lived in a typical suburban Miami neighborhood with nice homes and green lawns—though I doubt any of them were paid off. Now that they had the restaurant up and running, my parents were trying to get into the real estate business. On the advice of our neighbors, who'd found modest success as landlords, my father had gotten his real estate license, and my parents had taken out loans and bought several properties to rent out.

My parents had credit cards, and they used them often: not just for everyday things like groceries and school clothes and gas but for big, fun things, like parties, a new living room set, and trips to Disney World.

When it came to our birthday parties, my mom always splurged way beyond our means. I'm talking more than just piñatas and cake. I'm talking magicians and bouncy houses. As the daytime party wound down and all the kids went home, the adult party would start, with enough rotisserie chicken and spiked punch for the whole neighborhood. All of this went on the credit cards, of course.

Then everything changed. In mid-2006, my parents started to seem stressed. They muttered over their morning coffees about how everything was "falling apart" and how they were having trouble paying the bills.

We stopped taking trips and eating out. Even the trips to Disney World came to an end. Sometimes my parents would work at the restaurant until two or three in the morning.

One night, a couple of weeks before my tenth birthday, I heard them talking in concerned, hushed tones. Mariana and I went downstairs and my parents invited us into the room. "You're getting big now," my mother began. "Big kids don't have birthday parties; they go to the movies with their friends and hang out. This year, Michael, you're becoming a big kid. Instead of a birthday party, you're going to go to the movies with your friends."

Something about her concerned face, the way my father stared at his shoes while she spoke, gave me a feeling of suspicion. "Okay, sure, let's do that," I said. It was fine with me, actually. I'd never had the sense that those parties were for Mariana and me, anyway. They seemed like they were more for my parents.

However bad the situation may have been, my sister and I didn't think much about it. I was a happy kid, known for my big grin. "Your mouth looks like a mail slot," my mom would tease with affection. "Both rows of teeth showing."

—

We had the run of the house every day after school, and we made use of it. From three-thirty p.m. till we got tired and turned on the TV (Mariana) and the computer (me), our parent-free home was the stage for our elaborate and ambitious games. I would usually take the lead.

For example, one day, when I was eight years old, I asked Mariana, "Do you want to go to Jurassic Park?"

"Yes!" she quickly responded.

We could have just pretended we were in a jungle, but that wasn't enough for me.

The problem? My house didn't look like Jurassic Park. We didn't live on a jungle island and there weren't any dinosaurs to be found. I had to get creative. I looked over at my dad's printer, filled with a small stack of blank sheets of paper, and decided they would be the key building blocks for my vision. Taping the sheets together to form several giant canvases, I used my crayons to create a massive brachiosaurus, some flying pterodactyls, fields of grass, and a scary cave.

I ran and gathered all my parents' houseplants and circled them around my dad's big recliner. I taped the cutouts to the walls of the room. "It's ready!" I told Mariana, five hours later. Climbing into my dad's big recliner, she closed her eyes and commanded, "Roller coaster!" I rocked and spun the chair for a while, Mariana shrieking and giggling. When we were all played out, Mariana went to watch TV and I gravitated to the old Dell computer we kept downstairs.

The Dell—and the portal to the Internet that it opened—kept me distracted from the ever-increasing stress of my parents as they strived to stay afloat in a financial system that even I could see was still totally foreign to them, even after all these years. I knew that they had bought the Dell for us—I assumed on credit, like everything else—because they wanted to give us everything we ever wanted. This was how my parents thought, anyway. I knew it was painful for them when we complained about eating beans and rice for dinner or when they couldn't afford to buy us new school uniforms and last year's were bursting at the seams. The Dell made up for all that, though, by feeding my curiosity and imagination. Whatever I was curious about was right there at my fingertips, waiting to be discovered. Google had existed since I was born, and there was never a time when I had to ask my parents, "Why this?" or "Why that?" I would just Google it.

Like most siblings, sometimes Mariana and I were close, sometimes we weren't. Either way, she was my link to the real world. While I was content to spend my afternoons lost in a paper-dinosaur land or exploring Antarctica through the Dell, Mariana was extroverted and social and always a step ahead of me in life—she'd long ago surpassed me in both height and common sense, even though I was a year older. *She* was the one who had to tell *me* there was no Santa Claus. No one could see through grown-ups and their tricks like Mariana.

When we were really little, our mom used to get us to do whatever she wanted by crossing her arms and counting to three in her mean voice: "*Uno . . . dos . . .*" There would usually be a long pause after *dos,* just long enough for Mariana and me to jump up and finally do what we were being told to. For years, I made sure we never let our mom (it was almost always her disciplining us) get to the terrifying numeral that came after that pause. It was simply understood: if Mami got to *tres,* it was over.

Until, that is, the night when five-year-old Mariana called our mom's bluff. It was bedtime, and we were playing on the stairs when we were supposed to be brushing our teeth. At the bottom landing stood Mami, arms crossed and wearing yellow dishwashing gloves. "*Dos!*" she yelled.

"Mariana!" I cried. "We have to go!"

Mariana scoffed, "Michael, it's fine, she's not going to do anything." Mariana grabbed my wrist, pulling me back.

I tried to shake her off. "Let's go!"

"But, Michael! What's the worst she can do?"

I had no idea, and I wanted to keep it that way.

"Think about it," hissed Mariana. "She's our mom! She's not going to hurt us."

That had proven *so far* to be true—but there was always a first time.

"Look, watch, I'll show you!" Mariana said. She spun to stare Mami down.

"*Tres!*" yelled our mom.

"*Cuatro, cinco, seis!*" Mariana shot back. "*Siete, ocho, nueve, diez!*"

Everyone froze. Time froze.

Finally, our mom burst out laughing. "Oh well," she said, drying her eyes. "It was good while it lasted."

Other than the old counting trick, our parents used different parenting approaches for each of us. So different, we might as well have been raised in two different families. *My* parents valued scholarship above all else. *Mariana's* mom and dad believed emotional intelligence was the ultimate trait. I was celebrated for being great at math, while Mariana was praised for her kindness. I gravitated toward technology—a stereotypically male pursuit—and my sister took little interest in it. She definitely didn't share my passion for anything and everything Apple.

My lust for the Apple brand hit its apex when I was ten years old, on January 9, 2007, the day Steve Jobs announced the first iPhone.

"Look! It's happening!" I pulled my mom by the hand from the couch to the old Dell to watch the momentous event on YouTube. "The iPhone is launching!"

My mom snickered and shook her head. My dad jumped in: "Apple products are so impractical—incompatible with everything! You really want *that*?"

I nodded my head vigorously. *Yes, yes, yes!* I could hardly contain myself.

My dad looked at me, confused. "You're ten years old—do you even receive any emails?"

My mom's Motorola Razr and my dad's Nokia smartphone held no interest for me. I was already an Apple guy, through and through.

"You're turning eleven this summer," said my mom. "Maybe your *tíos* will pitch in for your birthday."

Thankfully, I had lots of *tíos,* and I immediately called all of them—Kike, Mario, Carlos, and Miguel—letting them know about my birthday wish in advance.

My uncles came through. Four days after the iPhone went on sale, I floated out of the Apple store with an opaque white plastic bag slung over my arm. Inside was the most expensive item I'd ever owned.

My parents added the phone to their family plan, so I had service, but back then, the iPhone was pretty basic—just a touch screen with which you could access an Internet browser, a camera, your email, your music, your calendar, and a few pre-loaded apps. You could message one person at a time, but I didn't have any friends with phones to text, and no one really used email. Still, the gadget was magnetic, addictive.

I'd never been one to sleep with a teddy bear—okay, I had a stuffed penguin—but I couldn't go to bed without my new iPhone.

Chapter 2

The Penguin Whisperer

IN THE FALL OF 2007, I began middle school with financial aid at Belen Jesuit, a private boys' prep school for grades six through twelve that my mom had dreamed of getting me into for years. Realizing that this was an opportunity to step out of my shell, I decided—to mixed results—to try to be more social.

Instead of being the kid whose homework everyone else copied, as I had been in elementary school, I became the kid who copied homework, showed up late for first period, and joined in the laughter when another kid pranked a teacher. This didn't make me popular, but I certainly felt it was better than my much quieter former self. And thanks to a fantastically addictive computer game I'd discovered called Club Penguin, this was enough. Club Penguin gave me a much more expansive social life. The world of the game was limitless, and nothing outside of it seemed to provide the same excitement. I had as many friends as I could want online, so it didn't matter that I had very few in real life. Yikes.

Acquired by Disney that same year for $700 million, Club Penguin was in many ways the first major social networking game of my generation. Users created their own penguin avatars, then waddled all over a virtual world, competing to have the most coins, the best igloo, the coolest avatar. Players could type messages to one another, which would pop up over the penguins' heads in chat bubbles. Club Penguin wasn't available for the iPhone, so I couldn't play it at school. But as soon as classes ended, I'd race to the school computer room to play alongside my classmates until my parents came to pick me up.

My Club Penguin friends lived in other cities and countries. They knew me only as my avatar, not as Michael, but that was good enough. It didn't matter that I wasn't athletic, or interested in girls, or good at being social; there would always be others out there who had similar personalities I could relate to. And more important, it didn't matter that I was fat. Over my sixth-grade year, the baby fat I'd been carrying since I was little had started turning into an actual weight problem. But who cared? On the Internet, I didn't have to worry about that. I could just be myself—the truest version of me. And so I dove in—way in.

One of my favorite hangouts was a WordPress blog called *The Army of Club Penguin*. *The ACP* was—prepare yourself for this weirdness—a military-themed recruiting page for virtual penguin accounts. A bunch of little penguin avatars, all dressed alike, would sign on to Club Penguin at the same time and walk around in formation chanting, "Army of Club Penguin!" over and over. Just as in the real army, the avatars were given ranks: soldier, sergeant, lieutenant, and captain. Wars were fought between different penguin armies. *Thousands* of kids participated, communing in unregulated chat spaces, where bad words were allowed.

But, at the time, there weren't really such things as apps.

In the summer before my thirteenth birthday in 2009, my mom sent me to Peru to live with my *tío* Kike for three months. At the time, I had been running my own WordPress blog that shared updates, guides, and walk-throughs about Club Penguin. I was really into this game. The only problem was that no one would visit it, so I would sit on my computer and refresh the page for hours to try and build up the view count. It wasn't really working. Nor were the YouTube commercials I created, "commercials" for my website to YouTube and linked back to my Club Penguin blog. It still wasn't working, so I knew I needed to come up with another way to make my Club Penguin blog a success.

A year earlier, Apple had announced something new for the iPhone—the App Store. Now people could build apps on their iPhones and distribute them through the store. In launching the App Store, Steve Jobs had said *anyone* could make an app and sell it. I hadn't given much thought to the announcement. But now, lying around my uncle's house with plenty of time to think, I realized that I could make a mobile app to promote my Club Penguin blog! The game itself was still not available on mobile, so I figured this was my opportunity to grab all the Club Penguin searches at the App Store. It would be a way for me to make my mark on the Club Penguin world, sharing the kinds of tips that were popular on Club Penguin fan sites, including the one I'd launched myself. I had no idea how to go about making an app, but if Steve Jobs said it was easy, then I was going to figure out how to do it. I started Googling.

By the end of January, I had a working app, and it felt valuable. Before I could submit it to the App Store, I had to purchase a developer license, which cost $100. So, I approached my parents, even though by that point things had gotten so bad they were in no position to help me. My mom knew I had been working hard on my creation, but neither of my parents could really grasp what I was doing. To them, it looked like I was playing all day long. It actually felt like that to me, too. But my mom could see how important the project was to me, and when I explained to her that I was going to charge $1.99 per download, she relented. "If you pay me back, that's fine," she said. "But if you can't, you're going to have to work in the restaurant washing dishes, because I can't spend that kind of money right now." She added, "*No se lo digas a tu papá*" ("Don't tell your dad").

I nodded. "I won't tell him, Mami."

The Club Penguin App was easy to access and it delivered what it promised: a thorough guide to the game, along with news updates on the latest changes to Club Penguin, and a built-in chat room for users to talk with one another whenever they wanted. I proudly sent in my $100 and submitted to the App Store. Then I waited. Within a few days, I got an email from Apple saying that I'd been rejected. The email said that the two images I'd uploaded for the icons—one with a little penguin on it, the other with the Club Penguin logo—didn't match; the small and large icons had to display the same image. I revised the icons so that both showed a penguin and sent it back in. And on March 2, 2010, my first app went live in the App Store. My parents were happy for me, even if they had no idea what it meant.

I'd been teaching myself about iTunes Connect, the online portal to view sales and track metrics for apps. I was checking it every hour the day my app went live to see if I'd gotten any downloads. I didn't see any, but I didn't know that the sales figures for downloads are calculated on the following day, not live. I had the sinking feeling that my app was a flop.

But I wasn't going down without a fight. I made my friends in the Club Penguin blogging community an offer: "I will place an ad for your website on my app, if you place an ad for my app on your website," I wrote. Then I sent them banners for kids to click on to download the app. That really started to create some buzz.

It was all so new to me. When I looked at iTunes Connect on day two and saw two columns and two rows of information, I figured two people had bought my app: my mom and my dad. It turned out that those two rows represented two *countries,* the United States and Canada, and at the end of each column, the number of downloads from each of those countries was listed. That first day, there were fifty-two downloads at $1.99 each, which netted me more than $100. On its second day live, my app was number 7 in the reference category. I ran to my parents' bedroom and shook my dad awake, shouting, "*Papi, mira, mira! Mi aplicación! Está en el puesto número siete!* My app is number seven in the Top Reference apps chart! Wake up!"

My mom peered at me groggily and said, "Wow, that's great, Michael, but your dad was up super late at the restaurant, let him sleep."

Every day, I checked the sales, and watched my app go from fifty to seventy to eighty downloads a day. By its first weekend, the app was getting one hundred daily downloads, making $200 a day. When I told my science teacher, he whistled and said, "That's more than I make."

The fact that I was making more money than plenty of grown-ups in my life was mind-boggling, but could it last? In the back of my mind, a voice had been whispering, *The Club Penguin App may be topping the charts now, but eventually it will fall—then what?* As well as things were going, my mind had already turned to how I could expand my business further. I needed to grow it as much as I could before the wind died down. So, I got to work building a few designer variations as fast as I could—a pro version for $4.99 that offered bonus cheats, a version in Spanish, and a lite version that cost only a dollar. Something for everyone.

I'd just submitted the new apps to the App Store when I got my first direct deposit from Apple, for $5,000. When my parents saw it, they seemed shocked that the money I was making was actually real.

"Michael, this is insane!" my mother said, sounding alarmed. "What have you done?"

"It's the app, remember? The one I built with the money you gave me."

My parents were too stunned to say anything else, but they exchanged a look that said, *We'll talk about this later.*

One night soon after, they were out to dinner with friends. "Apparently, Michael made this app thing, which is at the top of the charts right now, and Apple sent him five thousand dollars," they shared. As incredible luck would have it, another diner at the restaurant interrupted to say that they knew someone who worked at a TV network and could be interested in hearing more.

A few days later, my mom and I went to the CNN headquarters for the Latin American division in Miami. Someone sat me on a chair and said, "Okay, you're going to look into that camera and pretend it's a person."

I said, "What? That's so weird. I can't do that." I could barely keep eye contact with people in real life. I searched for my mom, who was standing behind the cameras, but couldn't read her facial expression because of the blinding lights in my face. When the camera began rolling, I just answered the interviewer's questions.

"What did you build?" he asked.

"Um, I made this app . . . ," I started awkwardly, giving him a tangled description. I had an accidental Justin Bieber haircut, which was embarrassing as hell, and I sat hunched over, hiding my pudgy thirteen-year-old body. I didn't feel like I'd done anything so special. When the host asked his final question, "Is there anything else you would like to say?," I thought about it for a few beats. "If there are other kids out there who want to learn how to make apps," I said, "send me a message on Facebook or Twitter and I can send you links."

Immediately after I left CNN's offices, my phone started to blow up. I got four thousand requests on Twitter and Facebook, and my parents started getting phone calls from all over the world. People wanted to interview me in Australia, Peru, and Colombia. Within a week, there were cameras all over our house, and my mom was on the phone fielding interview requests. After that, the interviews became a regular part of our lives. Every month or so, a news crew would turn our living room into a TV set or I'd go to a network studio for another interview. It was always the same set of questions in the same order: "How old are you? What made you decide to make apps? How did you learn to do it? How much money are you making? Is it true that you're supporting your family with your earnings?"

In the beginning, I'd straight-up tell reporters I made $10,000 a month, sometimes more. After a while, I got tired of the question and learned to dodge it with: "More than I ever could have imagined!"

When it came to the question about supporting my parents, I'd nod, grinning. While my mom hated for her family back home to keep hearing that I was supporting us, I knew I couldn't sidestep the issue. My role as family breadwinner was one of the things that made Latin American audiences hopeful about my story. Many Latin American parents hope to raise kids that one day could be able to help provide for the whole family. The family unit is very important in Latin American culture, a belief my parents made sure to instill in me. It was one of the main reasons reporters wanted to talk to me. But that didn't make it any less weird or uncomfortable. To be providing for my parents at such a young age was head-spinning and profoundly reshaped my relationship with my mom and dad. It was impossible to have a normal childhood while also keeping them afloat. But most of all, I was excited that I had a platform to let other kids know the exciting secret I'd discovered: a place existed where kids could make real money, building stuff they loved right out of thin air. I wanted everyone my age to know that if they'd ever wanted to try coding but thought it would be too hard or they weren't smart enough, they should think again.

"Get ready, Mariana," my mom would say. "They might want to put you on TV, too!" But my sister couldn't relate to my excitement at putting on a show for the TV cameras. Whenever a news crew arrived at the house, she'd lock herself in her room with her friends. The more the crews appeared, the further away Mariana seemed to drift from me. Not that

I had time to worry about it. My main concern was, *What do I need to do next to keep this all going?* Because *this* seemed to be where the possibility lay, not at school. At school, all that mattered was how many facts I could memorize (not many, as my test scores showed). No one there cared about what I actually *created*. But outside the walls of Belen, I felt I was able to express my true self through coding. The energy I would put into my apps would bounce right back to me in the most exciting and fulfilling way.

I decided to make another app. And this time, it would be a *real* game—based on Club Penguin, of course.

A real game would take more advanced coding than I'd learned so far. I bought a desktop Mac and dove into YouTube tutorials on how to create a jumping game, the kind where you tilt your phone left and right to make the characters jump. There was a popular one called Doodle Jump. I thought it would be a fun challenge to see if I could build a game with similar mechanics, with illustrations of Club Penguin characters bouncing up and down on little platforms, climbing higher and higher through the world of Club Penguin. Hundreds of hours of trial and error later, I finished it.

The application process was much faster this time: I submitted the app, it was approved by Apple, and it quickly climbed the charts. On the first day, it sold five hundred copies, priced at $2.99 a download. And the sales didn't let up.

But other parts of my life weren't going so well. I spent my lunch hour copying my classmates' work, so I never got a chance to eat lunch and was always starving after school. Every day I'd ask my mom to bring home McDonald's, even though I never actually said the words "Can you get me McDonald's?" because I was too ashamed. I knew the food was bad for me. And in the back of my mind, I knew we couldn't afford it and that I should just eat food from the restaurant. So I went through a ritual with my mom where I would say, "I'm super hungry," and she would respond, "Well, what do you want?"

Continuing the charade, I would answer, "I don't know. What can you bring me?" And then, after she reeled off the menu, I would say, "No, I don't really want that." Eventually, my tired and overworked mom would throw up her hands. "How about McDonald's, then?" she'd say. "Sure, okay, McDonald's," I'd mumble. Soon I was a full-blown addict, eating a chicken wrap and large fries twice a day.

Temporarily, at least, those fast-food chemicals helped me forget about my down-sliding grades, my up-sliding weight.

In May of 2010, the bank was threatening to foreclose on our house, and my parents had already lost all of their rental properties except for one, a little town house right in a neighborhood near our home. On top of that, their credit cards were almost maxed out and they couldn't keep up with the payments. The phone company was threatening to turn off our service. The restaurant was failing. Worst of all, my mother's eyes had stopped dancing when she spoke, and my father hadn't cracked one of his stupid jokes in months; each night when he came home from work, he went straight to his recliner to stare glumly at the TV. It didn't seem fair. At the same time that I was having my windfall, my parents found themselves in deep trouble.

A few months later, an administrator from my school called me into his office and informed me I was behind on my school payments. When I got home I questioned my mom, who informed me that she'd made an emergency withdrawal from funds I'd made from the App Store. I'd never seen a penny, because everything went directly into an account my parents managed. "It was necessary to pay the restaurant employees' salaries," she said. "Last month was worse than ever, but things will look up soon." The worry in her voice said otherwise.

Before long, my desperate mother was using my money to pay the employees' salaries twice a month, just so the doors could stay open. The waitstaff must have known this. After years of mostly ignoring me when I'd come to the restaurant, they now made a big point of asking how my apps were doing—trying to figure out how much longer my mom would be able to pay them, I figured.

My mom also asked if she could use my money to pay thousands of dollars to lawyers to try to save our house. She also used the money to pay for food, electricity, Internet access, gas, clothing, and—eventually—the portion of my Belen tuition that wasn't covered by financial aid.

"Just until we get back on our feet," my mom kept saying. "We'll pay you back when we can."

I wanted to be a good son. And besides, I didn't need all that money. At thirteen years old, all I wanted was a new iPhone or an Xbox, but that was about it. I certainly didn't need to spend $10,000 a month, and unfortunately, I'd never been taught the importance of saving for the future. "You don't have to borrow it," I'd say each time my mom asked. "Just take it."

Big mistake. My parents, clearly uncomfortable asking me for the money, eventually took me at my word and just withdrew what they needed, when they needed it.

Though at first I didn't mind sharing my money, what bugged me was that my parents wanted it both ways: I may have been the family breadwinner, but I was still being treated like a kid, expected to follow their rules. Now when my mom would try to parent me in the ways any typical parent would, I found it intolerable.

"Hey, Michael," my mom said timidly one night, cracking my bedroom door. "It's after midnight, and you've been on your computer all day. You haven't brushed your teeth yet, you haven't showered. Did you do your homework?"

Fuming, I hunched lower over my keyboard, not taking my eyes off the screen, where I was working on a new update for the Club Penguin Game. "Mami, you don't understand. I'm doing what I need to do, okay? It's all good."

It wasn't all good. After two months and $24,000 in profits, my apps had seen a rapid decline in sales. It was partly due to a shift in the marketplace: the App Store was no longer a free-for-all, where a handful of rogue players like me could clean up by selling games for $2.99 to $4.99. Now it was flooded with free games that made money through in-app purchases, charging players for accessories or to buy new skins for their avatars and virtual currency tokens. I was beginning to learn that most apps have a short shelf life; people use them less and less over time.

"Well, all right then," said my mother. I could feel her trying to let it go. She never could. "It's just that . . . if your grades get worse, you won't get into any colleges. What if your apps don't work forever? Then what are we going to do?"

I swiveled to glare at her. I no longer had it in me to try to appease my mother, and I was defiant about the fact that my grades had slipped from A's and B's to C's and D's. "Who gives a shit about homework?" I said through gritted teeth. "You said the car payment's overdue, right? Just let me do my work!"

Working on my apps had originally been relaxing. However stressful life got, when I was building something, I forgot my problems and felt calm and focused. Everything else just faded away. But now that my apps were the only thing saving our house from foreclosure, it was a different story.

Adding to the pressure was my growing fame in Latin America. This was mostly thanks to the dozens of big names who had interviewed me, including Jorge Ramos, and Don Francisco, who had a big show filmed in Miami called *Don Francisco Presenta*. Don Francisco was basically the Oprah of Latin America, and he'd interviewed *me*. There was no way I was worth his time. I still couldn't believe it, let alone all the interest that followed. There were profiles in major Latin American newspapers, an hour-long story about me on a Sunday night news show in Peru, and a string of video interviews with morning and late-night talk show hosts.

As the one who fielded all the media calls, my mom was always in a state of anxiety. Maybe she believed the publicity was good for app sales and wanted to book me on as many shows as possible—but she lived in dread of answering the phone. "I never know if it's someone who wants to interview you or a debt collector!" she'd cry, throwing up her hands.

It got to be a common thing for reporters from Spanish-language TV shows to follow me around school to see what my life was like. Kids who saw the footage in Latin America exploded my Facebook page with messages telling me how inspired they were by what I'd accomplished. But at school, my strange fame isolated me. No one even called me by my name anymore. "There goes the App Kid!" they'd call as I slumped across campus with another crew in tow. Some kids would try to grab their fifteen seconds of fame by jumping on camera with me; other people steered clear, probably not wanting to get in the way.

In one way, I wasn't so different from my classmates. We were *all* App Kids. You know how in the movies, kids are always walking through school hallways chatting with each other? And at lunchtime they're in the cafeteria, gossiping and shouting greetings? That doesn't happen when a school has iPads. During lunchtime, Belen kids lined the hallways, sitting on the floor, looking down at their screens. Groups of friends sat next to each other, all playing games on their own.

At Belen, students barely used bookbags or lockers, mostly just iPads. Students were meant to use them to take tests, do homework, and take notes. But because the teachers had no clue how these newfangled things worked, the students ran circles around them. Our history teacher would say, "Okay, guys, let's start class," and we would turn on our iPads. But we weren't looking at the daily lesson. To my left, a kid would be playing a mini-golf game. To my right, a kid would be texting in a group chat about a party that weekend. And in front of me, someone would be posting a photo of the whiteboard to the private Facebook group that we communicated on.

One day I got an idea for how I might be able to do something I actually cared about at school: replace that Facebook page with an app featuring student news, photos of the school, and a secure portal where students could look up their grades. Using a computer program called Xcode, I drew up a sample landing page to show the school principal, Father Phil. He was a Jesuit priest who could usually be found standing outside his office door or at the back of the assembly hall with his hands clasped behind him. He was kind, but my school was strict: if you didn't stand to pray in morning session, you were in trouble; if your tie was too loose or your top button was undone, you were in trouble. Would I be in trouble for mocking up a school app without getting permission first? It was worth the risk.

The morning I finished the prototype, I pasted a wide smile on my face and approached the principal, holding my phone out to show him my big idea. "Hi, Father! I'd love to make an app like this for the school, if you're interested!"

Father Phil squinted at my screen, grinning. "What's this, then?"

"It's an app, just for Belen students! It would be a great way for us to stay up-to-date on assignments and maybe even talk to the teachers!"

Nodding slowly, Father Phil patted my shoulder in an *Isn't that cute* kind of way and said, "Well, well . . . why not?"

"Really?"

"*Mmmm.*" He was looking past me now, at a couple of troublemakers down the hall, his grin settling right back into place. "Let me think about the proper channels . . ." He started down the hall, hands still clasped tightly behind him.

Proper channels? Belen didn't even really have a computer science department. Our school administrators seemed to think of programming as an after-school pastime, not the key to our futures. Their attitude was: school is for learning the *real* things—history, science, and math (the on-paper kind)—that will get you into college.

"Who should I talk to, Father?" I called after the principal, following close on his heels.

"The IT people!" he answered as he hurried toward his targets. "They'll help."

Dejected, I slumped against a wall. Belen's "IT people" were a handful of people who managed the school's iPads and stopped in whenever the Wi-Fi broke down. In other words, I felt it was pointless. The principal would never see the value in my Belen app, so it would never happen.

"Oh well," I said under my breath. It was fine. I had about a dozen app ideas in my head, just waiting to become real. Next!

Chapter 3

Growing Pains

EVENTUALLY, I DID MAKE a handful of IRL friends at Belen. The closest was a Cuban boy named Lucas who shared my obsession with tech and Apple and seemed to like me in spite of my one-track mind. Whenever Apple announced a live event, Lucas would come over to my house to watch on my iPhone. Whenever a new phone came out, we would camp out in front of the store so I could buy it. Having the latest iPhone was key to testing my apps. Though I had no access to the money I'd made—and had no idea how much of it my parents had spent—my mom always found a way to scrape together the funds.

Lucas was extremely organized and had excellent grades. He did his homework as soon as he got home, and when he grew tired, he went to bed. I, on the other hand, was a complete disaster at school—stressed and sleep-deprived from working on my apps until three a.m. every night.

We came from similar working-class families and were both strivers in our own ways, but sometimes Lucas and I clashed over our different approaches to getting ahead. The first time I asked if I could copy his homework, Lucas answered with a firm no.

"Why not?" I pleaded.

He responded, rightly, "Because I put work into this and

you didn't. So why would I let you copy it?" After that, I never asked to copy his homework again.

Sometimes I sensed a more subtle divide between us: for Lucas's entire life, he'd been told that if he got good grades and did well in school, he would succeed, yet next to him was his best friend, who was getting dropped from all his honors classes and had even been suspended for copying homework once—still making money hand over fist.

Because Lucas was my best friend, and I was the App Kid, people at school assumed he was riding my coattails. This couldn't have been further from the truth, but all the same, they started calling him my shadow or Michael 2. I didn't pay as much attention to the teasing as I should have. I should have stood up for Lucas, but I just blocked it all out, too focused on my next creation. Whenever we hung out together, I'd go on and on about how stressful it was trying to keep my apps at the top of the charts. Or how my parents had used the last thousand dollars of my money to pay the bills. The fact that Lucas had problems of his own didn't even cross my mind. Miraculously, he kept on putting up with me.

One time I asked Lucas to do an interview for a TV segment on me. He was shy, but it seemed he really wanted to do it, and I was excited to see him excited. The night the show aired, he and his family all huddled around the TV, excited to see his face onscreen. But it didn't take them long to realize that the producers had axed his portion of the interview from the show. The next day he came up to me at school and said, "Hey, did you see the segment?"

I said, "No, I hate watching myself on TV." I never watched myself; I couldn't stand the way I looked.

"Well, they cut me out," Lucas said.

"Huh," I responded. "No way. That's so weird."

I asked my mom later that day about it, to see if she could help me figure out why. "Maybe they cut him out because his Spanish wasn't very good?" she suggested. In retrospect, I wish

I'd told Lucas how sorry I was that he'd been cut from the show. I wish I'd told him how much I appreciated his time and friendship. Sometimes I wonder if we'd still be friends today if I had.

Being the App Kid gave me cover to avoid a lot of things that normal teenagers were supposed to want to do, like party and date. Being the youngest kid in my grade, I was certainly behind when it came to dating. Plus, I had other, better things to do, I told myself. I had my apps. I'd never given much thought to girls, despite my mom's attempts at matchmaking. For years, she'd been trying to convince me that I'd had a lifelong crush on a pretty girl from my kindergarten class, Sofia. Every time we'd watch old videos of my grade-school birthday parties, my mom would say, "Oh, there's Sofia, the girl you always loved! How is she doing now? Do you still think about her?" The truth was, I had never thought about Sofia, but it was always easier to be with my mom than against her, so I'd just shrug and mutter, "Sure, sometimes," and change the subject.

My mom couldn't wait for my sister and me to grow up and give her grandchildren. Whenever the family went out to our favorite Cuban restaurant, La Carreta, for dinner, she'd bring up how much she was looking forward to eating there one day with us and all her future grandkids. She missed her family in Peru and wanted to re-create the big, raucous meals of her childhood here. I really wanted that too.

On one of those La Carreta nights, from out of nowhere, my mom said, "I can't imagine what it would be like to have a child who was gay and didn't bring me grandkids!" She quickly added, "I don't have a problem with gay people. To each their own. But, Micky, can you imagine if one day, Michael brought someone home to meet us, and instead of, 'Mami, Papi, this is Janie,' it was, 'Mami, Papi, this is *James*?'" My dad pretended to have a mini heart attack, and we all laughed. This was how my

dad always dealt with uncomfortable conversations, by ham-
ming it up.

"Don't worry, Mami and Papi," I said. "I want you to have
grandchildren."

I knew the statistic that approximately 5 percent of people
identify as LGBT. For the most part, society was beginning to
be more accepting. But so far at my school, no one had come
out. The possibility that I could be in the 5 percent had certainly never crossed my mind before my mom brought it up
that night. I was fourteen years old. I'd never had a crush on
anyone, let alone a boy. Although I did sometimes find myself
looking at boys in my gym class, thinking, *Huh, that guy has
actual muscles. I wish I looked like that.*

My pudgy body was the outward manifestation of all my
insecurities. I was definitely a different species from the swar-
thy, muscular middle-school jocks who got all the girls. Mariana was always saying that I could get girls, too, if I exercised
more. And part of me thought that might not be such a bad
idea, if only to fit in. But too bad, because exercising and sports
were off the table. If I didn't try at sports, I couldn't fail at
sports.

Not surprisingly, I lived in dread of the yearly humiliation
that was the Presidential Physical Fitness Test, especially the
pull-up test. Pull-ups were my kryptonite. I had never been
able to do a single one. This was dread-inducing enough on a
regular day in PE class, but on fitness test days, it was practically
paralyzing. There we'd be, all lined up in front of the pull-up
bar, me at the very end of the line, postponing my fate. One by
one, the boys in front of me would approach the bar, leap up,
and lift their chins to the bar—once, twice, three times, sometimes even four. There were always a few kids like me whom
everyone expected to fail. I was grateful not to be alone and
would be overcome with resentment whenever one of those
sure-to-fail boys would surprise us all and make it to the top.
When my turn finally came, I'd start by trying to talk my way

out of the test. "I can't do pull-ups," I'd tell the coach. "So you can go ahead and fail me." This never worked, of course. "You have to try," the coach would insist. With that formality out of the way, I'd then approach the bar, feeling two dozen pairs of eyes boring into my back, and do my thing: grab the bar, hang there with shaky arms for long enough to show them that I'd meant what I'd said, then drop and walk away.

I took my eighth-grade fitness test failure particularly hard because I was starting to really care what my classmates thought. They were going out with girls, and I was getting left behind. So what did I do? I made up a girlfriend. Since I went to an all-boys school, this seemed manageable. But at some point, a school dance loomed, and everyone kept asking, "Are you going to bring her?" I told them I wasn't, and I was really sad, because my girlfriend was moving to Oklahoma. (Don't ask me why Oklahoma, it just came out.)

I did go to one dance in middle school. It was the big eighth-grade prom, and I went with my sister's friend Julia, who was Ecuadorian and liked me. At least according to my sister the matchmaker. My mom was overjoyed about the date. She even bought a corsage for me to give Julia. I remember pinning the flower to her dress and thinking, *Maybe this is the beginning of me getting interested in girls.*

My mom drove us to the dance, with my sister in the front seat. Mariana was slouched against the window, depressed because she'd wanted to go but couldn't find a guy in my school to take her. I would have gladly traded places with her and stayed home coding. But instead I did what I was supposed to do and escorted Julia into the gymnasium, which was all done up with balloons and strings of lights. The teachers had set out fruit punch and cleared out the bleachers to make room for the students, who were huddled together in circles. The song "Crank That" by Soulja Boy boomed through the speakers. *Watch me lean then watch me rock / Superman dat hoe / Yeah watch me crank dat Robocop.* Julia and I did the dance you had to do whenever you heard that song, and then we went to the corner of the gym and drank fruit punch and did some more awkward dancing. That's when another one of my sister's friends walked up and started dancing with us. She was a super-tall girl, and she towered over both Julia and me. Suddenly, she grabbed my head with one hand and Julia's head with her other hand, said, "Oh goddamn it, just kiss already," and smashed our faces together. That was my first kiss.

I found out later that my sister had put the tall girl up to it. "Michael needs a girlfriend at all costs," she'd said. "You've got to make sure he kisses her." It sort of worked—for Julia, at least. She messaged me a few times after that, inviting me to the mall. We went a couple of times. She always wanted to hold hands, so I would go along with it. But I just felt so awkward the whole time. Maybe I just wasn't the relationship type. *To hell with this,* I thought. *I'm going back to my apps.*

Chapter 4

Stress Tests

BY THE TIME I was in ninth grade, my mom and I were having nightly fights about money—the tens of thousands of dollars she'd taken from me, the thousands more she needed to pay off the latest creditor, the computer upgrade I needed but wouldn't get if she and my dad took my next Apple check . . .

"Michael, stop making your mom cry!" my dad exploded one evening, bursting in on one particularly loud fight in the kitchen.

"Why am *I* the bad guy?" I fired back. "I give everything to this family!"

"Ha!" my dad boomed. "You—you're just a selfish asshole!"

The words hit me like a punch, but my mom hardly seemed to notice as I stormed upstairs.

The next day, Saturday, my mom knocked on my door. I thought by the way she tiptoed in that she wanted to smooth things over. "Papi wasn't as angry as he seemed," she said, pinching a dirty T-shirt from my floor and dropping it into my hamper.

I nodded. "I know. I just hate it when he calls me names." Nearly all of the time, my dad was a quiet and sweet man. But he'd suffered a lot growing up. Losing his brother when he was a young man must have affected him deeply, but he had been raised to believe that being a man meant keeping his emotions in check. Even today, he almost never talked about his past, especially about being all but disowned by his family. All of that he kept bottled up inside, where it would build and build until he would simply explode—like a steam-release valve on a pressure cooker.

"Well," said my mom, "you know what would help him, don't you?"

"What?" I asked, a bubble of hope rising up in me. I'd never believed there was *anything* I could do.

"Ask him if he wants to go to the movies. You know he likes to go to the movies!" suggested my mom. And with that, she turned on her heel and walked out of my room.

I stared after her, confused all over again. This wasn't going to solve anything, and it didn't answer the question in my head. I just didn't get it: Sure, I was a teenager. I was grumpy a lot. But was I really such a bad son?

But almost as quickly, my dad's mood would usually turn around. "Movie, Cocolocho?" he offered, poking his head into my room an hour after blowing up at me that Saturday.

This was his nickname for me, a nonsensical term of endearment he'd never explained. *This* was the dad I got 90 percent of the time, the guy who liked to keep things light, even superficial. He stood looking out my window at our quiet suburban street. By the slump of his shoulders, I could tell that he was suffering.

Fine; I would try harder to be the good son he needed me to be, whatever that was.

"Sure, Papi," I said, turning off my screen.

That afternoon, my dad and I went to the movies and sat in silence. That was our way of making up. But I couldn't concentrate on the story playing out in front of me. His words just kept coming back to me: "selfish asshole." Did he really think that? Did he not know that Mom had spent over $100,000 of my money? It was possible. My mom controlled the purse strings. Until the big kitchen blowout, Dad had always vanished when the subject of my app money came up. There were times I wanted to bring the issue up with him, ask if he thought it was fair, what Mom was doing. But my mom had warned me more than once not to trouble Dad with our money problems. "It hurts him to think about it," she'd say. "Let's try to make his life better, not worse." So I chose not to rock the boat, which seemed fine with my dad.

Whatever my dad knew, Mariana knew even less—not how much I was making on my apps, and definitely not how much of that was paying for our lives. She'd always been shielded from the reality of just how bad our debt was, thanks to our mom's supernatural ability to pretend like everything was fine, even as everything was falling apart in front of us. But even if Mariana had known the whole picture, my sister wouldn't have taken my side. Ever since the TV news crews had started coming to the house, sending her running to her room, I'd felt a chasm growing between us. Before that, she'd always been game to let me hang out in her bedroom and tag along to the mall with her friends. But now she made it clear that I wasn't her clueless charge to look out for anymore. In Mariana's eyes, I was a selfish private-school brat who made our mom cry. In my eyes, I just wasn't cool enough to be allowed to hang out with her and her friends. We didn't dig deeper than that.

One day I called Tío Kike in Peru to ask for advice about to how to handle our money troubles. Tío Kike was on the opposite end of the spectrum from my parents when it came to finances. A scrupulous saver, he'd managed to save enough of his small salary each month to build a comfortable nest egg. My dad was always making jokes about how cheap my uncle was, but I thought he was a genius for building such a nice life with so little. "The best thing to do is not to give them any more money," my uncle advised me over the phone. "If you give them more, they're just going to spend it. Try to help them another way. No one ever taught them how to use money, so you should teach them how."

My uncle had a point. My parents were even less financially savvy than I was. They had no sense of what it meant to save, and they saw credit cards as free money that they could pay back at some point—hopefully. Still, with my teenage mouth and my mind on a million other things, I was definitely not equipped to lecture my mom and dad about how to budget and save. I'd have to start standing up to my parents in my own way.

The first time I tried, my mom had just picked me up from school. She pulled into our driveway, turned off the engine, and sat frozen for a while, gripping the steering wheel. Eventually she turned to me and said, "When your next check comes from Apple, we'll put it all toward saving the house." Then she burst into tears, sobbing, "I don't want to lose the house, Michael!"

I hated it when my mom cried. It made me want to cry too. I normally would've agreed, just to make the tears stop. But this was crazy. Supposedly my mom had been using my money to pay our mortgage for a year now, and it wasn't helping. Maybe the house was just too expensive for us. Something had to change.

I bit my tongue to distract myself from the tears prickling my eyes. Then I grabbed her hand and said as firmly as I could, "Mami, you need to find another way to—"

She didn't even let me finish. The next thing I knew, she was running into the house and slamming the front door.

When I brought the issue up a few days later, my mom wouldn't look me in the eye. "I'm going to pay you back, I promise," was all she'd say.

"I don't care if you pay me back," I tried. "We can forget about all the money you've spent. I just want to make sure that from now on you learn how to manage the money better, so we don't have to be in this situation again."

But there was no teaching my mom how to fish. Though she never came out and admitted it, I knew that she'd gone ahead and used the money from my bank account anyway. This made me angrier than I wanted to admit to myself.

In the months that followed, I kept trying to help them figure out their finances. I offered to help my mom understand how much money she could spend by listing out all the expenses and earnings of the household. She grew frustrated with my requests. Eventually I all but stopped speaking to my family. After school, I'd grab an armful of snacks from the pantry and head straight to my room to work in silence. Sometimes I'd hear my parents whispering in their room down the hall: "He's eating so much. He's getting fatter. He's getting angrier and ruder." I surely wasn't the nicest person to be around in my first two years of high school. But I never heard them whispering about the position they were putting me in by asking me to take on their debts. This only made me angrier, and hungrier.

My relationship with my mom thawed out in June of 2012, the end of my sophomore year. That was when she accompanied me to Santa Cruz, Bolivia, to do a press tour about my apps. The tour was organized by a woman whom I'll call Maria Carmen, a celebrity talk show host for a major Bolivian network. Maria Carmen had interviewed me in Miami when I was twelve, and she thought Bolivians were ready for a follow-up story. "Are you still helping to support your family with your apps?" she'd asked when she reached out. Reluctantly I'd said yes, and Maria Carmen had booked the tour right away. Her ambitious plan was for me to do a bunch of interviews with different TV shows in her network, speak at a conference, and cap off the trip with a big sit-down interview on her show, which was like a Bolivian version of *E! News.*

Maria Carmen was waiting for my mom and me when we arrived six hours late at the tiny Santa Cruz airport. With her trademark mane of straight auburn hair, her smooth bronze skin, and her fancy, sparkling red dress, she was unmistakable.

I was feeling a stress headache coming on, like my skull was being pressed in a vise. But still, I managed to paste on a happy face for Maria Carmen. My exhausted mom was beaming, too. She was a master at quickly switching out her emotions when she needed to, a skill I'd apparently inherited.

"Welcome home to Bolivia, Michael Sayman!" Maria Carmen said in her bold yet soothing host voice, rushing toward us with an ultra-white, made-for-TV smile. She hoisted her own equipment up off the ground and expertly set up a shot as her assistant fussed with the microphone.

"*Gracias,*" I replied. I'd learned from doing interviews with the Latin media back home that both Bolivians and Peruvians would engage in playful arguments about whether I was more Bolivian or Peruvian. During one newspaper interview, a reporter had even asked if my "heart was torn" about an upcoming soccer match between the two countries. "I can't answer that!" I cried. "That's like asking, 'Who do you love more, your mom or your dad?!'" I truly didn't have a favorite country. Even though I'd spent much more time in Peru with my mom's family and didn't know my Bolivian family as well, I'd never have picked a side. It was an honor to be loved by both.

The next thing I knew, Maria Carmen and her cameraman were ushering me toward a gathering of curious onlookers. Maria Carmen thrust her microphone out to a random girl about my age in the crowd. "Hi there!" she said to the girl. "I'm here with Michael Sayman, the Boy Genius of Apple. Are you surprised to see him here in Santa Cruz? What do you think of him?"

The girl and her friends blushed and giggled. They were clearly awed to be in the presence of a national star like Maria Carmen, and just as obviously clueless as to who I was. Still, the girl played along, gushing, "Yeah, he's awesome, I'm so impressed. It's a big inspiration." Satisfied, Maria Carmen packed up her mic, hoisted several bags of equipment over her shoulder, and strode for the exit. "*Vámonos! Vámonos!*" ("Let's go! Let's go!") she called back to my flustered mom and me.

We followed Maria Carmen and her cameraman to her dusty SUV, where she grabbed the wheel, revved the engine, and took off racing along a potholed dirt road into the city. I was convinced that she was a superwoman. "We've already missed one interview because of your flight," she said to my mom and me in the backseat, "but we'll make it to your next one if we hurry. And then after that, you're going to be a guest on our most popular late-night talk show." As she drove, Maria Carmen rattled off talking points she'd prepared for me, did her makeup, and styled her hair—only swerving onto the shoulder once or twice, which seemed miraculous. I could tell by my mom's white-knuckled grip on her door handle and the tight smile on her face that she was freaking out inside, just like me, about the crazy schedule, not to mention the crazy driving. But how could we complain? Maria Carmen had already secured several front-page stories about me in the upcoming Sunday papers. It seemed like her plan to make "the Boy Genius of Apple" a star in Bolivia might just be working out.

And that was good news, right? All of this was good. So why did I feel so terrible? Oh yeah, because the upbeat, generous kid I was pretending to be was a total phony, a cover for the one inside who was miserable, whose family resented him, who was exhausted by the constant effort of keeping up with his own creations.

After three days of back-to-back interviews, televised sightseeing tours, trips to schools to talk to kids, and the conference, my mom and I flew back to Miami, exhausted. Back at home, I went straight up to my room, fell on my bed, and checked my followings on Facebook and Twitter. Both had grown exponentially—to over fifteen thousand on Twitter and thirty thousand on Facebook.

—

By the summer of 2012, I was making about $12,000 a month. But that income was hardly secure. I felt like a stock on the public market, where uncontrollable events could send my value through the roof—or just as easily send me tumbling again. That's exactly what happened. By the fall, after a few killer months at the top of the App Store leaderboard, the Club Penguin Game fell to the bottom of the U.S. and Latin American charts. My profits were down to less than $1,500 a month. The interviews I did in Latin America had very little impact on any of the sales of my apps, as most of my revenue came from the United States.

And there was a new problem to deal with: Disney. They had acquired Club Penguin in 2007, not caring much, at first, about the fact that people like me were creating apps about their games. Now, as the giant company was preparing to roll out their own app, that had changed. I received a notice from Apple informing me that all developers, outside of Disney, needed to remove any apps related to Club Penguin from the store. I had already started brainstorming app ideas unrelated to Club Penguin that I was more interested in. So one by one, I took them all down.

My mom noticed almost immediately. "What's going on?" she started to ask. "Why do your apps keep getting pulled?"

Casually, I told her I'd been removing them myself. "I have to," I explained. "Apple sent out a notice saying that Disney's making their own Club Penguin app."

Her face turned into a mask of sheer panic. "How are you going to pay for things?" she exclaimed. "What about college?"

I felt a flush creep up my neck. "What do you mean, how am I going to pay for college?"

"Michael, I told you, I used the money for the restaurant," she said. "I spent it all on salaries! We just *have* to make it through until the economy gets better and people start eating out more!"

So I was a year and a half from graduating from high school, with no money to pay for college. At the same time, the bottom had fallen out of the app market. People no longer wanted to pay for apps; they were spending money only on in-app purchases, a relatively new world that I knew nothing about.

As shocking as my mom's announcement was, though, I'd already been secretly contemplating my future without college. Why stumble through four more years of a traditional education when my self-education as a programmer was what seemed to impress the world? Now I probably had no choice. I would have to adapt, get even better at coding, step up my act. If I could build a free game that stood on its own, maybe it would get acquired by a company that would hire me along with it. That was how it usually worked, as I'd learned from reading the tech industry blogs. It seemed like a solid backup plan to me: come up with an irresistible app that would catapult me straight from high school into a real job. Great! But what?

Chapter 5

Up with 4 Snaps

Draw Something is an endless turn-based game where you illustrate a given word for your friend to guess, then you switch turns. In 2012, Draw Something was one of the most popular apps in the world; within months of launching, it sold to Zynga, along with its production studio, OMGPOP, for $183 million. As I generated and discarded idea after idea, I kept coming back to Draw Something for inspiration. I thought, *What if I could create a new kind of guessing game, tied to an activity people my age love to do, like . . . hmmm.* What did we love to do, besides go to the movies and hang out at the mall?

Hoping to organically unlock a game idea that the big app developers, for all of their research and market testing, hadn't yet arrived at, I started to observe and analyze how my sister and her friends used their phones. They weren't into Draw Something, but they all loved to play a game called Hay Day, which was a lot like FarmVille, the popular social networking game that simulated farming. Combined, my sister and her friends probably spent hundreds of dollars a year in virtual coins on Hay Day, just for the pleasure of tapping on random buttons. Another thing I noticed they did was text one another pictures instead of writing out their messages. Adults liked to take photos to commemorate special occasions or to preserve a memory, but for kids like us, who grew up with cameras and storage on our devices, there was nothing precious about photographs. Taking them was as easy as talking or breathing. One day, I saw my sister texting a friend a series of pictures she'd just snapped. "Guess the word I'm thinking of?" she wrote. That's when I knew I had my idea.

I wanted to make a multiplayer game where the first player would send a friend four pictures, and the friend would have to guess the word they were thinking of. For example, if someone sent you pictures of French fries, nachos, buffalo wings, and cookies, you might guess the word "munchies." With luck, the players would get hooked and continue playing with new words, sending more photos back and forth.

Whenever I thought about creating an app, I'd spend weeks thinking up a name, brand, and design. The brand is the personality and message that a company wants to convey to its target audience. It's a lot like your personal style: the clothes and jewelry and hairstyle you choose to wear when you go out into the world. Design is more about the usability and functionality of a product. Along with most every other tech designer in the early 2000s, I loved a design style known as skeuomorphism. This is where digital interfaces mimic their real-world counterparts, down to their textures, drop shadows, and reflective effects. Early Apple products relied heavily on this style; their on/off switches looked like real-world knobs, their calculator buttons seemed to have beveled edges, and so on. This was the style I began to work with while designing my new idea.

I didn't have a name for it yet, but I knew I wanted my game's aesthetic to blend the thoughtfulness of Apple products with the emotional appeal of Nickelodeon shows like *iCarly* and *Victorious*. I downloaded those soundtracks, put on my headphones, and got to work sketching a rough version of my game in PowerPoint.

Until I had my visual sensibility down—and I could clearly imagine kids laughing at their phone screens, enjoying my game, and telling their friends about it—I didn't get into the nitty-gritty specifics of how it would work or build anything. I had to feel that spark of confidence first.

The way I got to that point was to run my idea by some test characters I'd created in my mind—a varied group with a mix of habits, personalities, ages, social groups, economic statuses, devices, and genders.

As I was dreaming up my photo game, my imaginary test characters were a ten-year-old girl who loved going to the movies, a theater kid who stayed up late after rehearsals playing games on his iPod Touch, and a group of cool kids who hung out in their school parking lot. I tried to imagine my game from each of their perspectives. I would then hit the play button in my head and watch the various scenes unfold. What did Ten-Year-Old Girl's face look like when she opened the app on her phone? What kind of interface made her smile?

Next, I dropped my test characters into various scenarios. I imagined Ten-Year-Old Girl sneaking a look at her phone in the middle of a movie because she got a notification from the game. What did the notification look like? How did she respond to it? The notification didn't interest her, so she put it away. I modified the text in the notification and replayed the scene. I pictured her running to the lobby to take a picture because she was so into playing that she couldn't wait until the movie was over. Then I asked myself, was that realistic? Would she do that? What would make her need to do that? Then I moved on to Theater Kid, imagining him sitting in class, bored, deciding what game to play with the fifteen minutes he had left of free period. Looking over his shoulder, I tried to visualize his home screen. I could see he had Clash of Clans installed on the front page, an online war game where users build an army and attack other clans' home bases. Then I spotted a folder with games like Candy Crush and Angry Birds, old games he hadn't deleted but didn't play much anymore. As he swiped through his home screen of apps, I spotted my game. He hadn't opened it since installing it the day before. Why not?

What could I do to ensure that he did? Did he think the game would take a quick five minutes to play? Would he prefer to play Clash of Clans instead? Why or why not? Sometimes my test characters would be super critical, which I found really helpful. If Theater Kid said he chose Clash of Clans because it was easier to play during free period, I'd ask, "But *why* do you feel it's easier? Tell me more."

After days of these imaginary conversations, I decided it was time to come up with a name. Since my photo game was built around friends sending pictures to friends, my first name idea was Pics and Friends. I liked that name enough that I spent hours examining it from my test characters' perspectives, even having them talk to one another about it.

I then had to run the name by a few non-imaginary friends and even some grown-ups I trusted, like one of my favorite teachers, Susan. Susan was in charge of our iPad program, and she was much cooler and knew a lot more about tech than most adults. One day I saw her coming out of the teachers' lounge, and with way too much energy, I ran up to her, shouting, "Hey, Susan! I came up with a name for the new game I've been working on!"

Susan spun around, looking like I'd just scared the crap out of her. "Oh! Hi. That's great, Michael. What are you going to call it?"

I was now walking in tandem with her. "Pics and Friends!" I blurted.

She thought about it for a minute as we continued walking. I was nervously smiling, anxious for her feedback. "*Hmmm,*" Susan finally said. "Maybe you should think of another one." Ouch.

I pushed myself further, and a week later, the name 4 Snaps came to me. *This one feels good,* I thought. I liked it so much, in fact, that I designed a logo. Then I pushed myself to get specific: *Okay, the game's obviously going to use four pictures,* I told myself. *You're going to take four pictures and send them to your friends. Let's do that.*

I was now ready to build my first online multiplayer smartphone game.

Up until that point, all my Club Penguin–related apps had been built for use by a single player, on a local device. I realized that in order to coordinate actions between two different users, and to save the photos they'd share, I'd need to connect 4 Snaps to the Internet. I asked my good friend Google how I was supposed to do that and found out that I'd need to store information on a server that lived outside my phone. This might sound obvious today, but to me at the time, it was quite the revelation.

Could I build a server? I wondered. I definitely couldn't afford to buy one. I didn't even know what one looked like. I soon figured out that there were fairly new hosting services, created by small start-ups, that charged a monthly fee of about $100 to use their servers. I wouldn't have to touch the servers directly myself. All I had to worry about was writing my code. The back-end service would handle the data for me: where it got stored, how to load it, how to parse through it, and searching and sorting. In short, it would do everything but build my game. I decided to go with a service called Parse because the website was pretty. (Hey, I was sixteen. That's how my mind worked.)

Slowly I learned how to build my first online multiplayer game. After four months of coming up with and building out a back-end design that created the illusion of a back-and-forth game between players, I started to test the game with my friends. When my sister said she loved it, I started to believe the game could be a hit. I needed to make sure it would make money, too, so I added some ad banners into the interface as I prepared to submit it to the App Store.

My mom was growing more and more skeptical with each passing month. "You'll be applying to colleges next year, and we're really struggling," she said. "Why are you building a free game? What if it doesn't work?"

I did my best to appease her, explaining that once the game was popular, I would make money through advertisements and in-app purchases that allowed players to unlock more words and get hints. I could tell my mom wasn't convinced, but as always when it came to my apps, she came around to trusting me. What else could she do?

As I was putting the finishing touches on 4 Snaps in May of 2013, a news crew from the U.S. Spanish-language network Univision called. By the end of the call with the team of three journalists, we'd arranged for them to start filming me for a documentary on my ongoing work.

They came to my house in July, just in time to film me submitting to the App Store for review. I was seated in my new "office," on a bar stool at the kitchen counter in the tiny town house where we'd lived since finally losing our house to the bank a few months prior. I'd offered to let my mom use most of what was left of the earnings from my old apps to pay for the floor to be redone with white marble tiles, as well as to redo the second floor of the unit with black hardwood. With mixed results, I was still trying to convince my parents to support themselves, but I also wanted to make sure they didn't feel all was lost. I couldn't fathom the pain my mom must have felt losing the home where she'd raised my sister and me. After that massive blow, I would've done anything to cheer her up.

"So, Michael, how do you feel now that you've submitted your new app to the App Store?" Marcello, the producer, asked—after reminding me to answer in complete sentences and to repeat his question before I responded.

I smiled, blinded by two bright lights as I started to speak.

"Look at Marcello, not at the camera," Rocky, the cameraman, interrupted. I nodded to Rocky and looked at Marcello. "I just submitted my new app, 4 Snaps, to the App Store, and I'm relieved! Now . . . I want to sleep!"

Everyone chuckled. Then Marcello got a serious look on his face. "Will you be continuing to help support your family with the money you earn from 4 Snaps?"

There it was again, the money question. I rubbed my sweaty

palms on my jeans, stalling. The only sound in the room was the whirring of my laptop, still cooling down from all the work it had done that day.

Marcello sensed my hesitation. "It's important to be honest about this stuff," he said in a kind voice, turning to look back at my dad and mom standing a few feet behind him. "Do you agree, Micky and Cristina?"

My parents exchanged a look. Then my mom nodded once, keeping her eyes low. Marcello turned back to me, repeating the question.

I took a deep breath. "Yes, I hope the app does well so I can continue to help support my family!" I said. Was that true? All I knew was I didn't want to see my mom crying anymore.

"That's super," said Marcello. "With so much responsibility, do you have any time for a social life?"

I laughed awkwardly. "Not really!"

And that was a wrap.

Outside, it was a beautiful warm evening. I considered an alternate reality where I was out there enjoying it, maybe playing basketball with my neighbors down the block. Did I want that?

Nah. It had been so long since I'd hung out with other kids offline, and one of my only friends, Lucas, tired of taking second place to my apps, had drifted away from me. While I'd gotten good at analyzing how other kids used social media to socialize, it had been a long time since I'd socialized myself—well, aside from sometimes working on my laptop near my sister and her friends, just to experience what it felt like to be around other people. Besides, exhausted as I was, I felt at ease for the first time in months. Friends, school—all that was overrated. So what if I'd failed most of my finals? Getting into a good college, or even going to college at all, seemed less important the more successful I was with my apps. Especially now that I'd crossed a milestone I never thought I'd see: inventing and creating my own game from scratch. Now I just had to wait to hear if Apple would accept it.

Chapter 6

Now That I've Built It, Will They Come?

SUMMER VACATION WAS ALMOST over and I was about to start my senior year when 4 Snaps was finally approved for sale at the App Store. I hadn't done any of the summer reading assignments or bought my uniform—but whatever. I had bigger things on my mind.

I'd never done much to market my previous apps—but I'd never been this desperate for money before. If I was going to reach my goal of selling 4 Snaps to a company, the product not only needed to be great but needed to generate serious buzz. In the past, I'd published my apps in the App Store the moment Apple approved them. This time, I felt like I needed to build hype around my creation before releasing it to the public. So I set a release date for a couple of weeks out and began putting together a list of tech journalists I'd followed through my obsession with Apple and tech news.

I still watched all the Apple events online, following iPhone releases and software updates with the kind of feverish interest sports fans have in their favorite teams. The bookmarks tab on my iPad at school was filled with tech blogs that reported daily on the latest rumors and news from Silicon Valley, and I checked them first thing every morning. Now I clicked on the "About" section of each tech blog I followed. From there, I copied and pasted every email address I could find to my list. Every one of those bloggers got the same email, starting with: "Hey! I'm

16 years old, and I created this app called 4 Snaps . . ." I was playing up my age, hoping it would help attract their attention. The first day I sent about one hundred emails. Then I waited.

A couple of hours passed with no responses. Sitting at my kitchen counter–slash–desk, I tried to ignore the raspy hum of our old refrigerator. It was on the fritz, but we were almost out of my app money and we couldn't afford to fix it. I hated this. I wasn't going to let this be our future. How could I increase my chances of a journalist responding? I looked back at my computer and began writing down everything I could think of to make my pitch more enticing. I decided to send out a second round of emails with prerelease copies of 4 Snaps and screenshots of the game. I spent hours getting it all ready and blasted my contact list for the second time that day.

While I braced myself for a flurry of interest, I turned to fixing some bugs (pieces of code that had the potential to fail) that I hadn't had the time to work on previously. The sun was setting outside, and my computer screen was the only light in the darkening room. I anxiously refreshed my email every few minutes, but nobody responded that day. It hadn't worked.

At one a.m., my family had gone to sleep and I was still in the kitchen, pacing in circles to help myself think. I realized that no matter what I did, my little emails weren't "legit" enough to get the attention of the tech bloggers. Most app launches from large companies included a well-produced teaser trailer. That's what I needed—a teaser trailer for 4 Snaps! I had no clue how to make one, but the idea of paying someone else to do it for me didn't cross my mind, and even if it had, I'd never have been able to afford a professional one.

The next day, I asked my sister to invite her friends over. I rented a camera from the local tech shop and walked around the block with the girls, filming them as they chatted and used my game. After editing the thing together on iMovie on my computer, I uploaded the video to YouTube and sent the link to another fifty or so addresses I found online. I was lucky that

time. Two journalists from smaller, relatively unknown websites responded with follow-up questions. Better than nothing,
I told myself.

With three days left until public launch, there were two stories about 4 Snaps in the works. It wasn't enough. As long as
there was time left, there were still emails I could send, tweets I
could post, and journalists I could reach out to. I kept reminding myself, *School starts in two weeks, and you won't have time to
promote the app then.* It was now or never.

I poked around the Parse website and found the email address
of their designer, who quickly wrote back.

I was frantically emailing another tech journalist when my
dad came downstairs, gave me a sad look, and went back to
bed. I was still wearing the same clothes from the day before.
Over the past year, my parents had witnessed my weight bal-
loon up to about 190 pounds. I couldn't even look at myself in
the mirror anymore. But as long as I was working on 4 Snaps,
I didn't have to think about the literal elephant in the room.
Sometime that summer, my parents had stopped asking me to
shower, get some rest, eat right. It was weird: I'd spent years
wishing they'd get off my back, but now that they finally had,
I couldn't help feeling sad. If my parents had given up trying, I
wondered, did that mean they'd given up on me?

While I waited on pins and needles to hear from someone,
anyone, I tweeted, "Can't hang out with my friends, must finish work on 4 Snaps."

A classmate I hadn't heard from all summer texted me
moments later: "Hey, are you taking the new AP Computer
Science class this year?"

"What AP Computer Science class?" I responded. I'd been
begging my school to offer one for years, but the powers that
be had never shown interest.

"They added it at the end of the year? Didn't you see the
email?" my classmate wrote back.

I'd never opened an email from the school, and for the first time, I regretted that. Was registration closed? What if the class was full? I needed in on this class. I shot an email to Susan, the school's iPad administrator who'd given me feedback on naming 4 Snaps. She was the only person on the faculty who'd understand how important this was to me. Hell, she was one of the few at my school who I felt seemed to understand the importance of computer science for my generation, period.

Susan gave me the address of the scheduling director, whom I quickly wrote, asking to swap my psychology class for computer science. I didn't really care too much about psychology and thought I was never going to need it. How wrong I was—but I'll get to that later.

At eleven p.m. on August 7, 2013, I took a deep breath and released 4 Snaps publicly in 182 countries on the App Store. Then I celebrated by shoving several Zebra Cakes—those delicious yellow carb bombs with cream filling covered in white icing and trimmed with fudge stripes—in my mouth at the same time.

Only then did it hit me: I'd only put ten word options in the 4 Snaps database.

The whole purpose of 4 Snaps was to pick, from three random words, one to take four pictures of—and there were only ten! I had already published it live. There was no going back; I had to act quickly and manually input more words before people started downloading the app.

By two a.m., I'd come up with one thousand new words and uploaded them to Parse, the back-end service I was using to host my app. By then, one of the tech blogs I'd convinced to write about the game had posted a positive article. I checked the App Store charts. I vividly remembered seeing my first app reach number 7 in the top reference apps back in 2010. Now I scrolled past the top ten, one hundred, two hundred . . . no

4 Snaps to be found. I kept scrolling down until I found 4 Snaps at number 1,078 in the Top Free Word Games category.

At three in the morning, I left the kitchen littered with my empty containers of McDonald's fries and Zebra Cakes wrappers and slowly climbed the stairs to bed, where I refreshed the App Store chart on my phone one last time. 4 Snaps had reached number 876 in Top Free Word Games. I finally fell asleep.

After a few hours, I burst awake, grabbed my phone, and checked the charts. 4 Snaps was still stuck in the high eight hundreds. I ate some more Zebra Cakes for breakfast and read the second article about 4 Snaps the minute it published. Scrolling nervously through the article, I realized that they hadn't mentioned my name or age, they'd just talked about the game. I'd always thought people paid attention to my stuff only because I was young. That the media attention I'd received and the press trips to Latin America were because I was a precocious kid. But this review treated my game like any other. It was a good sign.

I spent the rest of that morning on Twitter, trying to convince the reporters who'd previously ignored me to hop on the hype wagon. It didn't work as well as I'd expected it to. Several people blocked me for being the most annoying person ever.

By one p.m., 4 Snaps had managed to reach number 157 in Top Free Word Games. I needed to do more to keep it growing. I texted my mom:

Me: Hey, how much money do I have left?
Mom: $600.
Me: That's it?
Mom: My other account has negative $20.

I had earned over $150,000 from my prior apps over the past three years, and this is what we'd come to. I'd spend $150 on promoting the game with ads on Facebook. If it worked, I'd go for broke and worry about my parents' overdue bills later.

But the conversions weren't great. Only about twenty people clicked on the ad. This wasn't worth it. My mom had told me there was only $450 left in my bank account. I knew exactly what she'd say now: "What are we going to do? Your app failed, and we have nowhere to go. We'll have nothing! What are we going to do?" This was a typical refrain, and it always made me sweat. What if we *were* one App Store payment away from homelessness? What if that $450 was the difference between our spending the next years living hand-to-mouth and having a steady paycheck?

I hit pause on the Facebook ad campaign just as my mom texted back to remind me about an orthodontist appointment. Both my sister and I had worn braces for years, and with them came the obligatory monthly adjustments. I despised these appointments. I could relate to our dogs, who would pee themselves every time they realized my mom was taking them to the vet. But I submitted because I could not wait to see what I would look like without braces. I told myself that the day I got them off, I would start caring about myself again. I would lose weight. I would make an effort on behalf of myself, not just my apps.

In the car, my sister sat next to me in the backseat, scrolling through Instagram. Peering over her shoulder, I noticed that advertisements were popping up on her feed. This was odd. Instagram didn't have ads (yet). I asked Mariana what she was looking at, and she said, "Some accounts that I follow always post about these apps, it's so annoying."

I leaned in closer. "Can I see that for a second?" One account she followed was all about shoes.

"How many followers does that account have?" I asked.

"Four million."

"Wow, that's really big."

"Yeah, I follow a bunch of them. One has tons of pink stuff. Another is about dogs."

"Hey, is there an email address in their bio?" I asked.

She peered at her phone. "Yeah, there is. How did you know?"

Ignoring her question, I asked my sister to click on a few of the accounts that were posting annoying "ads." Then I had her forward the email addresses she found in their bios.

By the time we reached the orthodontist's office, I'd already shaken off my worries about spending the last of my money. In the waiting room, I emailed the people at those accounts (today, of course, we'd call them influencers): "Hey, I have this new app called 4 Snaps. I'd love to advertise with you guys. What are you charging?"

Throughout my appointment, as my teeth were cinched and jabbed with various torture devices, my phone buzzed nonstop in my pocket. Once I was back home, I opened up the emails on my laptop. I had uncovered a giant underground network of advertisers. One wrote, "How are you? This month, we are holding an 'Awesome August' special deal. $70 for 4 posts. $120 for 8 posts (twice a week). Posts stay in our account for at least two months. We have over 158K followers who would love your page and your products."

I knew that most of these accounts were blasting my sister with posts about annoying apps. I didn't want her to have the same experience with mine, so I thought, *How can I make this better?* I decided to create ads that were relevant to each account. For the one that was all about shoes, I grabbed four pictures of shoes from that Instagram and added the 4 Snaps logo with the comment: "Can you guess the word for this one?" The ads got great responses, generating more than a thousand 4 Snaps accounts.

And just like that, I felt like I was riding a rocket into space. The thrill of seeing months of hard work pay off was something I could finally bask in, even if no one around me knew what was going on.

A couple of days after launch, 4 Snaps continued to climb up the charts, thanks to all those Instagram promotions I had paid for. The game had reached two thousand users—doubling in less than twenty-four hours. I couldn't stop there, so I begged my mom to find another $300 for me somewhere. Somehow she managed to scrape up the money and deposited it into my account. Immediately, I purchased more Instagram promotions.

As I write this today, I can't resist stepping in to offer a more current perspective on advertising for any fledgling app developers who might be interested. Back when I was launching 4 Snaps, there were some Facebook ads but no sponsored posts on Instagram. So, I went to the influencers directly and asked how much they would charge to post about my app. (That figure has increased dramatically. Today, it could cost anywhere from $1,000 to $1 million to post an ad that I paid $80 for back then.)

Something that hasn't changed: an influencer's paid post should never interrupt their users' experience. People don't click on things that annoy them! The post should be relevant to what the users are there for. And it should be so engaging that people are drawn to comment on and share it. Hypertargeted advertising has always worked well for me.

The Facebook ad platform is a clear-cut service that works very differently from the vague influencer market that I was tapping into. If your ad doesn't perform very well, meaning it isn't being liked, shared, or clicked on a lot, guess what? Facebook won't take your money. They'll choose not to show it to people. Facebook just wants to show people ads that they are actually going to like and interact with—so make your ad speak as directly as possible to the people you want to see it.

I get asked a lot, Can advertising push an app to the top of the charts? The answer is yes—but only temporarily. I don't recommend spending widely on big advertising campaigns.

Instead, start by appealing to the smallest possible audience—one that's very narrowly focused and specific to your niche. Once you've successfully connected with that audience, then you can start looking at adjacent markets. These users might not be your exact target audience, but with a few tweaks to your app, a couple of new features, maybe you can expand to include them. And once you've taken over *that* market, then you can keep on expanding outward from there. By continually expanding your reach to wider and wider audiences, you may end up with a very different product than you started out with. And that's okay! As long as you always remember who your original fans were and make efforts to speak to and include them, your product will continue to be loved by those early adopters—and hopefully millions more!

As the week crawled by, my app continued to rise, from number 157 to number 50 in the Free Word Games category. Even though the app wasn't making any money at this point, because it was free, I knew it was on the right path.

And soon enough, things started to happen for 4 Snaps. The first week of my senior year, it became the number one word game in the App Store. But the biggest thing that happened didn't seem all that big at the time. I got an email from a woman at Parse, asking if I'd be willing to make a two-minute video describing how I'd built my app and how the service had impacted my life.

"Sure!" I fired back.

I was never one to turn down an opportunity to talk about 4 Snaps, and this opportunity was extra exciting because Parse had recently been acquired by Facebook. That sent an excited shiver up my spine. Facebook may not have been popular with my generation, but I loved it. A nostalgic kid, I especially loved cataloging my most important life events on the Timeline. The day they'd launched that feature in 2011, I'd gone into our storage, dug out my dad's old SD cards with all the old photos of Mariana and me throughout our childhood, and started creating my first digital memory book.

The same night I got the request from Parse, I recorded my video. I was wearing my blue-and-green-plaid pajamas, figuring about five people would watch it. That's not what happened.

What happened was someone played my video for Mark Zuckerberg. Every week, as I later learned, Zuckerberg gave a talk to his employees and sometimes, to close out the event, he would show a video of some regular person raving about one of Facebook's products. Parse had been acquired by Facebook months before, and it was their turn to be featured—in my video, as it turned out. So, Zuckerberg streamed me in my pajamas to his entire company. In Menlo Park and Austin and Dallas and Seattle and London and all around the world, every single Facebook employee saw me talking about my app. I later learned from the Parse CEO, Ilya Sukhar, that Zuckerberg turned to him while the video was playing and said, "Hey, I think we should hire this kid."

Chapter 7

Big in Peru

ABOUT A WEEK AFTER Zuckerberg saw my pajama video, I was sitting in my precalculus class, not listening to my teacher, when an email came in from Facebook, inviting me to apply for an internship. A second email arrived minutes after that: "Mark Zuckerberg would like to meet you, so we'd like to have you fly out." My teacher's voice grew even more distant. This couldn't be real. I banged my forehead on my desk once to verify that I was actually awake. Yep, I was.

"What happened?" whispered the kid sitting in the row next to me, poking me in the shoulder with his pencil. Speechless, I turned and handed him my iPad. He scanned the email, stood up, and blurted to the room, "Mark Zuckerberg wants to hire Michael!" My classmates started to freak out. The teacher marched over and took the iPad away. "Stop playing around!" he snapped.

I shrunk down in my seat. For the rest of the class, I sat there sweating, thinking, *I need to respond! I need to tell them yes, or they're going to think I'm blowing them off!* At the end of the lesson, I nervously asked for my iPad back and ran from the classroom. My attitude, along with my grades, had gone from bad to worse in senior year. It wasn't that I didn't care about my future; I was just feeling clearer than ever that good grades and college had very little to do with it.

"Yes, I'd love to!" I wrote back to Facebook from the hall-

way outside my classroom. Mariana's friends were always telling me I should run my own start-up when I graduated, but I
already knew that all I wanted was stability. After years of living with my mom sounding alarm bells that we were about to
lose the electricity in our home, run out of food, or lose the
restaurant, I did not want any more risk. So, I couldn't have
cared less about having a start-up. I wanted to work for a big
company that paid me a salary. I wanted to feel confident that
I would be fine, no matter what.

In October, I got two pieces of great news: First, I'd gotten
the Facebook internship! Second, I was being invited to Peru
to speak at a tech conference. I'd grown up spending summers
there with my extended family, but this trip would be different, a real business trip. I asked to not be paid to speak at the
conference, but they'd cover my airfare as well as my mom's.

The trip was the perfect opportunity to drum up interest in
4 Snaps in Latin America. I was determined to use my visit to
make it as successful there as it was in the States. We'd hit number 100 in the Top Free Overall category, with over a hundred
thousand users. Even though 4 Snaps was a free app and wasn't
bringing in any money, I still held out hope of making it so
popular that a big company would buy it for millions.

I always brought my mom on work trips to help me stay
organized and remember to eat and sleep, and because they
were always good opportunities for us to spend some time
together, improving our relationship. I was really going to need
her for this one. The agenda for my three days in the country
was booked solid from six a.m. to ten p.m. every day, in half-
hour slots.

While I still needed my mom's support, she still depended
on mine, too. I'd all but stopped trying to take a stand about
my parents spending my money—it just wasn't worth the tur-

moil it caused. I was, however, more tuned in to what my mom was spending. Each week, when Apple deposited what little money came in from my former apps, I would try to sit down with my mom to decide which overdue bills to pay first. She would usually tell me she was too busy, but I had to try. Of course, in retrospect, I now know that this was an absurd situation to be in: a child fighting with my parents about their finances—and my money. But at the time it seemed like a normal, if painful, conversation.

As we came in for a landing over the rooftops of Lima, my mom quietly touched my arm and said to me in Spanish, "Hey, Michael, we need to repaint the restaurant. It will cost a couple of thousand, but Papi and I think it's worth it. What do you think?"

I frowned. By now I was aware that the restaurant was losing $4,000 a month. When my money wasn't enough to cover the employees' salaries and operating costs, those expenses went on credit cards. The math on keeping El Pollon open just wasn't sound. "How is repainting going to make a difference?" I said.

My mom pressed her phone into my hand. "Look! This is what we could do." A friend had mocked up some images in Photoshop of what the restaurant would look like painted. "It will look more modern," my mom insisted. "If we do it, maybe people will want to come."

I sighed. Even after the crushing losses our family had suffered in the recession, my parents still refused to see that the American dream they'd fallen love with as young immigrants didn't come with a guarantee. My dad had been sure that his ambition to become a successful video and sound editor in television could come true if he just worked hard enough. He was so sure, in fact, that he'd given up the financial support of his family to come to the United States and do work that he loved—instead of what his family wanted him to do. When the opportunity arose, he'd leave his career to follow his dream:

to have his own business with my mom. And for a few years, when the restaurant was booming, my parents *did* experience the good life they'd seen on American TV shows while growing up in Latin America. But that life, the way *they'd* achieved it, wasn't sustainable, and it never would be. Why couldn't they see that?

"I don't know," I said, trying to keep my resolve. "Maybe you and Papi should just close already and find other jobs." I felt like a brat. It was horrible looking into my mother's eyes and telling her to close the business she and my father had started. But the restaurant was losing so much money that I doubted any paint job could fix it.

As the wheels of the plane scraped the runway, we sat back in our seats and retreated into silence. We would have to pick up the conversation another time.

Several camera crews, including a local Univision team getting footage for my documentary, filmed us as we stepped off the plane. The Latin American news outlets had been following me since my CNN interview when I was thirteen, and as a result, I wasn't pretend-famous there anymore. As I exchanged an awkward hug with my shy *tío* Kike and my eight-year-old cousin, Ariana, I noticed a group of curious onlookers.

After three years of doing publicity for my apps, my mom and I were pros, with our roles down pat: I was the happy Boy Genius of Apple, and my mom was the proud, supportive parent, nudging me if I forgot to smile or thank a supporter for coming out to see me. She was always concerned about what other people might think of us, especially when it came to maintaining the image that we were solidly middle class. We were still open in interviews about how I helped to support my family—it was probably the part of my story the press loved best. But I wasn't supposed to let on just how bad things had gotten. Even when we lost our house, my parents didn't want anyone to know, and they were always careful not to argue about our financial problems in front of the Univision people. Those fights were saved for two in the morning or when we were alone in the car together.

After the airport greetings, my mom and I were whisked into a van. It was time to show people what they wanted to see: the South American kid who'd grabbed his piece of Silicon Valley. Someone who'd made it.

Thirty minutes later, we were standing in a tiny ceviche restaurant, surrounded by the Univision crew, a cameraman from a show called *Día D,* and two people in charge of figuring out my schedule. No one else was there. Did they close the whole place down for us?

Someone put me in chef's whites. I had no idea what I was doing, what I was supposed to say, whom I was supposed to talk to, or what was going to happen. I met the chef. My smile was really turned up now. A half-dozen servers appeared and stood in a line behind the chef, who said, in Spanish, "We're just going to have you prepare some ceviche! It's going to be great!"

"*Espera! Qué?*" I answered ("Wait! What?")—I hadn't spoken a word of English since we landed. "*Yo prepararé un ceviche?*" ("*I'm* going to prepare some ceviche?")

"*Por supuesto!*" boomed the chef. He slapped me on the back. "*Te va a encantar!*" ("Yes! You're going to love it!")

They were filming me from a weird angle that would make me look extra fat, but what could I do? Just kept smiling. As long as I had a smile on my face, I could navigate this. The chef handed me a bowl of diced raw fish and tomatoes and said, "*Mezcla esto*" ("Mix that around"). I mixed it around for three seconds, and the chef was beside himself: "*Lo máximo! Felicitaciones!*" he said. "*Preparaste un ceviche! Lo hiciste! Y te salió buenazo!*" ("The best! Congratulations! You made your ceviche! You did it! And it came out great!")

Someone handed me an award, an actual medal, and a hard-cover cookbook. The servers applauded. My mom nodded and smiled. But I knew on the inside she wasn't smiling. She was tired and worrying about her restaurant, but she was here, and she had my back.

Now the chef was making a speech. Something about the Boy Genius of Apple. I didn't feel like a genius. I felt like a lucky kid who made an app. And now I had made ceviche in three seconds. They wanted me to speak, so I said, "Thank you so much for this amazing food. It's delicious! It's incredible! I'm so proud that I got to learn how to make ceviche with my mom. We're going to try it at home. It will probably turn out terrible, but we'll do our best!"

One of the people in charge of scheduling said, "Okay, time's up. Next place." We didn't get to eat the ceviche. All the food was just left there. We didn't even touch it, and I was starving.

We were brought to a stadium to admire some statue. Again, I had no idea where we were or what we were doing. Out from behind the statue appeared my uncle and Ariana. I wondered if I'd fallen asleep in the van and this was a dream. "Where did you guys come from?" I said, because I'd thought we'd said goodbye for the day at the airport. It turned out that the *Día D* program wanted B-roll footage of us walking around the city. They wanted to show me with my Peruvian relatives. We walked and walked, the cameras in front of and behind us, my blushing uncle and my mom and my little cousin and me, just out for a stroll.

We went to dinner—a family dinner, with dozens of people I'd never met before but was supposed to be related to. I couldn't really speak to anyone freely; I had to be over-the-top optimistic. Even though I didn't want to deal with the stress of trying new foods, I had to make faces like I loved it.

Next we had the late-night talk show. I just did it. I just got through it.

In the morning, we were picked up from my uncle's house for the big conference. Hundreds of students gathered in the university quad to greet me. I met with the president of the school and got a little tour, with the cameras following along. My mom never had to nudge me to smile anymore. My smile was so stuck, it hurt.

My speech was mediocre at best. I shouldn't have waited to write it on the airplane. I talked about the state of the App Store and how you could make money there. It was that basic. If I had given this speech in Silicon Valley, I'd have been laughed out of the room. People would say, "Why are you talking about this? I could Google this." But surprisingly, everyone here responded with, "Wow, thank you so much." They were more grateful and more gracious to me than I deserved. As soon as it was over, students crowded around me, asking questions: "Where can I download this program? How can I do what you did?" Their curiosity was incredible. I knew a lot of them didn't even have a computer at home, let alone access to good Wi-Fi. So I tried my best to explain.

Back at my uncle's house, I stumbled upstairs to my late grandparents' bedroom. My mom and I were sleeping there, surrounded by photographs of my grandmother and grandfather, and a guardian angel headboard, which is customary in Peruvian culture—nearly every bedroom has an angel sticking out over the headboard, including my bedroom back in Miami. The whole room was flooded with photographs of our family, in black and white and in color, some faded to beige. Photos of my sister and me as babies were littered throughout the house: they were on every side table, stuffed into every drawer, and posted all over the walls of the hallways. It was as if this house belonged to us. I fell onto the bed, dead. My mom turned on the little TV and flipped to the news. I was being featured on three different news channels. "Look, look. Here you are! Look! Look! They're talking about you! Michael! Michael! Look!"

I covered my head with a pillow, unable to take in one more drop of stimulation. All day long—for years, actually—I'd been pretending to be an extrovert. But all of this attention, all of these people, they'd drained me completely. I just wanted to go to sleep.

It wasn't until I got home and checked Facebook that I realized how much my trip to Peru had changed my life, launched me forward in ways I never anticipated. Kids from Spanish-speaking countries, as well as others from India, France, and all over the world flooded my account with messages. Most were Latin American. They told me stories about their families and how proud they were to know that somebody who shared their heritage had made it in tech the way that I had. They admired me, fat or not.

As I was scrolling through hundreds of new message notifications, I picked one from what looked like a middle-aged woman from Peru. It read:

Hi, "Boy Genius of Apple"!
    I saw you on the "Día D" program last night. I have two daughters who live with me in Miraflores, Lima, Peru. I made sure both of them were in the room to watch your segment. You're a genius! . . . You have inspired me to push harder. And my daughters, too. One of them is ill; we're praying she gets better in time. She told me she wants to make apps like you do one day. I wish you the best of luck. Don't forget your roots and where you come from, Michael. God bless you.

How do you respond to something like that? I couldn't send her some one-liner I'd repeated over and over. I wanted to be eloquent; I wanted to say something meaningful. The best I could come up with was:

Thank you for your kind words. Please pass this message along to your daughters:

The world needs more Latina coders! And you don't have to be a genius to make a successful app or grow up to be an engineer. I am definitely no genius, in spite of my silly nickname. But here is what you have to be: You have to be tenacious, above all else. You must believe in yourself to the point where others think you're delusional. It was easier for me, in Miami with my fast Internet and good technology, than it will be for you. But if you are determined—*súper determinada*—you will succeed. I honestly believe that. And I believe in you! Love, Michael.

Chapter 8

Meeting Mark Zuckerberg

AFTER PERU, THINGS REALLY took off. 4 Snaps had reached almost a million users in the United States, and a few larger companies seemed interested in acquiring it. Two weeks after my trip, I flew to California with my mom to meet Mark Zuckerberg, at his request. My mom had no idea who he was, even though she had a Facebook account for sharing pictures with family back in Peru. Days before the meeting, she'd quickly Googled Zuckerberg's name; the only detail that stuck out to her was the fact that he was Jewish, like my father.

We took an Uber straight from the airport to the campus, where we were met by a recruiter named Emily and two intern coordinators.

Walking onto the Facebook campus in Menlo Park was like walking into Disney World, my favorite place on earth: there were colorful buildings; basketball courts; restaurants serving every kind of food; vending machines stocked with battery chargers, cables, headphones, and keyboards—all of it free for employees. There were gyms with personal trainers; complimentary dance, yoga, and aerobics classes; barbershops and hair salons offering high-end haircuts; on-campus doctors and dentists who could see you at any point during the day; and complimentary nutritionists to help you find a balanced diet. Every floor of every building boasted a micro-kitchen with multiple coffee machines; refrigerators filled with milk, cheese, water, and sodas; and all kinds of snacks, including three kinds of popcorn. A bike shop on campus allowed employees to borrow bikes of their choosing for an indefinite amount of time, free of charge, of course. When you had to do laundry, you just dropped it into one of the laundry bins scattered across the campus, and your clothes would be returned to you at your desk, washed and folded.

I don't know whose jaw was closer to the ground, mine or my mom's. "Too much, too much!" my mom kept saying. Her English wasn't very good and she was struggling to convey her disbelief to our guides. "I teach my son to make his own bed and do his own laundry—for him to never lift a finger?"

Our guides just laughed. "We believe that keeping our employees happy encourages them to work harder," explained Emily, high-fiving two women in aviator glasses as they passed by.

It was about the tenth time she'd high-fived someone while we'd been walking around, and I finally had to ask what was up. Emily pointed to a giant LCD screen in the middle of the courtyard where we were standing: "#HighFiveFriday" scrolled across in neon letters. *Ohhh.*

"I want to work here full-time," I whispered to my mom. I'd always followed Facebook in the news and I knew a bit about the "Move fast and break things" company culture, but until that day, I'd never realized it would be so . . . happy-shiny! It was definitely where I belonged.

I'd had a queasy stomach all day, wondering when I'd get to meet Mark Zuckerberg. Finally, when the campus had mostly emptied out—it was Friday, and people apparently left early for the weekend—Emily got a message on her phone. "Okay, guys!" she said, already walking away. "It's time."

My mom and I chased after her, into a towering glass office space with an open floor plan. "Are you prepared?" whispered my mom in Spanish. "Do you know what you'll say to him?"

"Nah, I'll just wing it," I whispered back, trying to sound casual. Why hadn't I prepared? What *would* I say?

"*Ay, Dios mío,*" said my mom, crossing herself.

We turned a corner, and there was Mark Zuckerberg, one of the richest people in the world, dressed in jeans and sneakers and a T-shirt, sitting at a simple white desk in a corner of the open floor plan. He stood up when he saw us. "Hi, Michael," he said. His grip was firm, and cold. Really cold—like my hand was wrapped in a Popsicle. The whole place was freezing, in fact (maybe to make sure the computers didn't overheat?), which was the only reason I wasn't sweating bricks at that moment. All I could think was, *Oh my gosh, that's Mark Zuckerberg! He knows my first name!* Zuckerberg looked almost as uncomfortable as I felt.

"Let's go inside and talk for a bit," he said.

"Yeah, sure, okay!" I gushed, following him into the fishbowl meeting room.

He sat down, picking up a soccer ball that was sitting on a giant beige table that could have come from IKEA. "Have a seat," Mark said, tilting back in his chair and dribbling the ball.

I sat down, waiting for my next command like a big dopey puppy.

Mark put his sneakered feet on the table. "Why did you make 4 Snaps?" he asked.

"I—I—" It was the easiest question in the world, but all I could think was, *I can't believe billionaires put their feet on the table!* In many Latin households, this is like the ultimate taboo, and it completely threw me. *Focus, Michael,* I told myself. *You're in this meeting right now, don't fuck it up. Just answer the question. This is such an obvious question! You get asked this all the time. Just answer like you always do. And be calm. He's so calm. Just be like him!* As my mind raced, Zuckerberg waited, looking at me expectantly. Finally I managed to explain that the idea for 4 Snaps came to me while watching my sister and her friends text photos back and forth within a text message group chat. "I love to observe how people communicate and play and then build new ways for them to do things they already love," I added. Then, "I really don't believe there's such a thing as an original idea, just new combinations of what's already out there."

Mark swung his legs off the conference table and bounced the ball between his feet. "Cool," he said. Was that his way of saying he thought I was an idiot? Or did he really think I'd said something worthwhile? By his expressionless face, it was impossible to tell. I bit my tongue and looked through the floor-to-ceiling glass window behind Mark, waiting for his next question. Outside was a lushly planted courtyard, broken up with several hulking cylindrical pillars. *Oh my gosh,* I thought. *Those must be in case someone tries to ram a car into the building!*

Zuckerberg interrupted my internal babbling with: "How did you decide that programming would be something you wanted to do for work?"

I should have said something smart. What I said was, "I don't like to work. I just like to have fun." Zuckerberg raised his eyebrows ever so slightly.

Oh no, oh no, oh no. Why did I just say that? It was a line I'd repeated in a million interviews. I had a file in my head of different answers to different questions, and the old "I just like to have fun" zinger was one I'd repeated so many times, it had just come out. Now Zuckerberg was going to think I was lazy. This was bad. Really bad.

I tried to clarify: "I mean, I like to code, and coding is fun, so it's like I don't have to work!"

That seemed to help. He nodded, bouncing the ball once on the table. "Are you into playing video games and stuff?"

"No, I don't have time to play games, I just like to make them." Another fallback line. I was so nervous that I was just spitting them out like an automaton. I was missing an opportunity to be myself, and it was all going by so fast. The rest of the meeting was a blur. And after fifteen minutes that felt like a split second, it was over.

Zuckerberg walked me out to where my mom was waiting. We shook hands again, and then Mark went to shake my mom's hand. "He's a bright kid," he said.

That's when, for some inexplicable reason, my mom said, "You know, my son is Jewish, too."

All my life, my mom had been fighting with my dad over what religion I was, insisting that I was Catholic, like her. But for Zuckerberg, she'd just tossed her religion under the bus. I put my hands over my face. I would have been happy if the earth had opened and swallowed me up.

But Mark was laughing, giving me a look like, *Moms, right?*

My mom wasn't done yet. "One more question?" she said, looking super embarrassed. We all stood there, waiting for her to come out with it. I think that moment lasted longer than any moment in my life. My mom stretched out her hand toward the spellbinding billionaire, but she couldn't seem to get the words out.

"Let me guess," Mark finally responded. "You want a picture?"

"Yes, please!" my mom said.

"Oh my gosh, my mom is so embarrassing," I mumbled. I was wearing a black T-shirt with a purple San Francisco–branded hoodie that I believed hid my fat rolls decently, but my mom wanted me to put on the Facebook hoodie we'd just bought in the gift shop instead. Not happening.

"Smile!" she said. *Please let this end,* I willed as I beamed my metallic grin, my chubby face flushing a thousand shades of red.

Still, my mom wasn't finished.

"Now"—she laughed nervously—"just one more, with me, too?"

Mark was being so patient about it all, but I could tell Emily the recruiter was freaking out about wasting his time. "Okay, last one and we're done!" she chirped. My mom handed her the phone, and she snapped one of the two of us flanking Zuckerberg. Then, before I knew what was happening, we were marched out to the lobby and waved off by Emily, who looked like she needed a drink or a hot bath or *something*. But she couldn't have been more relieved than I was that the day was over.

Chapter 9

Bye, Belen

FOR ALL MY SELF-TALK in recent months about how my apps were more important than college in the big picture, a part of me still wanted to go—to learn computer science from real computer scientists. I'd ended up getting into that new course Belen offered, but it was taught by a teacher who knew less than I did about mobile app development. The best thing I'd gotten out of it was that there were names for many of the concepts I'd come to on my own, through trial and error. I now knew, for example, that the blocky timeline I'd made when I was planning out 4 Snaps was called a Gantt chart.

Anyway, it was my time of reckoning: college applications were due the first week of December. Soon I'd find out if my C− average had killed my chances—or not. I was actually optimistic: I'd gotten really good scores on the SATs and the ACT. And I figured that if I wrote a college essay telling my story and explaining why I hadn't excelled at school, the admissions people would understand why I was different, why they should take me. After all, if a college accepted a student with straight A's but nothing else on their résumé and rejected me just because my grades were bad, that would be messed up.

A few days before my first application deadline, my mom appeared in my bedroom doorway, wringing her hands. "Michael, what happens if you don't get into college?"

I shook my head. "It's fine, Mami, I've done big things. I've created apps that have supported our family. I've been inter-viewed on TV. I've met Mark Zuckerberg!" I didn't tell her that my school's college counselor didn't share my confidence. "Your chances of getting in aren't very high," she'd warned me.

With my mom reassured, I went back to focusing on my essay about how I'd learned to make apps as a kid. But when I was done, it looked nothing like the moving showstopper I'd envisioned. I'd written it in a last-minute rush, and it was a mess. Then there was the question of teacher recommendations—I'd felt too embarrassed to ask most of them. I only felt comfort-able asking my statistics teacher—one of two teachers I loved at the school (the other being the teacher who ran the Model United Nations club)—who had agreed to write me a letter. Though I had a D in her class, she could still see my promise, often stopping by my desk to offer words of encouragement like, "My son and I saw you on TV the other day. I'm so proud of you! Just keep doing what you're doing."

It was partly thanks to her encouragement that I went for it and scraped together the funds—nearly $400 in total—to apply not just to community college and a couple of mid-tier East Coast schools that my college counselor had recommended, but a handful of Ivies as well. The dense, confusing financial aid applications were the hardest part. My parents found them even *more* confusing than I did thanks to the language barrier, so I filled them out as best I could and sent them in. Then I waited.

In March, whatever hopes I'd had that the universities would look beyond my crappy grades to the real-world work I'd done and clamor to have me were dashed. The bad news all came in at once: rejection, rejection, rejection. Only the commu-nity college next to my school and a mid-tier college from Rochester sent me acceptance letters—and I got into Rochester only because I'd met with a recruiter who'd been impressed by what I'd done with 4 Snaps. The letter said my grades weren't there and I was going to struggle, but that they were making an exception because they liked my "story." Not that much of an exception, though: I didn't qualify for financial aid because of my grades. So, if I wanted to attend, I'd be paying the full $50,000 annual tuition.

According to Belen, which boasted a 100 percent college acceptance rate, that was exactly what I should do. Other kids, at this point, might have turned to their parents for guidance, but that wasn't an option for me. Early on, when the restaurant was still doing well and my parents weren't financially dependent on me, they had been in control. But over the years, as I'd taken on more and more responsibility for our finances, I'd stopped asking my parents how to live my life. I parented myself. So when it came time to make a decision about college, I didn't ask them what they thought I should do; I simply asked myself. And I already knew the answer. I couldn't afford college—I didn't want to take out student loans and pay them off for twenty years—which meant I had to do everything I could to get hired at Facebook after my internship.

Still, I wasn't ready to tell my parents I wasn't going to college, so I spoke to the admissions office at Rochester and told them I would give them an answer soon.

Meanwhile, a week before high school graduation, Belen sent my parents a letter. My mom's hand shook as she held it out to me. As my eyes moved down the page, I felt my neck and cheeks flush. The letter was a threat. If I didn't pay my overdue tuition of seven hundred dollars "immediately," I would not be allowed to graduate with my class.

Tears blurred my vision, and I quickly turned away, blinking. I didn't want to cry in front of my mom. Any sadness I felt instantly converted to anger or faux indifference. I wore the mask in front of everyone: teachers, classmates, and family. I even lied to myself about the idea that I could ever be vulnerable. Feelings were for little kids—not the man of the house. I felt a familiar tightness in my chest, followed by a rush of heat between my ears, as though a furnace had been lit inside my head.

Spinning to face my mom, I said, "Why didn't you pay? You didn't even tell me!"

"We needed the money to pay bigger debts!" she cried.

Recently, they'd finally shuttered El Pollon. The family business was over, done.

"Oh, Michael, I'm sorry!" She sank to the edge of my bed and put her head in her hands.

Crumpling up the notice from Belen, I let it drop into the garbage. "It's fine," I said coldly. "Screw them. I don't need the diploma, anyway." I knew I was being a jerk—I'd known all along my parents were using my money to pay their bills—but I didn't feel like comforting my mother in that moment.

"I don't need it. I don't want it," I continued. "Not from this school."

My mom looked at me like I'd lost my mind.

"What are you talking about, Michael? You don't need it? That's not an option! You need your diploma!" A deep groove of worry had formed in the middle of her forehead.

"Don't pay the school," I said, starting to pace. "If they can't see we're in a dire situation . . . I hate them!" Before I could stop them, the tears were sliding down my face. Too shocked to brush them away, I heard myself say in a little-kid voice, "But you said you'd pay it."

"Michael, I said I'd try. But we didn't have it!" I could tell she was right on that edge—deciding whether to be the strong one or make me be.

And. There. She. Goes. My mom began to cry. She wiped her eyes with her fingertips so as to not ruin her makeup. I shook my head. Was this how other families functioned? Everything always had to be perfect on the surface: my mom's manicure immaculate, our car waxed and gleaming, the front lawn of the town house trimmed as evenly as Astroturf—even though, when you peeled back that top layer, there was nothing but dust. My mom went on and on about how she just wanted me to go to college and get a good education, but underneath her words there was no substance, no plan to pay for it. That was up to me to figure out.

"I wish Belen would be more forgiving with you," my mom said. "They know you are special!"

I shook my head. "I'm not special, Mom. What are you even talking about?"

"They know how hard you worked to get the Facebook internship!" my mom insisted. She'd lowered herself into a chair and was rubbing her temple as if a headache was setting in.

"Yeah," I said, a little more softly now. "That's the problem."

As I walked out of the room, I added, "I'll see what I can do, but don't count on it." *She doesn't understand,* I said only to myself. I was furious with my mom for putting me in this position, but I didn't want to make her feel worse than she already did. The restaurant was shut down, and as hard as she tried to keep up a good front, my mother's spirit seemed to have shut down with it. Some days, she would drive by our old house just to catch a glimpse of the life we used to have. Both my parents were slowly falling into a depression; I could see it in the way they bickered, then fell into glum silence. The other night I'd caught my mother sobbing while she watched a sitcom on Univision. I couldn't bear seeing this. It made me feel devastated and heartbroken to see her this way, but at the same time, I didn't know how to comfort her. All I wanted to do was fix this. Somehow.

I'll call the school official who happened to be taking me to task that day Mr. Thanos, after the coldhearted character from *The Avengers*—because honestly, he scared the daylights out of me. Not because he yelled at students, but precisely the opposite. Mr. Thanos never raised his voice or registered any emotion at all, even when faced with a tearful seventeen-year-old begging for a chance to graduate.

So there I was, sitting with Mr. Thanos, pleading for mercy. I'd tackle my financial issues later; first, I needed to make up for all the work I'd missed while preparing for my internship interviews and traveling to give speeches in South America.

"Please, Mr. Thanos. I'll do anything if you just give me a chance. I'll take more tests, do more assignments—anything!"

Mr. Thanos leaned back in his too-small desk chair, lasered me with his dark brown eyes, and smirked. "What was it they called you on TV? The Boy Wonder of Apps?"

"The Boy Genius of Apple," I offered, not knowing better than to correct him.

"Ah, yes," said Mr. Thanos. "The Boy *Genius* it was. Shame you couldn't have applied some of that genius to your studies here at Belen. It's a bit late now, I'm afraid. Even if you did pay your unpaid tuition, there'd still be your subpar grades, not to mention . . ."

A pause filled the room as Mr. Thanos hunched over to open a drawer, pulling out a manila folder labeled "Facebook." Uh-oh.

Earlier in the year, the administration had discovered the Belen Student Facebook Group, a private page where kids would share homework assignments, dumb memes—and complaints. We weren't planning a coup or anything, just commiserating about what many thought was bad leadership at our school. Which of course should have been well within our rights. But the administration didn't think so. As punishment, they'd canceled our senior prom. I'd also heard rumors that kids who'd posted especially "disruptive" commentary might be barred from walking in graduation. I'd never been singled out, though, until now.

Mr. Thanos handed me a page printed from the Facebook

group, pointing to a comment I'd written. I don't remember exactly what I said—probably something about how I wished the president of the school would take my apps more seriously.

As I returned the sheet of paper to him, my hand shook just as much as my mom's had when she'd read the letter from Belen a day earlier. I tried to steady my voice: "Mr. Thanos, please, I didn't insult anyone! It's not that bad . . . is it?"

Mr. Thanos was eye-lasering me to my chair again, though he remained unnervingly calm. "You won't walk in graduation," he said after a long pause. "You'll attend summer school to make up for your many absences. You'll pay your tuition. *Then* we'll talk about a diploma."

I burst into tears right there in front of him. After a few embarrassing sobs, I wiped my nose on my sleeve, blinked, and in the bravest voice I could muster I said, "I can't go to summer school. I have an offer from Mark Zuckerberg! To intern at Facebook!"

Mr. Thanos pushed back his chair and stood up from his desk. "Mark Zuckerberg can wait."

So, that was that. Authority had spoken. I went straight home, called Mark Zuckerberg, and told him I couldn't do the internship—summer school was more important.

Ha ha. Hell no! Kidding, obviously.

I ended up going to the school president and convincing him to let me walk in graduation—even though I wouldn't be graduating, now or ever. He relented on the ceremony but made it clear that I wouldn't be getting my diploma until I finished paying the tuition. That was fine by me. I'd quickly gotten over caring about that piece of paper and what it signified. Something about stepping out of the heavy school gates after my meeting with Thanos—out of Belen's walls and into the blinding blue afternoon—had made everything clear. All that mattered was the internship, the chance to move on. And letting my mom get her picture of me in a cap and gown, of course.

—

"Michael, wake up! You have to get ready!" With a snap and an excruciating burst of light, my mom opened the blinds on my bedroom window. The night before, while I'd been hunched over my computer in bed, she'd carefully ironed my navy uniform and gown, laying them out for me on my chair.

I dressed quickly and was sweating through the synthetic fabric before we even got to the car. It was a typical boiling-hot, disgusting summer day in Miami, and my family stood outside our black Mazda SUV fitted with an all-black interior with the doors open and the AC on to let it cool down enough to be safe. "Ugh!" I moaned, tugging at the collar of my robe. "I just want to take it off!"

My sister rolled her eyes. "Let's just go already." She wasn't looking forward to living alone with my parents. With me gone, my mom would have even more energy left to worry about my sister's grades, which had never been that great, either. Pushing me aside, Mariana plunked into the backseat, then immediately screamed, "Ow! The seat belt burned me!"

On the ride to the graduation ceremony, my mom lectured me again about how I was supposed to keep my diploma folder closed for the pictures so no one would see that it was empty. She was nervous, applying and reapplying her lipstick in her compact mirror as she talked. My dad was quiet, but when he glanced at me in the rearview mirror, I could tell from the tilt of the lines around his eyes that he was smiling. That was a relief. I hadn't seen those laugh lines in a long time—at least not since my parents had given up the restaurant. Some men had come to look at the chairs and tables yesterday. The restaurant's new owner had decided to keep it exactly as it was, which depressed me even more. Soon the sign on the façade would advertise some other family's business and there was no changing it back. I wondered what my mom and dad planned to do for work. Did they expect me to give them my salary from the internship? We hadn't talked about it. Because if we didn't talk about it, it wasn't a problem, right?

At the ceremony, I walked across the stage and smiled at my mom. True to their promise, Belen had withheld my diploma, replacing it in the decorative folder with a gigantic phone number scrawled across a sheet of white paper in blue pen. I recognized it as the office number for the school.

Afterward, when my classmates and I posed for pictures, I did my best to pretend I actually belonged there. I'd been so walled off from my peers all those years that I didn't even know the names of half the kids surrounding me. And if I'd *wanted* to go to a graduation party that night, I wouldn't have known where to find one. In my periphery, I could see Lucas, one of the only true friends I'd ever made at Belen, hugging a pretty dark-haired girl. Had he gotten a girlfriend? Since he no longer bothered to talk to me, I wouldn't have known, but I'd heard through my mom that he'd gotten a full scholarship and was planning to study computer science.

Finally, the group picture-taking was over with, and the other kids broke off to pose with their real friends. As my mom fluttered around, bragging to anyone who'd listen about my internship, I was grateful that some of the other parents came up to talk to me. "We heard about Facebook!" they'd say, patting my sweaty back. "What an achievement, congratulations!" I willed myself to be cool about it—to reply with a simple "Yeah, thanks," and a shrug. But I couldn't help beaming and gushing back to every parent who approached me, "Thank you so much! I'm so excited! I can't believe it happened!"

My mom tore herself away from the other parents and came trotting over to me, her high heels sinking in the grass. My dad trailed behind, wearing the pleasantly detached look he gets in big crowds.

"Micky, take one of me and Michael," said my mom, putting

her arm around me and squeezing. Then she looked into my eyes and said sweetly, "This one with the book closed?"

I held up the closed folder and my dad took the picture.

"Okay, Mami," I said, pulling away. "You got what you wanted. Can we go now?"

She squeezed my arm. "Yes, we can go. Thank you, Michael. That's all I wanted."

We celebrated at our family's most-special-occasion restaurant, a Benihana-style Japanese place where they set your food on fire. And then we went home, all smelling like smoke and garlic. My mom went straight to her bed to post pictures from the day from her phone to Facebook, and with the little energy I had left, I tried to stop her.

"Mami, don't post those! I look fat!"

"Michael, don't worry, I'm going to Facetune out the fat. The family is expecting them today, I can't keep them waiting!"

"Ugh, I'd rather you just not post them."

Ignoring me, my mom started uploading my photos into the Facetune app. "Look, I'll just do a little here, a little there . . ."

I gave up. I didn't have the energy to argue.

The only extended family members who cared about my graduation photos were surely fast asleep in their beds in Peru, but there was no point in arguing. As I trudged up the stairs to my room, my mom was already calling after me, "Michael, your aunt Cecilia says congratulations and that you look so grown-up! And your uncles Miguel, Kike, Mario, and Carlos all congratulate you as well!"

"Okay, Mami. Tell them I say thanks," I called back.

"Make sure you like their comments, okay? Can you go to Facebook and do that right now, Michael?"

"*Okay,* Mami!"

I was about to close my bedroom door when she shouted up again, "Oh, listen, Michael, this is really nice . . . Michael, are you listening?"

"I'm listening!" I replied, gripping the knob on my door so

hard my knuckles showed white through my skin. I thought I
might actually die if my mom didn't stop soon.

"It's from one of your cousins! He says, 'Michael has great
things ahead of him! I bet he will be a millionaire by thirty!'"
my mom shouted up to me. "That's nice, right?"

"Yeah, Mami, that's nice," I said quietly. I could care less
about becoming a millionaire. I just wanted stability.

Chapter 10

The Countdown Starts Now

"Promise me again, Michael."

"Oh my gosh, Mami!" I puffed out my cheeks and rolled my eyes. "I promise I won't forget about you!"

My family was saying goodbye to me outside the security checkpoint at Miami International Airport, and each one of us was acting 100 percent true to form: My mother was making a spectacle; I was embarrassed; my dad was patiently waiting his turn to speak; and Mariana, annoyed that my departure was making her late to a nail appointment, was only just barely tolerating all of us.

"*No puede ser!*" my mom lamented. "My baby's only seventeen!" She was starting to cry a little bit.

My dad sighed, patting her on the back. "Come on, Mami, don't get like that. He's almost an adult, and he'll be back in a couple of months!"

"Yeah, Mami, he'll be back before you know it," said my sister.

"I'm okay," sniffed my mom. "I'm fine . . . It's just that I'm remembering you when you were tiny and I held you in my arms." She began to mime rocking a baby with a faraway look in her eyes.

I slung my bag over my shoulder and reached around her to hug my dad. "Bye, Papi."

"Bye, son. Good luck with——"

"When you were little, you loved your candy!" interrupted my mom. "Remember, I used to buy you those long, swirly lollipops? They were bigger than your head!" Now she was laughing and sobbing at the same time. "Do you remember that, Michael?" I needed to get on that plane before Mariana spontaneously combusted with embarrassment.

"Of course I remember. Bye, Mami, I love you," I said again, hugging her. "I promise, I'll send you pictures all the time, okay?"

In the security line, I turned to look back over my shoulder. My sister and dad had already disappeared, but my mom was still standing there. I gave her one last little wave and turned around, my thoughts already three thousand miles away.

The official start date of my internship, which came with a free apartment, was still a week away, but I'd left early and booked a hotel so I could attend the Apple Worldwide Developer Conference. WWDC is a yearly summer event where Apple announces new software and products, and big-deal engineers give lectures on how to work with the new features. Imagine a couple thousand programmers all being raptured up to techie heaven at once, and you've pretty much nailed it. I was almost as excited about WWDC as I was about starting at Facebook.

The Univision documentary crew had flown out separately to film me at the event. They'd booked rooms at my San Francisco hotel, which my mom was happy about. She'd come to trust the crew, as we all had. Over the three years that Marcello, Charline, and Rocky had been occasionally checking in on me for Univision, they'd become like a second family to me. Marcello, in his forties, was the oldest, and the one who usually interviewed my parents and me for the documentary. I thought of him sometimes as a younger, cooler version of my dad. Rocky was in his early twenties and in charge of doing all the camera work for the production, along with piecing together all the clips in postproduction. He was always the person I could count on to talk to. He gave me a window into what life was like as an independent young adult. Charline was in her late twenties. Her role as the executive producer for the documentary was to coordinate the logistics. I could always trust Charline to tell me if I had food in my teeth before a shoot, or to talk me down if I was in a fight with my mom. So as excited as I was to be out on my own, I had to admit I was happy the three of them were with me in this strange new city. San Francisco was a world away from Miami and so totally other to me, with its crazy hills, uptight Victorian houses, and bone-chilling summer fog.

In a downtown diner packed with twenty- and thirtysomethings, Marcello placed his 1080p professional-grade camera on the table and high-fived me, grinning.

"Got your sleeping bag?" he asked.

"Heck yeah!" I pointed to where I'd stashed it under the table at my feet.

Charline pursed her lips, looking out the window at a man in ragged clothes stumbling through an intersection. "Are you sure you want to do this? What if you get mugged?"

"Oh, don't worry, there's plenty of security," I reassured her. I planned to spend the night with the other hard-core attendees who lined up in lawn chairs around the block the night before opening day. When the doors opened tomorrow at eight a.m., we'd be the first inside, stampeding into the main hall to nab front-row seats to the keynote address by Apple's CEO, Tim Cook.

Charline had managed to score permission to film me at the event—no small feat, as Apple is very strict about whom they let into the conference. They don't allow big cameras, so a fourth crew member she'd sent for the day filmed me on his phone.

"You sure you don't want to stay out with us?" I asked Marcello, licking ketchup from my fingers.

Marcello smiled. "Sounds . . . fun, but I'm sure we'll get what we need on our visits."

After I fueled up on enough greasy diner food to take me through a winter in Patagonia, the four of us walked to the Moscone Center, a monolithic glass building flanked by a row of flapping flags. A long line of shivering programmers, the majority wearing identical black WWDC-branded hoodies and square-framed glasses, already snaked to the end of the block. I joined up with a couple of guys I'd met on Twitter, grateful to see familiar faces.

"Dude, you didn't bring a chair or anything?" said Oliver, a skinny blond twenty-year-old programmer.

"Nah, just this." I yanked my mummy bag from its case.

"You can take turns in my chair sometimes," said another kid in the group. "Sidewalk's cold."

"Cool, man, thanks," I said as Marcello filmed us. I could sense that he was enjoying this moment, seeing me getting along with people around my age.

Throughout the long night, my Twitter friends and I traded stories about our apps, ate pretzels, and basked in our shared excitement. It felt good to be around kids who spoke my language, who thought of me not as the App Kid but as just another kid who liked to code. This was what I'd been missing the last four years: solidarity. The relief of knowing that there were some places in the world where I fit in.

At eight a.m., the doors opened, and I threw myself, laughing crazily, into the stampede. Marcello, who'd returned just in time to catch the mad rush on video, joined me inside for the keynote lecture. "You guys don't mess around." He laughed, shaking his head.

The lights dimmed, and Tim Cook appeared on the stage before a prominent Apple logo at the center of the massive wide-screen displays. He began the keynote by highlighting the diversity of their developer conference attendance that year. There were record numbers of nationalities, young adults, and online participants. As Cook spoke, I was already plotting my next move: to get a picture with him. To state the obvious, Cook is like a god to programmers. For us, getting a moment with him is as monumental as a tween girl getting to meet Beyoncé, or a die-hard tennis player scoring a selfie with Federer.

When the keynote speech ended, I rushed to the main hallway, where what looked like a hurricane of bodies swirled around Cook and his orange-shirted security guard. Tim was moving toward the exit, and the swirl of kids in hoodies was moving with him. "Over here, Tim!" they shouted, waving their phone cameras above their heads. "We love you, Tim!"

I knew I had to get to him before he made it to the door, but I wasn't going to get anywhere chasing after that mob. Instead, I intercepted them from the front, then began pushing my way through the bodies to the eye of the storm. Once I finally elbowed my way to Cook's side, I reached past his burly security guy, sticking out my hand and gushing, "Oh my gosh, hi! I'm Michael!"

Cook returned my handshake. "Where you from, Michael?" Everything about him said understated success.

"I'm from Miami!"

"Cool," he said, giving me a friendly smile. "The Heat are doing quite well, aren't they!"

I had no idea, had never given a shit about basketball. What if it was a trick question? "Go, Heat!" I raised my fist in the air. "Um, Tim, could I get a picture with you?"

The second he nodded his consent, I was leaning into him and raising my phone, grinning from ear to ear. *Snap!* I thanked him and was off. I'd gotten my fifteen seconds; it was time to give someone else a chance.

After pausing to tweet the Tim Cook photo, I made a beeline—with Marcello running alongside, filming—for the pressroom. I wanted to see if any reporters might be interested in hearing about 4 Snaps. The app had been steadily marching down the charts since I'd stopped promoting it to turn my attention to preparing for the internship. But now I was reenergized about 4 Snaps—as if some of the Apple CEO's magic had rubbed off on me during our handshake.

For the rest of the conference, I was a whirling dervish. I chatted up several reporters, getting 4 Snaps back in the press and sending it a few spots higher on the charts. I did a podcast interview with a guy whom I'd met previously on Twitter—and who would go on to build and sell a product-review website that would make him a millionaire. I'm pretty sure I never stopped smiling for the entire event. But unlike the fake cheer I'd plastered on for my various press appearances in the past, my happiness was authentic. Now that I was thousands of miles away from home, my family's financial worries felt far away, too, and all I could think about was the future—*my* future—and how impossibly, thrillingly wide open it was.

I was still grinning the day the conference ended and I Ubered to my new apartment in Mountain View, in the heart of Silicon Valley, near the Facebook campus. Stepping out of the car, I hurried along a red terra-cotta pathway through a Spanish-style complex with lush lawns, past a sparkling swimming pool that I'd obviously never use, and up a flight of stairs to the sunny two-bedroom I'd be sharing with my mystery roommate. What was the first thing I did in my brand-new place, with my newfound total independence? Order a pizza, of course.

My roommate arrived as I was scrolling through my phone and polishing off my sixth slice. He was tall and skinny with round glasses and carried himself with a slight hunch, as if to apologize for his height. "Hello, my name is John," he said with a thick accent, dropping a giant, bulging suitcase. John, I learned, was from China, had attended a prestigious Ivy League university, and would be working on infrastructure at Facebook—back-end stuff that even I find boring to talk about because the only people who interact with it are other programmers. I had a feeling I'd see very little of John over the next three months, since both of us would spend the vast majority of our waking hours on the Facebook campus. But that night, we both tried to put our best foot forward. John had heard about a Korean place that served boba. I didn't know it at the time, but boba is practically a sacred drink in Silicon Valley. People debate over which spots serve the best version of it with almost as much intensity as they argue over whether to use tabs or spaces as indents in writing code.

The boba place was packed with interns from Facebook, Google, and Apple. It was a tiny shop about the size of my mom's kitchen, with close to forty people squeezed inside and another two hundred or so in a line stretching all the way around the block. We could barely hear each other over the din of the crowd. When I finally got my boba tea, John excitedly asked what I thought of it.

"I love it!" I said, giving him my best fake smile.

John tossed out his empty cup and glanced at my full one. "Should we go home and prepare for tomorrow?"

"Yeah, gotta prepare!" I faked a final sip, then discreetly tossed out my tea.

Back at home, we closed our bedroom doors. While John compiled his Internship Goals spreadsheet or whatever highly organized task he was doing, I stayed up all night watching TV on my computer, posting, tweeting, and checking 4 Snaps. I was hardly unconcerned about the challenges ahead, though. Ever since I'd boarded the plane to San Francisco a week earlier, a ticker-tape mantra had been looping through my mind: *The countdown starts now. Three months to secure a full-time offer. Get planning. The countdown starts now . . .* But, unlike John, I had no idea how to prepare for the biggest day of my life. And sleep? Who could *sleep?*

At six a.m., I finally let my phone drop to the mattress. At seven-thirty a.m., I vaguely heard the click of the front door and John's footsteps receding down the pathway. The Facebook shuttle came every half hour until nine a.m. and then only hourly after that. I was supposed to check in with my internship coordinator at nine, which meant I could squeeze in another forty-five minutes and catch the eight-thirty, no problem. My last thought, before falling back into a deep slumber, was that I should probably set an alarm.

Chapter 11

All Set?

NEVER DID SET THAT alarm. Now it was ten and I was an hour late for my first day at work. Sweat dappled my T-shirt as I charged through the Facebook campus, zigzagging by clusters of annoyingly relaxed workers. Why was everyone moving in slow motion? Just thirty minutes earlier, I'd jolted awake, looked at the time on my phone, and shouted some words that would've sent my mother straight to St. Thomas Catholic Church to light a candle for my soul. After grabbing a dirty pair of jeans from the floor, I'd caught the last shuttle of the morning with seconds to spare.

I skidded to a stop in front of a temporary booth marked "Intern Registration." "Hi, hi! I'm sorry I'm late!" I panted to the women at the booth, covering my mouth. I hadn't even looked in the mirror before running out the door. Why hadn't I grabbed a toothbrush kit from one of the free vending machines all over campus? Who knew what was stuck in my braces?

"Don't worry, you're good," said one of the women. She had long brown hair, sunglasses, and a T-shirt that read, "What's on Your Mind?" like the placeholder text in the new-post box on Facebook. I couldn't tell if she was smirking at me or if her mouth was just permanently like that.

"Are you Michael Sayman?" said the other, who looked to be

in her late thirties and had wildly curly hair with highlights—more Jennifer Lopez, less surfer girl.

"Yeah!" I panted. "How'd you know?"

"We heard there was a really young kid starting," said the woman with sunglasses.

Did I really look that young? Bummer.

"Welcome to Facebook, Michael!" said the curly-haired woman. "I'm Selena and this is Sarah. You can still catch some of the commencement address. Go on in!"

I slunk into the back row of a crowded meeting room as a guy in a crisp button-down was explaining how to take advantage of the thousands of perks and benefits that would be available to us for the next three months—from endless free dining options to state-of-the-art health services to gym memberships, yoga on the lawn at sunset, and on and on. He gestured at a giant rack stuffed with Facebook-branded backpacks. "Make sure to grab one of those later. It'll come in handy for the new laptops you're about to receive!" The room erupted in hoots from the nearly four hundred programming geeks anticipating that new tech in their hot hands. Earlier, we'd given the intern coordinators our preferences: PC or Mac? Android or iPhone? I'd picked Apple everything, of course. I couldn't wait to get my hands on my new stuff.

I wished my old friend Lucas were there to see all this. It seemed like a million years ago that we'd watched live-blogged Apple product presentations together. We'd been true Apple fans together, feeding off each other's excitement about the promise of tech. And then, well, I guess I'd chosen that tech over Lucas's friendship. I was pretty sure that was how he'd see it, at least. It hadn't been an active choice, just plain laziness on my part. I'd let my one real friend slip away because of my intense focus on developing apps. Where was he now? Probably working a summer job to save for college—the path I hadn't taken. If we still talked, it would've been cool to know what that path looked like.

My attention snapped back to the speaker at the front of the conference room. He was holding a hand in the air and reminding us to walk *slowly* and *carefully* to the laptops and bags without trampling one another. "Everyone got it?" he said.

"Got it!" four hundred engineers yelled back.

"Okay, then! Go on and—"

Before he got to "grab 'em!" we were already on our feet and running for our free tech. It was like Christmas morning on steroids.

With my own gorgeous, shiny, top-of-the-line, maxed-out fifteen-inch MacBook Pro in my hands, I was suddenly gripped with terror that I didn't belong here with these twentysomething kids from fancy universities. I heard them talking about programming at a level of sophistication that I didn't understand. And with good reason, as most of them had developed their skills under some of the best computer science professors in the world. Meanwhile I relied on question-and-answer sites like Quora and Stack Overflow to keep up. My application must have been put in the "yes" pile by mistake. Some overworked intern coordinator had messed up. At any time, someone could—surely *would*—tap me on the shoulder and demand that I hand over the goods and leave. The possibility filled me with dread, and with it came a conviction that I would have to work extra hard to pull the wool over their eyes and make it look like I knew what I was doing.

I couldn't stop gawking at my surroundings. Facebook was in the process of building a new campus designed by Frank Gehry—but I couldn't imagine how anything could beat our tree-lined Main Street, which I'd learned was in fact modeled after Disneyland. No wonder I felt so at home in this place. I loved its multiethnic restaurants and old-timey barbershops and candy stores and soft green lawns to lie down on when you needed a break.

Inside was nice, too, but sadly less Disney-like. My desk was one of hundreds in a sprawling, industrial-feeling space. To encourage collaboration and egalitarianism, Facebook Just Said No to walls. There were no private offices, not even for Zuckerberg himself—though he did get a designated conference room. Colorful murals covered almost every hallway, and workers sat around in beanbag chairs in glass-walled meeting rooms with names like Tangled Earbuds; Like, Totally; and Not Found.

A few days into my internship, I plunked down my new backpack and said hi to Jake, my manager, who sat next to me. He was on the Parse team within Facebook, where, thanks to my early connection with the platform, I'd be working, too.

"You made it," said Jake, a tall, skinny Asian-American guy who wore a uniform of blue jeans and a plain black V-neck T-shirt.

"Yeah, sorry!" I looked at my watch. Ten-twenty. I'd overslept again and Ubered to work.

"Hey, it's your internship," said Jake. "Let's go to Tangled Earbuds and figure out a project for you."

Jake had seen the embarrassing pajama video that had been my entrée into Facebook, so he thought of me as a game guy. In the meeting room, he explained that he thought my experience would lend itself to building a game module—specifically, a generic, turn-based game model that any developer using Parse could plug into. The idea was to save people from having to reinvent the wheel every time they built a new game.

"What do you think? Sound like a fit?" he asked me. I scratched my head. I'd heard that at Facebook, they were really into letting people follow their passion, and this module thing was definitely not mine. This was infrastructure, what my roommate, John, lived for. Me, I got lit up creating things for users. I was way less interested in thinking about what some imaginary programmer wanted and needed than what an imaginary gamer wanted and needed. But I didn't have a better idea, and Jake's sounded . . . well, at least it sounded useful. A premade back-end module was definitely something I could've used when I was building 4 Snaps. Maybe it wouldn't be so boring if I imagined I was building it for my past self?

I told Jake that it sounded like a great idea.

"Great! Then we're all set?" said my manager, obviously impatient to wrap this up. His Android watch was buzzing on his wrist, and he rocked up and down on his toes, like he was warming up for a sprint.

I felt a little bit like throwing up, like at Belen every time I'd walked into a final exam I hadn't studied for and knew I'd fail. But I switched on my TV smile and said, "All set!"

Scene: The Facebook offices, two weeks later.

Jake: [*At his desk, glancing over at my screen*] Morning, Michael. What are you up to?
Me: Oh, you know, just getting started!
Jake: It's three p.m. Have you been working on the module?
Me: Kind of . . .
Jake: [*Staring at me with a blank expression*]
Me: I mean, yes! I'm totally on it! [*Pulling up a single line of code*]
Jake: [*Turning back to his work*] Cool.

Twenty minutes later . . .

Me: [*Clicking away from same line of code to Facebook Messenger, beginning to type . . .*] Hi, would this be a good time for that cup of coffee?

This is how my life looked, more or less, for the first month and a half of my internship. I knew how irresponsible I was being. I could see the big picture: If I wowed Jake and his bosses, hopefully even Zuckerberg, I stood a chance of getting hired full-time at Facebook, which was likely my *only* path to financial security given my lack of a high school diploma or college plans. This internship was my golden ticket. I cared, I cared, I cared—desperately—about succeeding. But I just couldn't get to that module. Instead, I spent the first month and a half of my internship meticulously programming and designing a transition animation for a volume button that would morph from an on to off state. No matter how niche or random that sounds, it was designing and programming animations for user interfaces that fascinated me. The code was just a means to an end. It wasn't what I was tasked with doing.

I knew myself better than to try to force the code for the module. As with any kind of writing, to code well you have to dig in and find your inspiration, even when it's buried so deep you feel like you're mining for diamonds with a blunt spoon. The problem was I couldn't even find my spoon. I was so used to working on my own apps that finding a balance between the aspects of programming that I loved and the ones that were required for this project was tough. Really tough. I'd get there, I told myself. And in the meantime, I had to do *something.* I decided to push forward on a different track, work the opportunity my internship presented from another angle. At the Apple Worldwide Developer Conference, I'd sought out a random programmer for advice on how to get hired in Silicon Valley.

"Should I just keep building my apps?" I'd asked him.

"Nope," the guy said. "You've already built a bunch of apps. You've got thousands of twelve-year-old followers. But it's the people *inside* your industry who will choose you for their teams or recommend you for jobs. What *you* need to do is network like a fucking boss." And then the guy walked away to talk to somebody important.

As daunting as it was, that advice stuck with me. I got into coding because I loved it, not to work my way to the top. But I often thought about how, if I'd never cold-emailed that Parse designer to pitch 4 Snaps, I never would have met the marketer who invited me to make the video that captured Mark Zuckerberg's attention. Who knew where I'd be if I hadn't networked? At my parents' place, probably—sitting at the kitchen counter, sweating over the next app that would make or break my world. I never wanted to feel that fragile and precarious again. I made a promise to myself to devote the rest of my internship to networking like a boss. I began by reaching out to market researchers, data scientists, and other people at that level, telling them I'd like to learn about their experiences. Rarely did someone decline to meet with me. Most people, I've found, will embrace the opportunity to be a teacher.

The secret, I learned, was not to talk about myself, beyond saying enough to reassure people that I was competent and worthy of their time.

A good networker is confident, don't get me wrong, but I tried to steer the conversation to the other person's accomplishments whenever I could. I asked: "How did you get your start here?" And then I shut up and listened. Most people love talking about themselves, so usually they talked for a while.

My favorite trick was to ask, "Would you be willing to introduce me to three people that you think I should meet?" at the end of each conversation. I'd ask for three names because I figured it would be easier for people to say "no one is coming to mind right now" if I only asked for one or two.

True to my vow to network like a boss, I sometimes had two or three lunches or bobas a day. I met everybody and anybody that I could. I had burritos with a Facebook chef, ate ice cream with a marketing manager for Instagram, had pizza with an admin in PR, and so on. Slowly but surely, I met someone who introduced me to someone who introduced me to someone who introduced me to the chief marketing officer at Facebook, Gary Briggs.

Gary was the first guy I'd met at the company who tucked in his shirt, a real grown-up with a friendly face and graying hair.

My nervousness about sitting down with such a senior person at the company went away the minute he shook my hand outside the conference room next to his desk.

"So, how do you think Facebook is doing, Michael?" he asked as we settled into a pair of armchairs inside.

"Oh!" I said. "Okay, that's a big question!"

Gary laughed. "Answer it any way you want."

"Well, you guys own the territory of long-term memory and significant moments posting," I started. "That's so awesome! And I'm a huge fan of the redesign. In the months you were rolling it out, I was constantly refreshing my page, and, like, every morning I would Google how to get the latest beta! Oh, and the single-column Timeline is super sweet. I update mine all the time!" As I paused to take a breath, I realized how unsophisticated and gushy I sounded. "Sorry, I'm just super excited to be here," I said.

"Hey, don't apologize," said Gary. "This is great! I have two teenagers. I wish I could get them to think this much about Facebook!"

"Yeah, I might be more into it than most kids my age," I admitted.

But as into Facebook as I was, it had become clear to me that there was trouble ahead for the company. "The truth is, people of my demographic are losing interest in Facebook as a product because of the long-term nature of the content that can be posted. Not to mention the stagnant friend graph of each user that I've noticed is challenging for people my age to come to terms with, given the life stage they are in. Friend graphs change rapidly during the later years of a teenager's life. Facebook doesn't provide an easy way for its users to feel like the product reflects that change," I explained.

"Anyway, I don't want to nerd out too much here, but I'd love to share more of my thoughts with you on what I am afraid Facebook will have to address in the near future. I had a lot of fun talking to you," I said, noticing we were out of time.

Gary nodded, looking thoughtful. "It's fun talking to you, Michael. We should do this again."

As I rode the shuttle back to my apartment that evening, my mom called to check in.

"*Hola, Michael! Cómo estás?*"

"*Hola, Mami, todo bien!*"

I was bubbling over with positivity, recounting my great conversation with Gary—the freaking CMO!

After a while, my mom said, "Michael, you sound *different*."

"Different how?" I said.

"I don't know." She paused. "Lighter. You sound lighter."

"You mean, skinnier?" I said. Thanks to my regular networking lunches and the two orders of pasta Alfredo I often ate daily, I was definitely not getting skinnier. In fact, I'd packed on the "Facebook Fifteen," the typical weight gain new employees experienced from eating all that free food.

"No, I mean, you don't sound *serious*," said my mom, in a way that told me she did not think this was a good thing. "Are you taking this internship seriously, Michael?"

I sighed. In my mom's eyes, work wasn't supposed to be fun. She had been raised to believe that career and pleasure were mutually exclusive things in life—basically the opposite of the Facebook ethos.

"Yes, Mami, I promise I'm taking it seriously." And I was. I went home exhausted at the end of every day from my rigorous networking.

"*Michael, me preocupas! No me dices nada de lo que está pasando en tu trabajo en Facebook. Estás seguro que todo te está yendo bien? Me preocupas porque sé que a veces eres desordenado. De repente eres muy confiado, no sé. Ten cuidado.*" ("Michael, you worry me! You don't tell me anything about what's going on at your job at Facebook. Are you sure everything is going well for you? You worry me because I know you're messy sometimes. Maybe you are very trusting. I don't know. Be careful.")

I was starting to feel exasperated. "*No te preocupes, Mami. La gente en Facebook está feliz conmigo. Por supuesto, me cuesta a veces debido a mi estilo de trabajar, pero me entienden y saben como soy.*" ("Don't worry, Mami. The people at Facebook are happy with me. Of course, sometimes it's hard for me because of my style of working, but they understand me and know how I am.")

She sounded entirely unconvinced. "Okay, Michael, *no más te preguntaba. Sabes que me preocupo.*" ("Okay, Michael, I was just asking you. You know I worry.") She paused, as if trying to keep a thought from escaping, then blurted, "*A veces me da miedo que te boten del trabajo!*" ("Sometimes I'm scared that they'll kick you out of work!")

"*Jaja, Mami, no me van a botar. De eso no te tienes que preocupar. Yo sé que te preocupas—no te preocupes. Todo está bien.*" ("Ha ha, Mami, they won't fire me. You don't have to worry about that. I know you worry—don't worry. Everything is fine.")

Then, to escape from her relentless lecturing, I did the only thing I knew how: I pivoted. "Remember you said I sounded lighter? Well, you're right. I do feel lighter."

"Lighter" was the perfect word for me, in spite of the extra Alfredo pounds. Since I'd gotten out of myself and started paying attention to other people, the viselike stress headaches I'd been getting since middle school had stopped coming. For the first time since I could remember, I stood up straight without any effort at all.

Chapter 12
_____

Shine or Fail

A MONTH INTO MY internship, I got to experience my first Facebook Hackathon. Growing up, I'd gotten this idea from the movies that hacking was always bad—like when evil geniuses took over the heroine's computer to ruin the world. And that *is* one kind of hacking. Malicious hackers are different from what we call hackers within the computer science world, people who enjoy researching and discovering new ways to build upon and improve code. So-called white-hat hackers are trained professionals who help businesses by finding the weaknesses in their systems. In movies, white-hatters are the arch-rivals of malicious hackers.

"Hacking" is nearly always a positive word in Silicon Valley. It isn't about destroying things; it's about coming together and solving problems and creating things. When you hack, you're not just following directions and working with a prescribed set of ingredients. You're using your own ingredients to put something together and make it your own.

At Facebook, I quickly learned, company Hackathons were (and still are) a revered tradition—and key to the company's business model. People put aside their official work and spent three days straight coding whatever they wanted. You could participate whether you were an engineer or a lawyer or a human resources specialist, and you could work solo or in a group. At the end of the three days, you presented your project, and the three best ones were passed along to Mark Zuckerberg for his review. A lot of big Facebook features—like the famous thumbs-up "like" button—had come out of Hackathons.

On a Wednesday morning in June, an announcement from the Hackathon coordinators popped up on my screen, above my gaming console project, which was still just that single line of code: "It's Hackathon time. Let your manager know they won't be seeing you for a few days if you're participating."

That afternoon, I followed a mass exodus to the orientation in one of the big group rooms, where we were greeted by the sunglasses-wearing, supernaturally perky Facebook activities director, Hannah.

"Hey, everybody!" she shouted to the room with extreme enthusiasm. "Are you guys ready for Camp Hackathona?"

"Yeah!" I hollered back with the crowd. Secretly, I was resenting the fact I wouldn't be able to schedule a single coffee or lunch date for three whole days. I was quickly realizing that my internship wasn't necessarily about writing some amazing code; it was about making sure that as many people as possible could see the value I was creating with that code. I was still high on the novel human connection thing that happened when I left my laptop at my desk and sat across a table from a person who was also doing their best to converse without looking at their phone, as people seem surprisingly willing to do when you get them talking about themselves. I'd spent so many years working alone on my apps that I'd forgotten what it was like, back in school with Lucas—or with Mariana and her friends—to laugh and share stories with flesh-and-blood people. I'd be surrounded by hundreds of people at the Hackathon, of course, but that was different. Not a lot of deep conversation happens between glassy-eyed programmers in full coding mode.

But the deeper reason I was dreading the Hackathon was that I was scared I wouldn't be good enough. I could really code only by using Google at every step, and I was sure that wasn't the case for the other programmers at Facebook, who all seemed to be better educated than me. (I would turn out to be wrong about this: *all* programmers look stuff up as they work! And certain aspects of my programming skills were unique to me.)

At the end of the orientation, Hannah began tossing T-shirts in the air, and I joined the mad scramble to catch one, feeling like an overgrown nine-year-old at a birthday party. The graphics on the shirt included the words "Camp Hackathona" with a drawing of a campfire that had yellow lines shooting out of it. I pulled it over my other Facebook T-shirt and waited for instructions.

"Okay, everybody!" called Hannah. "Find your group and come up with your ideas! Then email us your project, and that's it! Is everyone ready?"

"Yeah!" we cried again. This activities director really was good at her job. I was starting to feel buzzy.

"Okay, go hack!" she cried.

I found three of my colleagues from Parse huddled on some couches in a lounge and asked what they were working on.

"Hey, Michael," said Victor, a lead designer at Parse. "We're thinking of creating a dynamic photo format to replace the old grid style for albums. It'll be like a collage, with size and shape variation, maybe some movement." He went on to explain that, through facial recognition software, photos of the most important friends in your network would be highlighted, and people in the outer circles of your group would get less real estate on your page.

An engineer at the company added, "It will be about telling a story, not just laying down a bunch of photos, but letting them interact. Hey, we could do some animation! Michael, you could bring something to this. Work with us."

Maybe he was being nice. Part of me feared that everyone in the group was thinking that having me on board would mean more work for them, not less. But I decided to suspend my fears and join in. Even if I knew I'd have a lot of questions.

Once Victor, our leader, had semi-patiently answered dozens of my questions, the four of us bowed over our screens and dove into writing code. This looked nothing like in the movies, where 3D graphics and animations were forever popping out of programmers' screens. How in the hell could anybody work like that, after all? It felt good to be working again, how I imagined fiction writers feel when they began the process of translating a story from their mind onto the page, only our language was Objective-C instead of English or Spanish or what have you.

Originally created in the 1980s, Objective-C was the first "true" programming language I'd ever learned. In 2014, it was still required to build products for iOS devices, so we all had to use it. It was super old-fashioned: most anything a newer language would handle automatically, Objective-C required you to input manually, using a ton of clunky square brackets. It was probably the wordiest language out there. Writing in Objective-C felt like taking thousands of teeny-tiny steps up a mountain, only to realize a few hours later that you'd climbed up a hill.

My team and I were already deep into that inchworm process when a flurry of activity in the courtyard drew us out of our screens. Under a dusky sky, a caravan of carnival-colored food trucks drove in and formed a circle in the courtyard. I abandoned my laptop and ran from truck to truck, sampling the free fare—a cup of mac 'n' cheese, a Chinese burrito, a slider or three. Stuffed and happy, I stayed up until dawn, tapping keys with my team.

Obviously, in hindsight, Facebook wasn't *altruistically* showering us with money and free food while we played on our computers. Hackathons have always been key to the company's business model. When two hundred or so engineers are freed up to pursue their passion projects, there's a very real possibility that a game-changing feature will come to fruition. (My team project, for which I can take zero credit, was later adopted and patented by Facebook. It's the basis for their albums today.)

At the same time, Hackathons give workers a break from their daily grinds to form new connections and recharge their creative batteries. Bottom line, they're ingeniously efficient productivity extractors.

If I'm sounding a little starry-eyed about Facebook for your liking, keep in mind that I started there in 2014. Sure, some reports of data breaches had begun catching our attention, there was your run-of-the-mill trolling, and mental health experts were starting to suggest to the world that maybe spending hours every day "liking" our happier, richer friends' posts wasn't all that great for our self-esteem. But the way most of us saw it from the inside, I think, was: Hey, when you have 1.23 billion customers (as Facebook did at the time—they've now surpassed 2.8 billion), not *all* of them can be happy customers. It was easier, then, to dismiss Facebook's missteps as unfortunate by-products of the company's "Move Fast and Break Things" ethos.

With that caveat, I want to take a moment to talk about why Facebook was, and probably still is, a great place to work.

If you've heard of Moore's Law, you know that computer processing speeds have doubled every two years for about half a century now (though that will probably end soon). Naturally, that acceleration has caused—and will keep on causing—massive shifts in the employment landscape. For all its mounting problems, Facebook has created a culture that helps workers not only adapt to but thrive on all this rapid change and discovery.

I wish more companies—*all* companies—would take notes on the creative ways Facebook engages and sustains their employees' passion for work. Imagine the innovations that could emerge if every sector of the business world cultivated employee happiness and growth instead of perpetuating the tired and completely outdated "Stick to what we hired you for" model.

Lecture over.

Despite our success in the Hackathon, I was worried about the project I was tasked with but not very interested in. "My intern is something, all right," Jake told a group of Facebookers a few days after the Hackathon wrapped. We were at a campus Mexican restaurant that served margaritas after five, and all the drinking-age people laughed extra loudly. I laughed too, nervously sipping my empty virgin margarita.

"I'm not kidding," said Jake, leveling me with a smirk. "It's been nearly a month and I don't really know what Michael does."

"What have you been up to, Michael, besides going out to lunch?" asked a senior developer named Kevin, whom I'd invited to lunch the week before.

"Uh—" I shifted in my chair. "I've been animating a couple of buttons that people could put on their pages to—"

"The fucking buttons!" Jake interrupted, pounding the table for emphasis.

Everyone laughed. I looked at the table.

"Well, I get really excited about implementing my own ideas, and I'm actually really proud of the subtle animated transitions of these buttons. But I haven't yet figured out how to get excited about this intern project."

Jake threw up his hands. "Says the seventeen-year-old intern!"

Kevin looked more sympathetic. "Are you saying you don't know how to get motivated, or you don't want to?"

I thought about that for a moment. "All I know is . . . if I can't get excited about seeing the finished thing in my mind, I can't seem to start."

Kevin snapped his fingers. "You should talk to my friend Andrew. He just got promoted to engineering manager, and he's a genius at talking people through stuff."

"That would be great!" I said, feeling Jake rolling his eyes. I knew he thought I was being a spoiled baby, but I didn't care. I'd been grateful for his hands-off approach to managing me at first, but now I needed some serious guidance.

Andrew was on my video chat screen, blowing his nose. He was visiting his grandmother in Michigan and had caught a cold, but he'd accepted my invitation to chat anyway, thanks to Kevin's referral.

"So you're saying you want to get hired full-time—but you don't know how to convince yourself to work?" he said, wrinkling his forehead.

"Pretty much, yeah," I admitted. I was obviously an idiot. An idiot who was wasting a stranger's grandma-visiting time with a stupid non-problem. I shook my head. "Sorry, you know what? I'll figure it out. I didn't mean to bug you."

"You're not bugging me," said Andrew, running his hand through his brown curly hair. "I'm a manager now, so this is my job, to help people." I breathed a sigh of relief. "And I can tell you that there's no way you're getting hired if you don't get your shit together, fast."

"Right," I said, swallowing a lump in my throat.

"How long would the module project take you to code if you were inspired?" asked Andrew.

"Oh, man, about two weeks!"

"And you have a month left?"

I nodded vigorously. He was actually taking my non-problem seriously!

"Here's what I think you should do," said Andrew firmly. "You should just finish this project in the two weeks you say it would take you, and then you can work on all the fun things you're excited about, Michael. That is, if you want to work at Facebook long term."

Eureka! Minutes—possibly only seconds—later, I found Jake working in a beanbag chair in one of the lounges. He stretched out his long body and looked up at me, hands laced behind his head, as I breathlessly laid out my new plan for total internship domination. I explained that I was going to build the entire gaming console in Objective-C and also in a cleaner code called Swift, so it would be more accessible. I'd thought of the Swift layer on my way over to him, and since it was my idea, I was actually kind of excited about it. I crossed my arms and waited for Jake's verdict.

"You're going to build it in two completely different languages." Jake sounded dubious.

"Yeah!" I said. "I'll make an Objective-C module for experienced coders and a Swift module for beginners. I'll build something for everyone!"

"Are you sure you can do this in a month?"

At this point, my adrenaline dipped just enough for me to realize that even though I was feeling pretty confident, I should probably lower his expectations, just in case.

"I'm not *sure* I can finish the second layer in time, but I am going to try my best," I told Jake, adding, "I am really, really hoping for a full-time offer at the end of this."

"Noted," he answered.

A lot of the interns at Facebook were really shy about wanting a full-time job. I think that coming from college backgrounds, they weren't used to having to advocate for themselves so much. Their approach was to be quiet and work hard and hope to be recognized and appropriately rewarded. As you've probably noticed by now, waiting and hoping has never been my tack.

I finished building the module in two languages in two weeks, somewhat surprising even myself. Then it was time for my final presentation to Jake and a few other managers, including the head of the intern program. This was going to be the easy part.

I was good at presentations. I owed this entirely to one of my sixth-grade teachers. She encouraged me, and a handful of other students, to join the Model United Nations club, which she helped lead. Outside of that, she was very open about the fact that she hated working with sixth graders. But since she was stuck with us that year, she would teach us what she believed was the most valuable thing anyone could learn in school: how to give a presentation.

My teacher would give us a new topic every week. Each student would have their turn standing in front of the class, talking nonstop for forty-five minutes on the subject with no photos or notes; behind us, we'd have a slideshow that we had to move through without looking over our shoulder once. Afterward, there was a fifteen-minute Q&A period, where the other students would compete to ask us the toughest questions possible, trying to knock points off our grade. We became really good at answering people who were trying to screw us over. Most important, we learned that giving a presentation is as much about emotion as it is about words. It was crucial to convey the emotion you wanted your audience to feel.

Another key thing my sixth-grade teacher taught us: always weave a story into your facts. So I talked about the difficulties I'd run into building 4 Snaps and how the simple, pared-down Swift module I'd just designed was exactly what I could've used back then.

After I took a round of questions, the group applauded. The surprised look on Jake's face was especially satisfying. I decided to take advantage of the moment and caught up with him as everyone filed out of the conference room.

"Hi! I hope you liked the presentation!"

"I did, good job," he said.

"Do you think you might mention to Anastasia how it

went?" I pressed. "Because I'm extremely interested in being considered for a full-time job." Anastasia, a tall Eastern European woman with a thick accent, was the head of the intern program. As the person who'd be writing my final review, she also held the keys to my future. I had already emailed her three times to let her know about my interest in staying on with Facebook. Her answers had always been vague and short. She'd intimated that the company didn't usually hire people full-time before they'd been to college—that Facebook didn't want to deprive young people of a chance to pursue higher education. In response, I'd *more* than intimated that I had no interest in attending college, whether or not Facebook took me on—pointing out that in the programming profession, skills were more important than pedigree. I could only hope that my lack of interest in college might come as a refreshing change, that maybe the company was sick of hearing *Harvard* this, *Stanford* that. I definitely was.

On August 25, 2014, the day after my eighteenth birthday, Anastasia called me into a conference room. I was so nervous and sleepless from worrying about whether or not I was going to get hired that I switched to autopilot the minute I shut the door, and I remember nothing about what happened next. Total memory wipeout.

When the meeting ended, I was in such a state of shock and relief that I couldn't have told you any of the details of the job I'd just accepted: that my title would be software engineer; I'd be making $110,000 a year plus bonuses, a whole lot of Facebook stock, and plenty of benefits; and I'd start in six weeks. All I knew, as I walked outside into the bright courtyard, was what mattered to me: I'd done it. I had a full-time job that would pay me twice a month. I would be able to save my money because I was eighteen, and it would be mine. I would finally be secure.

Chapter 13
————————

Bitter/Sweet Independence

THE FIRST THING I did after getting hired was sprint outside the building and call my mom and dad. I'd told them that my meeting with the intern head was today, and my mom picked up after half a ring. "Michael?" Her voice wobbled like it always did when she was nervous. "Did you get the job?" Before I could answer, I heard a click, and my dad's booming baritone came through the line. "*Hola, hijo!* What's the news?"

"Yeah, yeah, I got it!" I said, bouncing up and down. They both burst into tears.

They were happy for me but probably also feeling a little guilty—and relieved.

The second thing I did after getting hired was post to Instagram and Facebook:

This summer internship at Facebook has been amazing, but it's not over. Facebook has offered me a full-time job as an engineer. The adventure is just beginning!

Right away, congratulations from my new colleagues began lighting up my screen. Even Mark Zuckerberg wrote to me over Messenger, saying, "We look forward to seeing what you build," which I wasn't expecting. By midnight, journalists from Bolivia, Peru, and Colombia had written to ask for interviews. It didn't occur to me that this could be a problem with my new, famously secretive employer, so I fired back to every one of them, "Sure!"

The third thing I did after getting hired was walk to my bank and open a brand-new account that no one but I could access. Because I'd been underage till now, the $21,000 that I'd made for my internship had gone directly into the account that my mom had full control of. I hadn't touched the money, because Facebook paid for my food, my transportation, and all my basic day-to-day expenses.

At the bank, I followed a nice woman into a tiny cubicle, plunked my Facebook-branded backpack on her desk, and handed her my never-used bank card. "Can we transfer what's in my old account to the new one?" I asked. I'd never even checked my balance, but I figured that since my mom hadn't asked for money lately, I should have a decent chunk to move from my old account to my new one. It would be a good foundation for the savings account Tío Kike kept nudging me to start.

The woman did some typing, then looked up over her glasses. "Sure. Your current account has a balance of seventy-seven dollars."

"What?" I yelped, suddenly on my feet. "That can't be right!"

The banker chuckled, shaking her head. "Have a seat, hon," she said, adopting a kindergarten-teacher voice as she walked me through the string of transfers my mom had made to her personal account.

"Oh," was all I could say.

"So, let's decide what kind of account you'll be needing, hon! Are you currently employed?"

The woman's eyes widened when I told her I'd be making over $100,000 a year. She made a call, and a guy in a suit appeared, leading me to a much fancier office. There, I was offered sparkling water and a slew of credit card and brokerage account options.

"Uh," I said, "I just want one where I can put money in and not really take it out, ever."

To the suit guy's great disappointment, I ended up choosing the kind of account where your debit card is declined if the account you withdraw from doesn't have any funds left over and where you get charged for making more than a couple cash withdrawals a month. Having never learned to save, I needed all the incentive I could get.

That evening, I called my mom and faux-casually informed her that I'd opened up a new Chase account, where my Facebook paychecks would now be deposited.

There was a pause, and then my mom said in an overly bright voice, "Good for you! That's great!"

"Really?" I said, relief washing over me.

"Yes, of course! You're eighteen, so that's the way it should be."

"Oh, well, cool!" So it was this easy to stand up for myself? I couldn't believe it.

"Maybe you can give me your password, just in case?"

I put my head in my hand, saying nothing.

"Ha ha, I'm just kidding!" my mom trilled. Whether or not she was, I knew right then that it would take more than a new bank account to help my parents build their own independence again. But hey, it was a start.

In one week, I'd be on my own. No more internship, no more free digs. The prospect of apartment hunting filled me with dread. Having no idea where to start, I put it out of my mind. When my internship wrapped up, I packed my suitcase; said goodbye to my roommate, John; and flew home to Miami. For the next month, I slept, watched TV, went to Disney World twice—I paid for my whole family's tickets, of course—went to the movies about a dozen times, ate a lot, and tried not to engage with my parents' ongoing financial dramas. They'd stopped offering me information about their financial situation, but I could see that things weren't getting any better. My dad's third attempt at a real estate career still hadn't taken off, and my mom was exploring the idea of starting a jewelry business. As my Facebook start date grew close and my apartment problem hadn't magically solved itself, I wrote a quick "looking for a room for rent" post on Facebook. Hours later, a guy I knew a little from the Internet but had never met in person messaged me that a room had opened up in his "hacker house" in San Francisco. *Wow, that was easy,* I thought. "I'm interested!" I typed back. "Details?"

The gist was that everyone in the house (he didn't say how many there were, and I somehow didn't think to ask) was in their early twenties. They were what you'd call Silicon Valley hackers—lone wolves who hate the idea of working full-time and code independently, making occasional money from selling their apps. The rent was $1,350, which I thought sounded very steep, but I was getting anxious to nail down my living situation, so a week before heading back to California, I confirmed with the guy that I would like to move into the hacker house.

One week later, I flew back to San Francisco and Ubered straight from the airport to my new home in the city at around ten p.m. It was in the center of the Castro District, a two-hour commute in rush-hour traffic to Facebook in Menlo Park. Most young Silicon Valley workers lived in the city and took the free Facebook and Google shuttles to and from work every day. I wasn't looking forward to commuting, but I figured everyone my age lived in San Francisco for a reason, so it must be worth it.

Regret kicked in the second I stepped out of the car. It was a freezing Sunday night and drunk, half-naked men stumbled out of thumping bars, hooting at the cold and tripping on homeless people, who lined the sidewalk in grimy sleeping bags and jerry-rigged shelters. "Shit," I said under my breath, trying to act as if everything were fine. Sirens blared and a string of cop cars sped past, running a red light. I gripped the handle of my suitcase tighter and stepped around the legs of an unconscious man who was sprawled under a cardboard sign reading, ANYTHING HELPS.

In Miami, you rarely saw people living on the street. It was just too hot. I'd heard that California had more unsheltered people than any other state. San Francisco and all of Silicon Valley had a particularly large homeless population, thanks to a housing shortage and the wealth bubble created by the rise of big tech over the last two decades. The average tech engineer here spent 40 to 50 percent of their salary on rent, not leaving much for savings, buying a house of their own, or eating out off campus. Some Silicon Valley CEOs, like Marc Benioff of Salesforce, had begun stepping up with their billions to fund hospitals and shelters, but obviously, it wasn't enough.

The GPS on my phone was telling me I'd arrived at my destination, but I couldn't see any residences, only restaurants and clubs and tattoo parlors. After walking up and down the block for twenty minutes, I finally flagged down a guy who was at least fully dressed and walking in a straight line.

"Hey," I said, trying to sound casual, "do you know where this place is?" I showed him the map on my phone, praying he wouldn't grab it and run.

"Right there, bro." He pointed to a dark, narrow staircase wedged between a gay nightclub and a grungy coffee shop, the bottom stair blocked by a guy in torn military fatigues and his equally tattered-looking dog. I stepped around them and found the key under the mat where my roommate had said he'd leave it. Super reassuring. As I fumbled with the lock, I felt the camo man's cold eyes on my back.

Inside, I walked into what looked like a crack den straight out of *NCIS,* except that the six or so scruffy-looking dudes who slumped on ripped couches were all typing furiously into laptops. The place reeked of garbage, and there were beer bottles and empty pizza boxes everywhere. A projector played an anime show from YouTube on a cracked wall. After I'd been standing there awhile, taking this nightmare in, a couple of the guys finally noticed me. They gave a "S'up?" and went right back to doing their thing. It was hard to see in the dark, but none of these guys looked like the profile picture of the guy I'd been talking to, so I messaged him, "I'm here." Right away, he wrote back: "Your room is the second one on the right." I looked around and didn't see any doors.

"On the right, where?" I typed back with shaking fingers. All I wanted was to shut a door between me and whatever this was and forget everything that was happening right now.

While I waited for an answer, the front door burst open and a bunch more guys stumbled into the room, pushing me against the wall as they started up a flight of stairs so small and dark I hadn't even noticed it. As the last guy in the group passed by the fat kid (me) trying to flatten himself into the wall, he did a double take.

"Hey. You the new guy?"

I nodded.

"I heard about you. Your room's upstairs. I'll show you."

I followed the guy to a cramped second floor, past a row of rooms stuffed with giant computer screens and more dudes, hacking and playing video games. It was stuffy and smelled like a thousand unwashed bodies.

My guide stopped in front of a closed door. "This is your room. Got the key?"

He waited while I fished it from my pocket, turned the lock . . . and stepped into a closet. I'm not lying: it was a closet, just barely a walk-in. Taking two steps across the space, I ducked under a narrow platform bed on precarious stilts, looking back at the guy in the doorway. "This is a room?"

"Yeah, this is your room."

"But is it *a* room?" I said. "It's just that it looks like a closet."

"You get what you pay for," said the guy, crossing his arms.

"But I'm paying a lot for this! Thirteen fifty!"

When the guy was finally done laughing, he said, "This is San Francisco, man," then shut the door behind him, leaving me alone in my closet.

I couldn't get out the door fast enough after my first night in the hacker house. It had been an agonizing seven hours of tossing and turning in my airless closet, the beat of the nightclubs throbbing through my dreams. For the first time ever, I jumped (okay, make that climbed) out of bed the minute I stirred semi-awake in the morning instead of going back to sleep three or four times. I quickly dressed, used the bathroom—careful not to touch anything; I'd wait to shower at the Facebook gym—and ran out the door without a word to the random people I apparently lived with now. This would be my routine for the rest of my time in the hacker house, which I already knew wouldn't last long.

God, I hated that apartment, and my dank, noisy San Francisco neighborhood, and the long commute to work, while I'm griping. My spirits would only begin to lift when the Facebook shuttle hit that last southbound leg of Highway 101, leaving behind the city fog and barreling into sunny San Mateo County with its rolling hills and ancient gnarled oak trees. Only then would my shoulders slowly come unglued from my ears, the fist in my stomach unclench. That's how it felt in those early days, anyway.

It felt like a place where everyone was filled with ideas and no one was just sitting around, waiting for luck to strike. They say in Los Angeles, everyone is working on a screenplay. In Silicon Valley in the mid-2010s, everyone was working on an app. Ask any Uber driver or barista or dog walker under thirty about their life, and they'd tell you about the million-dollar app idea they were going to make happen just as soon as they could afford to take the time. Ask any software engineer if they thought tech was going to save the world, and they'd tell you, *Duh, of course.*

I wasn't sure if that was true, but even still, Silicon Valley brought out the optimist in me.

When you join Facebook as a full-time employee, you go straight to boot camp. For two months, your job is to learn about how Facebook works, from the infrastructure out. There are courses in diversity, advertising and monetization, well-being, and how to take advantage of the millions of available company perks. You're assigned to a boot camp mentor, who ushers you through the orientation process and becomes your de facto advisor.

During that two-month window, each boot camp engineer, as they call the new workers, is up for recruitment. Managers from all over the company compete to lure the best programmers to their teams. It's like pledge week in the university Greek system, only the pledges hold all the power because every team needs as much fresh blood as they can score. Once a boot camper accepts a team's invite, they're expected to stick with that choice for at least a few months; then they're free to switch teams if they want to.

A few teams invited me to join them in my early weeks, but I dragged my feet on accepting an offer because I wasn't excited about the projects they were working on. Thanks to my internship, it was fresh in my mind that I shouldn't say yes when my gut said no.

My gut was telling me to hold out for a team that was working on the problem I'd been noticing since my internship: the Snapchat threat. In 2014, Snapchat was just becoming really popular, and everyone I knew loved it. But while Snapchat had every teenager in America in its thrall, Facebook was a non-player in most kids' social media lives. Sure, we used it for school meetups and other adult-sanctioned activities, but it wasn't where we went to hang out and be ourselves. Facebookers had to be panicking about this, didn't they? Not really. On the one hand, Facebook had acquired Instagram for $1 billion in 2012 and had recently forked out $19 billion for the messaging app WhatsApp. But in spite of these acquisitions, they still faced a formidable challenge in trying to capture and appeal to younger users. The prevailing attitude I saw from some people at the company was: *Nothing to worry about. We're unstoppable. Snapchat is just some random app that some teenagers use.*

Deflecting pleas from Jack, my boot camp mentor, to "just pick a team, any team!" I devoted all my time to dreaming up my own project, an app that Facebook could use to compete against Snapchat's massive teen market. Jack loved the concept.

He put me in contact with his manager, and I did the same presentation for him. That manager said, "I want Chris Cox to see this."

Chris Cox, the chief product officer, loved the concept, too, and quickly scheduled a time for me to pitch it to the top company executives, including Zuckerberg himself. I was a tangle of nerves walking into that meeting. Zuckerberg and the others were already seated on couches when I arrived, and they looked up from their phones at me in unison, like a single organism with eight heads—holding eight very valuable brains. Beneath their cool professionalism, I deduced from some of the execs' flexed jaws and erect postures that they were as nervous as I was. They were counting on me to sell my idea to their boss so they could take credit for seeing its promise and nurturing what might be key to Facebook's understanding of the teenage demographic.

"Hey, Michael, have a seat," said Cox, pointing to an empty spot on a couch next to a TV monitor.

I eyed the spot on the couch, trying to decide what to do. Every other time I'd presented my concept, I'd done it standing in front of my audience. My sixth-grade teacher, the Yoda of presentation-giving, had taught us that standing was key, the best way to convey the excitement and energy you wanted your audience to feel. The sixth-grade method had never failed me before, and I needed every edge I could get. But then again, Andrew, the engineering manager who'd helped me get my shit together as an intern and had since become my go-to guy when I needed help navigating the Facebook world, had warned me against standing up today. "When you're pitching a product," he'd said, "you might want to take it down a notch, be a grown-up at the table."

"Hey, Mark," I said. "Do you remember me? I'm Michael Sayman."

"Yes, of course I remember you," Zuckerberg answered, though his expression gave me no indication either way.

I was so nervous, there was no way I could do this sitting down. "Is it okay if I stand up?" I asked the billionaire.

"Um, sure," he said.

Some in the room laughed, and everyone else looked confused. But as I launched into the presentation with excitement and passion and energy, I could tell from the VPs' and directors' relieved expressions that they were happy. Also possibly amused, but I didn't care.

When I finished, all eyes turned to the leader, waiting for him to speak.

Zuckerberg was in no hurry. He looked out the window. He looked at the ceiling.

"Well," he finally said. "I think—I think this is interesting . . ."

The directors and VPs nodded, leaning forward in their chairs.

"But overall I don't really see how it's any different from, like, Instagram," our leader continued. "I guess the concept is cool, and there are parts of this that I really like, but I don't know about the whole thing."

Silently, I cursed myself for not sitting at the table like a grown-up. I'd blown it. Now what? Was it too late to sit down? Maybe I should just thank Mark and leave. Or let him leave first? I never knew the etiquette. I looked at Chris Cox, who was rubbing his neck with a pinched expression and seemed floored by this outcome.

"Mark, maybe we at least try it," said Chris eventually. "Personally, I love it. It's so different."

Now Zuckerberg was looking past me to a giant TV screen that mirrored the squiggly illustrations, emojis, and logo ideas I'd scribbled during my presentation. Was he grimacing? Oh God, I'd made a fool of myself. My presentation was unprofessional, a joke. If only I'd done a formal slideshow instead of showcasing all those crazy strategy funnels. What a mess. My stomach did flip-flops as I berated myself.

"I'd like to think about this more," Zuckerberg said in his über-calm way. Then he turned back to his phone, already on to the next thing.

A few days later, I got word that Zuckerberg had given me the green light to start a new team at Facebook focused around addressing the teenage demographic. And so I began the process of recruiting engineers from boot camp to join *my* team.

I knew the success I was having at the company was not about my being super smart. I had the advantage of being one of the youngest people at Facebook, and now I wanted to turn that advantage into something more. Facebook was started by college kids—Zuckerberg and some friends—*for* college kids, which was its secret to nearly instant success. To understand what their audience wanted, the founders hadn't needed focus groups and data analysis—they'd just looked to themselves and their friends. But by the time I got there, the people who'd built the product were now in their thirties, most with little kids. And they had kept on building products for themselves, not the *new* youth market, which they needed to retain their edge.

Realizing that no one seemed to be paying attention to this

really credible threat, I put together a presentation on teen social media habits and invited everyone I knew in the company to listen to it. Before I started my "Teen Talk," as I was calling it, I asked my mostly thirtysomething audience to take a little quiz about teen culture, with questions like: "What are acceptable use cases for the word 'lit'?" and "What band was founded by this top teen influencer?" As I'd predicted, everyone bombed. F's all around. This was understandable, I assured the audience. Now at least their eyes were open to how little they knew about the youth market and what that crucial demographic wanted from social networks. Then I went through each of the different social networks and explained how teens used them. Like: we posted on Instagram once a month, we almost didn't post on Facebook at all, we used Twitter occasionally, and we loved Snapchat and used it all day long.

The communication tools we use in our formative years will shape how we communicate and view the world for the rest of our lives. After explaining this concept to my audience, I reminded them that my generation, who grew up with iPhones, communicated differently than theirs—who'd grown up using phones strictly for talking—did. Using Snapchat to say hello to a friend who was standing in the same room as us felt natural. Spending a year chatting on the Internet with someone we'd never met in real life felt natural. To us, there was nothing sad about seeing our phones as extensions of ourselves.

People liked my Teen Talk so much that they asked me to give more talks, with different topics and focuses . . . The presentations got slicker, and within a month I was addressing rooms of several hundred product managers, design leads, and engineers while many others watched online. Little by little, Facebookers started to admit, *Yep, maybe we do need to do more to address our younger audience.*

Building on that momentum, I began posting regular "notes" to the company-wide Facebook page about teen engagement. Every day or two, I'd fire off another one.

One evening, I was riding the shuttle home and overheard two apparently fresh-out-of-college brogrammers—one in a Stanford hoodie, the other decked in MIT swag—talking about me:

"Hey, did you read that new note from the Teen Talks guy?"

"Facebook has so many users. It can't possibly be that bad."

"Yeah, it's like, Thanks for the biz dev advice, kid!"

"Right? Talk to me when you've been in the business for a few years."

[*Laughter.*]

The next day, I unfollowed every one of my adult Facebook friends, including my coworkers, for one day. With only my teenage friends left, I refreshed the feed. There was nothing there. Well, a few ads came up, of course, but no posts.

I took screenshots of my lonely feed and wrote a note about the experiment, titled, "This is what Facebook looks like for someone my age." Then I refollowed my coworkers and posted the note to the internal company page.

Another time, I had all of Mariana's friends take screenshots of their phone home screens to prove that the Facebook app was placed farther away from their reach on their devices than other social apps. (Snapchat, of course, was at the front and center of everybody's.) After I posted about that, Chris Cox asked to use my screenshots for his own presentation on teen engagement. But it's hard to tap into the teen brain if you're not, in fact, a teenager. An older coworker who knew what I was working on suggested we create a "teen zone" on Facebook where teens could have fun! I almost died when I heard that. A teen zone? LOL. No teen wanted to be put in a zone.

It was a catch-22. Being the youngest employee at Facebook was my biggest strength but also my greatest weakness. No matter how much a leader like Chris Cox valued my perspective and followed every internal note I published and talk I gave, it was still a constant battle just to be taken seriously.

One thing I came to expect at Facebook was that the "grown-ups" in the room would automatically assume any idea I presented had come to me on a whim. "Cool idea," they'd say. "It's great that you're passionate about it. But we need data to back it up." As a result, I got better at bringing a whole lot of data into every pitch.

While I was still a bit of a bratty teen, titling my internal posts with "TeenZone" to be tongue-in-cheek (I'm pretty sure it never occurred to my co-workers that I was using this expression sarcastically), I got better at listening. I made a big effort to hear what other people had to say and ask for feedback (always a good way to rattle someone trying to take you down a notch!). And I learned to emphasize that my age wasn't a weakness but rather a strength.

Using the new momentum I had, I started pushing VPs and executives to pay attention to the Snapchat threat. At the time, the culture and mindset of many was to be dismissive of Snapchat. But I knew in my gut it was a bad idea to discount the social media giant.

Chapter 14

Diversity Training

A FEW WEEKS AFTER Mark Zuckerberg gave me the green light to allow me to assemble my own team of three engineers and a designer, I started recruiting engineers. Andrew, who had morphed from my mentor into a friend—we texted constantly and grabbed dinner at least once a week— introduced me to one who was considered one of the best in the company. When he agreed to become my lead engineer, I took that as a vote of confidence in my project. I was also intimidated by the guy, who was known for extremely efficient code that could be reused across multiple products.

I was now expected to act like a product manager instead of a coder, but I had no experience running a team. I knew how to get people on board with my ideas, but I found it chal- lenging to help others carry them out. Mainly because I was inexperienced at scheduling and setting proper expectations.

"Hey, Michael," my lead engineer would say with a note of concern in his voice. "How are those mocks coming?" A mock is a critical part of the interactive design process that my engineer should've had from the get-go. It's an illustration of the interface elements that will exist on key pages of a game or website, a map for every member of the team to follow. As a visual thinker, I didn't have had any trouble collaborating with my designer to whip out mocks for my project. But no sooner would we draw something up than I'd trash it and start over.

What no one knew: I was taking so long to finalize these critical product design mocks because I'd started to lose confidence in the idea itself.

What if Zuckerberg had been right? What if it wasn't different enough from Instagram? The more times I redrew the mocks, the more I grew to understand the underlying root of the problem we were trying to solve, the more the doubt grew inside me, choking out my inspiration.

My indecision and novice management style were trying for all of us. But while my team members had no trouble going home every evening and brushing off the day's stress with beers or salsa dancing lessons or time with their kids, I lived with my doubt 24/7. It was turning me into a neurotic mess. At six p.m., my team would clear out, and I would continue working well into the night, my only company the evening cleaning crew. After even *they* left, I'd find myself sitting in the dark, waving my hand in the air to catch the light sensors, and eating protein bars for dinner. I had no hobbies. I didn't play any sports. Work ended when I was too tired to keep my eyes open and started the minute I opened them again. Not only was I in charge of this team and the product we were building, I also spent countless hours developing my monthly Teen Talks and a TeenZone bulletin, which thousands of the company's product leads and engineers subscribed to. Separately, I helped the executive team at Facebook strategize over the Snapchat problem, joining in on meetings where everyone but me was a VP or chief officer of the company. And to top it all off, I was helping Zuckerberg learn how to use Snapchat by snapping back and forth on the weekends.

My computer screen was a mess: filled with screenshot designs I planned to use in my talks, mocks for the product my team was building, and all kinds of unanswered meeting invites from product leads across the company. I also spent hours trying to predict Snapchat's next moves. Many of the predictions I presented at various product strategy meetings ended up proving to be accurate, and my credibility within the company grew as a result.

Afraid of burnout, I sometimes took to working from home or at a campus café, ignoring my buzzing phone. I couldn't ignore the Facebook comms team, though.

"So, it's the *Today* show, now, is it?"

The VP of communications was speaking to me from a giant monitor on the wall of the conference room where members of his team flanked me around a table. Facebook's chief technology officer was also there, I think to offer me moral support. He had been extremely supportive of me, always seeking to understand me. I was glad he joined in. I'd been summoned to discuss an invitation I'd received to appear on the *Today* show—an invitation that everyone in the room but me thought I should decline.

Admittedly, I'd been receiving quite a few press inquiries. After I'd posted on social media that I'd been hired at Facebook, a slew of South American reporters had asked to interview me about being the youngest hire ever at one of the best-known social media giants. Given the lack of diversity in Silicon Valley, and at Facebook in particular (where Latinos made up less than 4 percent of the workforce), it was a pretty big deal to a lot of South Americans that one of their own had climbed so far so fast.

Journalists who'd been covering my story since I was twelve continued to focus on my headline-grabbing backstory: how I'd helped my parents get through the Great Recession. My sense was that because my parents were no longer standing in the room where I was being interviewed, these reporters felt more comfortable probing beyond the feel-good narrative they'd been promoting for years. When they'd ask, "How was it that you decided to help your parents?" I'd give them a steely look and say, "Why wouldn't I?" Then I'd steer the conversation to what

I wanted to talk about: how I was proof that anyone, from any background, could code.

I often thought about a fifteen-year-old girl I'd met on one of my trips to Bolivia. "I've been watching you for a long time," said the girl, who'd traveled from a small town four hours away by bus. She gave me a woven bead bracelet that she'd made with a phrase written on it in Spanish: *Ni En Broma Digas Que Es Imposible* ("Don't even joke that it's impossible"). It's a quote I liked to use to close my lectures in Latin America. She remembered it, and it meant something to her.

It seemed only right to me that I should continue to share my story with other kids whose dreams had never fit the mold. But the VP had a point. "You work at Facebook now," the VP on the screen was saying. "You can't just go on TV and say whatever you'd like."

I could feel sweat trickling down the sides of my rib cage, which, on the bright side, was starting to make its existence known—I was starting to lose some weight!

"Michael," said the CTO, "I know your motives are genuine, but I think he's right. Maybe it would be better to sit this one out."

I told the comms team that I wanted to do *Today* to help make Facebook seem more welcoming to young, diverse programmers. They didn't seem very excited about the idea, though. It was a known fact that even off-camera opportunities to share stories about working at the company were usually nonstarters. I thought that Facebook, like most of Silicon Valley, could use a story like this to encourage more Latinos to pursue careers within their industry.

In truth, the comms team probably didn't want to take a risk with a slightly loudmouthed newly hired teen. And their cautious mentality had its reasons. It was how Mark Zuckerberg had worked since his Harvard days. And it was how they still worked, rarely allowing anyone but Zuckerberg and occasionally the COO, Sheryl Sandberg, to talk to the press. And even *they* did so only in very specific circumstances. Thank God I'd known enough to decline to pass along the Univision crew's request for an interview with Zuckerberg. Marcello, the producer, had pushed hard for that, warning me that without a big name to anchor it, my years-in-the-making documentary would be reduced to a fifteen-minute video on the network's off-brand Fusion channel. (That's exactly what ended up happening.)

Still trying to gauge whether a chance to be on the *Today* show was worth battling the intimidating forces of the Facebook comms team, I pressed on. "What if I don't talk about anything we're working on, just about how I learned to program and how I got here and stuff?" *And stuff?* Ugh. I needed to get it together.

"So, you want to promote *yourself*?"

"*No*, that's not it!" The words came out slightly louder and a lot squeakier than usual. My voice was still changing, and when I got stressed, it was particularly hard for me to calibrate my tenor.

I willed my voice to come out low and steady: "I want to promote coding. For other kids." *Other* kids? Good one, Michael. The last thing I needed was for them to be reminded of my age. This was not going how I'd hoped.

The CTO cleared his throat. "Michael, why don't we pause here? We can look at future opportunities down the road."

Nodding, I pushed my chair back, pulse racing, and walked *calmly, calmly, calmly* for the door. I had to get out of there before I made this any worse.

I beelined down the hallway, trying not to hyperventilate. I was sick and tired of being the youngest person in every room, the kid at the grown-ups' table.

You have so much more to learn, was the message I was getting. Yep. That much was clear.

—

"I'm thinking about reaching out to Maxine," I said to Andrew. "What do you think?"

Maxine Williams was Facebook's global chief diversity officer. Andrew had been counseling me for months on how to better communicate with my thirtysomething colleagues. "Try listening more than you talk," he'd offer, or "Maybe if you were more selective, and less like a machine gun firing ideas randomly all over the place?" Now he was referring me up the ladder of wisdom.

Like everyone else at Facebook as far as I could tell, I revered Maxine Williams. I'd see her around campus, casual but elegant, smiling and waving to everybody. She had what was considered one of the most important roles at the company, one she described as "expanding the funnel of people applying for positions at Facebook." The statistics, she had publicly admitted, were grim: Few Latinos and African-Americans even bothered applying to the company. As a result, the population at Facebook looked nothing like the population of the United States—which was a problem not just at Facebook, of course, but all across Silicon Valley. Maxine tried to tackle this head-on, by visiting high schools and low-income communities and encouraging kids in those demographics to pursue careers in computer science—and to ignore everyone who told them it wasn't possible.

When it came to employees' personal relationships with Maxine, she had a fairy godmother vibe, a way of making each of us feel like we belonged. I often thought about a story she'd told my boot camp group at a mandatory seminar on diversity. Her story started with something like "I'm from the Caribbean, but I don't know how to swim. Do you know why?"

The room of mostly white faces stared back at her. Maxine nodded patiently. This seemed to be the audience reaction she was used to.

"Were you afraid of the water?" someone offered. Maxine shook her head. That wasn't it.

"Did you live far away from the coast, so you never got a chance to learn?" asked another new hire.

"No, no, I lived right by the ocean," said Maxine.

Finally, an African-American woman in the room raised her hand. "Was it because of your hair?"

"Exactly!" laughed Maxine. "You're the only one who gets it!" She explained to the rest of us that saltwater presented challenges to her Black hair.

I came from a home where terms like "institutional racism," "microaggression," and "safe space" weren't spoken in any language; where someone's Peruvian mom might say stuff like, "Don't worry, Mariana, you can always marry a rich guy!"; and where kids still used "gay" as a put-down, so diversity training was an eye-opener.

While I knew that Maxine was more insightful than your average person at Facebook, or probably anywhere, I was surprised she was willing to take so much time with a low-level noob like me. Maxine's job, as far as I understood it, wasn't to life-coach employees. She had bigger things to deal with, like growing Facebook into an inclusive and globally diverse utopia. Or something like that.

But she seemed excited to help. So I went to see Maxine. We took our meeting strolling through the courtyard on campus, like most people did. (Because, of course, no one had an office at Facebook.) I told her about how I couldn't seem to connect with my colleagues and how no one seemed to want to take me seriously. Maxine nodded thoughtfully as I spoke, her gold earrings swinging almost hypnotically.

"This is really interesting, Michael. I think your biggest problem is the fact that you are avoiding this confrontation. Talk to your coworkers, sit with them. Share your feelings so they can hear how you feel directly from you. It matters so much more to hear it from the person who is hurting, rather than to hear it from some third party, right?"

As we passed the yellow Hackathon crane mascot, Maxine

explained how I would benefit from learning how to talk to my coworkers, rather than passing a problem up the management chain. First and foremost, she felt, we needed to learn how to communicate with one another. I thought about this, and how whenever someone pushed me, my first urge was to push back. What if instead, *I* took a step back and tried to see the problem from their perspective? I spent so much time sitting behind my computer screen, I sometimes forgot that I wasn't just pushing back against ideas and products all the time; I was pushing back against actual humans.

"Still," said Maxine, "there may be something to what you're saying about how people see you. I agree that some of that feedback isn't fair."

"You do?" Finally! Someone got it!

"I do," said Maxine. "Now, let me ask you something . . ."

"Ask me anything!"

"What do you think is going to happen in a few years, when you start to grow facial hair and your voice gets a little deeper, and you start to look more like an adult—maybe even grow a couple gray hairs?"

"Hopefully, the problem will stop," I said.

"I'm hopeful that it stops for you as well," said Maxine, laughing. "And I'm sure it will. But think about this: What if you couldn't grow out of it, and you knew they would always perceive you this way?"

I wasn't sure where she was going with this, but I was trying to stay with her. "That would, uh, suck?" I said.

"Women actually experience what you're experiencing permanently," replied Maxine. "Their entire lives. African-American men, as well. If they speak strongly, they're being 'too aggressive.' If they're quiet, they 'need to speak up more.' No tone lands well for them. So you're lucky, Michael, that you have the opportunity to grow into a fair-skinned thirty-something dude in the future."

"I never thought about it that way," was all I could think of to say.

"And hopefully sometime in the future, you'll put your understanding of what other minorities and other genders go through to good use."

I had to stop walking for a minute to recalibrate my thoughts. I was one of the lucky ones. The complaints I'd come to Maxine with suddenly seemed trivial. "We have to fix this," I said to Maxine. "I don't want to wait!"

Maxine smiled at me. I'd surprised her. "I'm glad you feel that way, and I appreciate your . . . passion. But the reality is that discrimination won't go away overnight. There are a lot more minds to change, first."

We finished our talk outside our office building.

"If you want . . ." said Maxine suddenly, "we have a program called Tech Prep. We send ambassadors into underserved communities to raise awareness about computer science and connect kids with free programming courses."

"Really?" I felt myself lighting up.

"Absolutely. You speak Spanish, right?"

I nodded.

"Done," said Maxine. "I'll vouch for you with the comms team."

I felt instantly deflated. Tech Prep was a comms team thing? Well, then it wasn't happening. Even though I'd finally caved and turned down the *Today* show, I felt the comms team was still wary of me. I was pretty sure they didn't want me representing Facebook to anyone, anywhere, ever. I should just forget it. Maxine wasn't *that* magical. Was she?

Chapter 15

Out on a Limb

FIVE MONTHS OF TINKERING later, I finally admitted the truth to my managers: the concept I'd sold them on wasn't strong enough; it was time to pivot. This was kind of the nature of the tech world. The approach was to forge ahead and then pivot as necessary. I'd been doing it with my own apps all my life, so I was used it. But it still felt scary to have to change course on something that Facebook had poured so much time and money into. My new concept was still teen-focused—but it would do away with other complicated elements I'd originally envisioned. More important, it would recapture the pared-down vibe of Zuckerberg's original, Harvard-days Facebook. The early Facebook had resonated with young adults in large part because it highlighted users' likes and dislikes at the top of their profiles. Over time, as Facebook morphed into a news outlet, it lost its appeal with younger audiences. My app would win them back by letting them share their favorite things via their favorite medium: video. It would be just like the Facebook of 2004, except all the different aspects of the user's identity would be represented by video clips—of their favorite restaurant, pet, song, or whatever.

My managers were incredibly nervous for me. They didn't have to spell out that I needed to bring Zuckerberg an idea that resonated with him or risk losing what was left of my credibility.

But Zuckerberg's reaction to my latest pitch shocked us all.

"This is really great and really smart," said the founder, grinning ear to ear as he studied the prototype—which was basically just a row of circles indicating where the "video highlights" would be depicted. "The video circles are perfect. Great job, Michael." Still smiling, he patted me on the back. My manager and several other executives in the room whooped. This was not the kind of reaction we saw from our boss often—or ever, come to think of it.

"Really?" I said, giddy.

"I'm excited to see where this leads us," said Zuckerberg. "Let's look into implementing it across all our products."

As the months wore on, though, a weed of doubt began to grow. Was my concept, which I'd renamed Lifestage, really strong enough to stand on its own? I was already having discussions with other product leads to integrate some of this into the existing Facebook and Instagram apps; perhaps it would make more sense as a feature, not a standalone product. Once again second-guessing my instincts, I made my programmers undo and redo their work every few months. It couldn't have been easy for them, taking orders from a kid. Especially a kid with no concept of work-life balance. I simply couldn't put myself in the shoes of an adult with other responsibilities and interests. One afternoon, I stopped by the desk of my lead engineer with yet another tweak to his work. Sam was one of the best engineers at Facebook; no one could write back-end architecture like him. He'd spent weeks planning and designing infrastructure for Lifestage that would keep the videos stable.

"Hey, Michael, what's up?" he said, looking up from his work.

I smiled. "Hey, I'm wondering if you have a minute." I paused. "I'm worried that some of the things we're working on are not going to work. We might need to make a slight pivot." He managed a smile as I rushed to add, "It's not going to be anything crazy—I promise!"

Although his frustration was visible, like the pro he was, he nodded and said, "No problem, I'm on it." Like the rest of my team, Sam was annoyed by my constant pivots but put those feelings aside because he believed my instincts were special. At the time I was something of a Facebook "celebrity," and while not everyone knew what I worked on, almost all ten thousand employees had heard about how important I was to the company's road map for teens. Sam knew my creative process was not linear or structured and believed that my skills in product made it worth his time to work with me.

Lifestage wasn't the only project I was working on. At long last, Facebook had decided to get serious about competing with Snapchat—particularly Snapchat Stories, collections of snaps that lived for twenty-four hours. So I was now helping to implement our own version of Stories for WhatsApp, Instagram, Facebook, and Messenger. I'd been yelling about the Snapchat threat ever since I'd given my first Teen Talk in 2014, and the executives had finally started to listen, including me in meetings and cc'ing me on memos about anything Snapchat related. I was brought in to review designs and meet with engineers and executive leadership to strategize about the company's overall goals for the product. Because Instagram Stories appeared at the top of the old feed, it wasn't necessary to build a new audience in a different app. As the unofficial gatekeeper of All Things Teen at Facebook, I was given a lot of latitude to express my opinions and my ideas were taken seriously. At times I clashed with other PMs, like the ones who believed that people should be able to upload content to Stories from the camera roll, giving them an opportunity to edit their photos first. As a huge proponent of unedited "raw content," I was very much against that idea, but ultimately, I was overruled. I did, however, find a way to incorporate Zuckerberg's beloved circular video highlights into the product.

—

Over the course of that year, as I focused more and more of my attention on Stories, I knew my Lifestage team felt frustrated by my distracted leadership. I just didn't know how to fix the problem. Lifestage whiplashed from the original concept Zuckerberg had loved so much, to an overworked design with too many categories.

Clearly, all the time I was spending on Stories, TeenZone, and the monthly talks didn't help when it came to where I was taking this separate app project.

Deep down, I was worried this app was destined to fail. The imaginary characters in my head had told me that this app wasn't really there; I just hadn't wanted to believe them.

I was power-walking around the campus rooftop garden, gulping for air as a mocking voice ranted inside my head: *You can't even build an app, you're just a big fake, Zuckerberg's going to fire you, your engineers hate you!* I burst into tears just as a tour group of teenagers led by a Facebooker appeared at the top of the stairs, of course. I'd come up here because it was so hot and windy, it was almost always empty. But now there were a dozen witnesses to my pathetic-ness. I ducked behind an oversize plant, tears streaming down my face, heart hammering. Only after twenty minutes did my heartbeat finally slow down, the knot in my stomach start to loosen. Then I headed home to wallow in my shame and self-pity.

I really needed to get a handle on that voice in my head. I was hearing it more and more lately.

At Facebook, they were always encouraging us to take advantage of their free mental health counseling. Apparently, something called Imposter Syndrome was super common among Facebookers. If you haven't heard of it, Imposter Syndrome is the persistent belief that you don't deserve to be in the job you're in, no matter how hard you've worked for the position. It's the unshakable sensation of not being good enough to be where you are right now—that you've succeeded due to some crazy stroke of good luck, not because of your talent or accomplishments. In fact, you believe that none of those accomplishments are deserved. You are a pathetic fraud, and the clock is ticking down to the moment when your colleagues and friends find you out and send you packing.

It was nice to know that I wasn't alone in feeling like the world's biggest con, but I didn't want to seek professional help. When I was growing up, my parents had always talked about therapy as a frivolous indulgence, a waste of money and time. Real people with real problems didn't tell strangers about their problems; they sorted themselves out, or better yet, as my mom liked to say, "*A veces, hijito, hay que dejar que Diosito se encargue de las cosas.*" In short: "Let Jesus take the wheel." What did I have to be depressed about, anyway? I had money. I had everything I'd ever wanted. I'd even gotten out of the hacker house and was living in a fancy two-bedroom in a sunny neighborhood in the city. What a spoiled brat.

The morning after the progress report meeting, I woke from an epic sleep to find blinding sun pouring through my bedroom window and my new roommate, Selena, pounding on my door.

"Michael? Are you getting up? We're going to be late for work." Selena was the very put-together project manager I'd met on the first day of my internship (she planned her outfits the night before). Comfortable, fashionable, and professional. A true adult. A few months ago, she'd posted that a room in her South Bay house was available, and I'd jumped to take it, not anticipating that living with a woman twice my age might have a weird mom factor to it.

No doubt about it, living with Selena was making me regress. As she went on knocking, I covered my head with my pillow, groaning like the high school kid my mom used to have to shake out of bed after I'd stayed up half the night on Club Penguin.

"Well, I'm leaving in ten minutes," Selena said through the door. I could hear the scuttle of her Yorkie's nails on the hardwood floor as she followed Selena around the kitchen.

After a while, the TV went quiet, the front door slammed. Maybe I'd skip work today. What was the point in going? How could I convince my team to believe in my vision if I didn't even believe in it myself? *No one will miss you, you lazy, worthless, fat piece of shit,* said the hater voice. *You could die, and no one would even notice you were gone.*

I called in sick.

Just as I was drifting back to sleep, where the voice hopefully wouldn't find me, my phone pinged with a string of texts from my sister:

Call me
Where have u been?
Are u ignoring me?

It had been only a couple of days since I'd been in touch with Mariana, but that was a long time for us. When I'd moved to California, we'd gotten closer, Snapchatting back and forth throughout the day about every little dumb thought that popped into our heads. In our last exchange, she'd sent a screen grab of an epic-fail video. Normally, I'd have fired back an LOL emoji, but I'd silenced my phone and fallen into bed as soon as I'd walked in the door last night. Figuring I'd better answer or risk Mariana getting my mom worried, I sat up and typed back:

All good. Call u later.

The phone rang in my hand. I sighed and picked up.
"Why don't you answer?" snapped Mariana.

"Sorry. I'm just really busy with work."

"You sound weird. Were you asleep? Where are you?"

I cleared my throat. "Just heading out the door for work," I lied.

"*Mmmm.*" I could picture Mariana's eyes narrowing. "How's that going?"

It was suddenly extremely important that I convince my sister everything was great. The last thing I wanted was to have my family worrying about me. All that would lead to was the usual lectures from my mom about how I shouldn't take Facebook's faith in me for granted and how I'd better shape up and count my blessings and keep up appearances and project a good attitude.

"Things are great!" I said. "In a couple weeks I'm going to Anaheim for four days. There's this giant YouTuber convention called VidCon. I can't wait."

I rattled on for a while about how I'd be meeting with all the big video creators and YouTube celebrities at VidCon to gather feedback from them on Instagram and Facebook's road maps. I was also going to introduce early prototypes of Stories to them. "Do you want any autographs?" I asked Mariana. She loved YouTube.

"When did you say it was?"

"Uh, starts Thursday after next." I looked at my phone calendar. "July twenty-third. Why?"

"Michael, you can't go."

I squeezed my temples with my free hand. The stress headaches had been coming back again. I just wanted to go back to bed. "Why?"

"It's a secret. Just trust me, you really don't want to go on this trip," said Mariana.

Eventually, I got it out of her that my mom had decided the family should pay me a surprise visit that same weekend. They'd already bought their tickets, which were nonrefundable and had probably cost my mom's entire earnings for a month.

I groaned. "I can't cancel it. It's all planned. I'm representing Instagram. I'm sorry, but Mami shouldn't have done this. I've told her before to not do surprise trips with me because of my crazy schedule."

"So you're going to ditch us? Waste Mami's money?"

I didn't have the energy for this conversation. I felt like an old man, not an eighteen-year-old in the prime of his life. "I'll figure something out," I told my sister. "Gotta run to work. Bye!"

God, it was bright in my room. Ever since I'd moved to San Francisco, I'd been bitching about the lack of sun, blaming it for my foul moods. I was paying out the nose for my room here because it was in a rare sunny location, and now I couldn't wait to get blackout shades. Squinting, I moved into the living room, where everything was beige and pastel, but I still didn't feel comfortable. I was particularly afraid to sit on the couch and mess up Selena's throw pillows. So many throw pillows. Just like at my parents', except my mom picked bright splashy colors, and my couch at home was broken in and inviting, with a worn leather ottoman wide enough for Mariana and me to stretch out on while we watched TV. I didn't want to admit it, but I felt suddenly homesick.

Selena's coffee table was glass and stacked with her favorite athleisure catalogs. Once I'd put my feet up on the edge of it and she'd scolded me like I was a naughty kid. I didn't even have my shoes on! Selena had trained me to take them off and leave them by the front door before I entered the apartment. I couldn't get used to that.

Until I moved to San Francisco, I'd never seen anyone take off their shoes inside a house. In my family or many others, it's considered dirty and disrespectful to do so. You might as well throw food on the floor. It's unthinkable. We even have a derogatory term for people who take their shoes off inside. We call them *patas sucias,* which means "dirty paws"—as in, "You're an animal."

Partly out of rebellion, and partly for comfort, I retrieved my sneakers from the hallway and pulled them on. That was better. After pacing around awhile, worrying unconstructively about the work I was missing, I sat on the floor and turned on the TV. As usual, a Wendy Williams recording came up. I'd hated the show when I first moved in, but it had grown on me, and I was on my third episode when Andrew texted: "Hey! I'm outside!"

He was on my doorstep, holding his coffee from Starbucks. Most people in San Francisco were more likely to get their coffee from the fatally hipster place down the hill where they brewed from cold beans in individual stainless-steel pots dipped in fairy dust or whatever, but not Andrew. He didn't care much for the whole hipster vibe in Silicon Valley. He was much more about practicality.

"Hey, man," was all I could manage. Behind Andrew, a street-light popped on. I looked at my watch: five-forty-five p.m.! How did that happen?

Andrew furrowed his brow. "Are you sick?"

It seemed easier to say yes, so I did, making something up about my stomach feeling bad. Andrew probably didn't buy it, but he didn't say so. A big reason why Andrew was one of the fastest-rising employees at Facebook—leapfrogging from engineer to manager to the director of a major division in less than three years—was that he was equally gifted at understanding technology and understanding people. Andrew always knew the right thing to say—when to offer constructive feedback, and when to steer the conversation in a new direction.

"Hey, wanna go to the sushi place?" he said now.

Fifteen minutes later, we were huddled in a corner table in a nondescript room eating California rolls with cream cheese.

"Feeling better?" he asked.

I nodded, pushing away my plate.

"Good," said Andrew, throwing down his napkin and settling back in the booth. "Now can we talk about what's really going on with you?"

I felt my face turning red. "Nothing's going on. I must've caught something, but really, I'm fine now."

The look on Andrew's face said, *Really? That's all?*

"Okay, fine," I said. "Mark wants me to rethink Lifestage. My engineers are exhausted from all the pivots. I feel like a failure."

For some reason, Andrew was smiling. He reached across the table and punched me on the shoulder. "I'm so proud of you!"

I rubbed the spot where he'd socked me. "You are?"

"Yeah," said Andrew. "You're partway there! Recognizing your failures is a huge step. Many managers would never admit that they failed, not even to themselves."

Andrew went on to say that I should be *excited* that my weaknesses were showing themselves to me. He said that plenty of promising people started off strong in their careers, but if they were blind to their faults, they plateaued, lost their edge. He said that the best, the smartest, the most capable and promising people in the world were those who were deeply flawed and knew it. They excelled only because they recognized those flaws, then worked their asses off to overcome them, getting stronger and smarter in the process.

"In a nutshell . . ." Andrew looked at my unwashed hair, my stained T-shirt, my whole sorry deal. "It's okay. It means you're already ahead."

I managed a tiny, awkward laugh. "Doesn't feel like it." I said. But silently, the whole bus ride home, I prayed that he was right.

And I did go to VidCon after all. Our team had all-access passes with a backstage setup to meet with Vine, Musical.ly, and Instagram stars. We tested out the prototype features we'd developed for Stories and polled them for suggestions on what features they'd like. I took it as an opportunity to understand more about their world and how they saw their fame and leg-acies. Later, some of those stars dropped by the Facebook/ Instagram headquarters to learn about our monetization model. I joined them for a tour of the campus. Walking next to the YouTube star Cameron Dallas, whom my sister had chased all over Miami when she was a teenager, I thought, *Damn. My sister is never going to believe this when I tell her.*

Chapter 16

Gut Intuition

MY WEIGHT HAD PLUMMETED from 190 pounds down to 129. I wasn't dieting, exactly, but thanks to the unease that was taking up all the space inside me, I'd stopped eating two fettuccine Alfredos for lunch and started eating smaller meals throughout the day. After stress, my health-fanatic roommate was the second-biggest factor in my weight loss. Thanks to Selena, I was learning what it meant to eat like a healthy person. Most days, after she drove me to work, we'd eat breakfast together on campus. Where I'd once piled my plate high with tater tots, eggs, and bacon, now I copied Selena and limited myself to egg whites, spinach, and a single tater tot every other day.

On top of eating much less, I was a secret gym rat. I was secretive about it because I didn't think I belonged in a gym, and I didn't want people looking at me. Still haunted by my childhood pull-up failures, I imagined my coworkers would make fun of me for even trying to be an athletic person. Every night after work, I'd sneak in the back door and beeline for a StairMaster that stood apart from all the others, facing a corner in the back of the gym. I'd climb on that thing until I could hardly take another step. Then I'd take the shuttle back to Mountain View, getting off several stops before my apartment to get more walking in.

One night, when I'd snuck out the back door of the gym and was making my way across campus to catch the shuttle, I ran into a super bro-y guy I hadn't seen since my internship. Nick smelled like eucalyptus cologne and was swiping through images of women on his phone as he walked toward his car.

"Hey, Nick," I said, falling into step beside him.

He looked up, did a double take. "Whoa, man, I thought that was you!" He slapped my back. "You look different!"

I shrugged. "Yeah." Nick was in his late twenties, about six foot five, and—like the majority of Silicon Valley tech workers, who have money to pay for trainers and eat right—annoyingly fit. I wondered if he was judging my newly scrawny body, if he could see the love handles I'd kept from my fat days through my baggy workout clothes.

As we walked across the quiet campus he told me he was on his way to a Tinder date. He pulled his phone from his pocket and showed me a picture of an athletic-looking Asian-American woman standing on a windy cliff, her long hair whipping across her smiling face.

"She looks nice," was all I could think of to say. She did look nice. I wondered what they would talk about. I tried to remember the last time I'd talked to anyone besides Selena or Andrew outside of work and couldn't come up with anything.

"You on Tinder, Michael?" he asked, tucking his phone into the pocket of his hoodie.

"Me, ah, not lately," I said. Ninety percent of the people I knew dated exclusively through apps, but I hadn't yet downloaded Tinder, or any other dating app for that matter. I told myself that I would as soon as I looked better. When I got rid of the love handles, then I'd download the app, go on a date, kiss a girl. Once I'd kissed a girl for real, my sexuality would finally come alive and everything would make sense and fall into place and I would finally feel complete. But not yet. I had to lose the love handles first.

Nick was looking at me funny, but we'd reached the parking lot, and my shuttle was thankfully approaching. "Gotta catch that," I said, turning. "Have fun tonight!"

"Hold up a sec!" said Nick. "You like to work out?"

"Oh, no, I don't exercise at all," I lied. "I can't even do a pull-up."

He didn't seem to have heard me. "I'm gonna Messenger you my trainer Jack's number," he said, pulling out his phone. "Give him a call. You've lost a lot of weight. He'll help you build some muscle." Nick slapped me on the back, adding, "Trust me, it'll change your life."

The very next day, I followed Jack the Trainer around for a tour of the gym's crowded, clanking weight room. I'd never had the courage to step foot in there before. A half-dozen lean Facebookers in state-of-the-art sweat-wicking gear were contorting inside various uncomfortable-looking machines. A woman with a sailor's biceps jumped to a high bar and effortlessly lifted her chin to tap the metal, again and again.

"So hit me with your fitness goals, Michael," said Jack. He looked a lot like one of the jocks who'd made me feel like a weakling back in grade school, but that wasn't his fault, I told myself.

"Oh, I just want to go on dates with girls," I said. That was what I wanted, wasn't it?

Jack laughed, running a massive hand through his crew cut. "Got it. Anything more specific? Were you looking to focus more on cardio or strength?"

I was trying not to stare at Pirate Biceps, floating up and down on that bar like she was made of helium. Her physique was as extraordinary as mine was pathetic. I thought of myself back at Belen, thrashing and red-faced, unable to lift my pandalike body a single inch for the Presidential Physical Fitness Test. Maybe all I needed was to kill that kid off, once and for all. Maybe all I needed was just one pull-up.

"There is one thing I'd like to be able to do . . ." I started.

"Hit me!" said Jack again. His eyes gleamed with excitement. I bit my tongue.

"Never mind. Forget it."

Who was I kidding? Pull-ups were my confidence kryptonite, and after all the "opportunities to better myself" I'd created for myself at Facebook, confidence was not something I could afford to lose more of at the moment.

Jack's face had fallen like I'd just stolen Christmas. "You sure, bud?"

"I just want to look good," I said. "Let's stick with that."

Five minutes later, I sat across from him in his tiny back-of-the-gym office as he went over the financials with me.

I stared at the screen. At $70 a session, that was of course $350 a week, or a cringe-inducing $1,400 a month. Was that completely irresponsible? I was making good money—great money, by most of the world's standards. But it somehow didn't go very far in Silicon Valley. What if I ended up following in my parents' financial footsteps and losing everything? Was signing on with this Jack guy my first step toward the flip side of the American dream? An image flashed in my mind: me, homeless and sprawled across a San Francisco sidewalk. I shuddered. Shit, was that some kind of a premonition?

Quickly, ignoring the weird feeling in my gut, I scribbled my "signature" on the iPad and handed it back to Jack. I was being dumb. Other than rent, I had hardly any expenses, thanks to the shuttle and the dining plan. This wouldn't hurt me. And Jack was older than me and had a certificate that said he knew what he was doing, so really, I was probably being *smart*. Besides, I was beginning to wonder if my gut really knew best. Following my instincts above everyone else's at Facebook had helped me in some projects and hurt me in others.

With apologies for the digression, here's something I didn't know then that I know now, as I write this: there's a difference between intuition and impulse. Intuition is the super-calm, clear guide that shows up when you're able to block out the noise in your life (for me, the noise is often the mean voices in my head, the jabbering or whining of my panic or stress voices). Intuition doesn't bark orders. It waits to be asked, "Does this feel right?" And then it answers—usually with a feeling. It's a clear, whole-body *feeling* of "yes," or "hold on," or "not this one"—not a bully shouting in your head, "Just do it, coward!"

Where intuition is our subconscious wisdom, impulse is our knee-jerk reaction. Impulse is pretty much always driven by some form of fear. It was my fear of not being dateable that prompted me to sign up for training with Jack on the spot, instead of taking a minute to consider whether there might be a better-suited trainer for me. Twice I'd stood up to Zuckerberg himself, because my gut told me my way was a better way than his. I'd thought this was being strong, but, well, my gut had been wrong about my initial concept.

Needless to say, things didn't go so well. I stayed with Jack for the next seven months anyway, following his instructions to "pile on the calories" in order to build muscle. Without guidance on what kinds of foods to eat, I went ahead and ate calorie-filled junk. And pretty soon, in spite of our grueling workouts, I'd gained back thirty of the sixty pounds I'd lost from my StairMaster days, albeit with some solid muscle gains too. Not that Jack or any fitness trainer could have changed this part, but ten grand in private workouts later, I still hated myself—still couldn't look in the mirror, still had days where, no matter how much progress I was making with my team on Lifestage or how often I reminded myself that *failing was growing,* I'd have to duck into a bathroom stall to cry.

Then Jack moved away, and Jasmine took over my training. Jasmine was a Vietnamese super-athlete with a heart of gold and a body made of something much harder. Where Jack was Mr. Boot Camp, Jasmine was all about happiness, excitement, and positive energy. I immediately felt comfortable with her, and within days, I told her about my childhood Presidential Physical Fitness Test humiliation and how much it would mean to me to do just one pull-up. In spite of all the muscle I'd gained, I still hadn't dared to even try.

Jasmine understood. She didn't rush me. She worked with me for months, helping me eat better by focusing on small but frequent high-protein and low-fat meals and bringing my weight to a healthy 145 before she asked me if I was ready to try *It*. I was, and I failed, many, many times, even with the helper bar. By then, I wasn't embarrassed about it anymore. Everyone in the gym knew me as the Kid Who Wanted to Do a Pull-Up, and I didn't even care. With Jasmine's support, the gym was no longer a place where I felt judged and watched. I realized that nobody there was happy with their body; everybody wanted to look better—that was why they were at the gym. So we just kept going back to the bar, day after day, and trying, and trying, and trying, until, one day . . .

"Michael, you did it!" Jasmine screamed. She was jumping up and down at hyperspeed, clapping her hands like a mom whose kid had just hit their first-ever home run.

My arms were trembling so hard I thought they might give out entirely, but I managed a second chin tap before dropping to the ground. As I looked around, trembling with exhaustion, I hoped nobody was looking at me.

Doing a pull-up didn't solve all my problems, but it was a turning point. After that, I walked differently. I had more energy. I believed in myself.

And I downloaded Tinder.

Chapter 17

Baby Code Monsters

THE COMMUNITY CENTER SMELLED like cafeteria food and kid sweat. It was vast and empty, except for me, two Latino Facebook interns, and the fifteen Latina moms who'd come—strollers and restless kids in tow—to hear my Spanish-language Tech Prep presentation. I'd been giving the talks for several months now, thanks in part to Maxine, who had miraculously convinced the comms team to let me do it. I loved it. I loved speaking Spanish with these determined, notepad-clutching moms. I loved the little kids who paid no attention and had no idea why they were there but understood from their mothers' serious expressions that it was something important. Because it was about their futures, like everything was.

The women sat in folding chairs with their overflowing purses at their feet, scribbling notes as I talked about the free computer programming classes and resources that were available to their families. The kids—all younger than ten, I guessed—chased one another around the back of the room, or played on their moms' phones, or, if they were really little, got jiggled and bounced on knees. Every few minutes, one would stage-whisper, "*Cuánto tiempo más?*" to a parent, who would shush them and wave them away. A couple of the kids spoke English to each other, but I got the sense, as usual, that the interns and I were the only fully bilingual adults in the room.

Tonight's presentation wasn't going very well. I was trying

to walk the mothers through the Tech Prep website, reminding them that we could connect their kids with free programming courses. But the cord connecting my laptop to the display screen I'd brought with me was frayed, and in spite of Raul the intern's best efforts, the projection kept blinking out. Not that the women had been getting much out of it, anyway. Even as they diligently took notes, I could see from their frowns and hunched postures that they were confused and overwhelmed by all the information I was throwing at them. More than that, I could sense that the hope they'd walked in with was turning to skepticism. Still, not being able to afford sitters, they had schlepped their young kids to this smelly, out-of-the-way community center at six p.m. on a Tuesday evening, probably coming straight from work, eager to learn what computer science was. More important, they wanted to know if it could be a realistic career path for kids like theirs—probably exceptionally smart, curious students who were underserved by the rigged educational system that resulted in a massive underrepresentation of Latino and African-American kids in the tech field. There was anecdotal data galore: all I had to do was walk around Silicon Valley, where I could see that most of the people cleaning the offices were Latino, and most of the coders were white.

It was my job to convey to these women that yes, computer science was available to their children, even if they couldn't afford classes or their own computers.

"Believe me," I told them, "companies all over this country are actively seeking more programmers from diverse backgrounds." As we'd practiced, this was where Raul clicked to a photo of young Latino professionals working on expensive laptops in an airy glass-walled office. I continued with my canned introduction: "My company, Facebook, is one of them. We're striving to greatly increase the diversity of our workforce. So I'm very happy to be here talking to you today. It's never too early to start coding!"

The women looked back at me, frowning. Their children were so small, years away from entering the workforce, and the world was changing fast. They were probably wondering why they should pin their dreams on some Internet site.

Which wasn't even what I'd meant. I pushed forward with the hard sell. "I'm not just talking about future opportunities at my company, or even in the tech industry. It's important to know that the career options for programmers are practically unlimited! By learning to code early, your kids will develop skills to help them be almost anything they want to be when they grow up. Programmers can find work in industries like health care, social services, agriculture, education, construction . . ."

The harder I sold, the more suspicious this crew seemed to grow. Some now listened with a narrow-eyed look that said, *Sounds too good to be true.* One audience member was already getting ready to leave, stuffing her toddler's arm into the tiny sleeve of a puffy pink coat. Another leaned over to whisper something in her friend's ear; the listener chuckled, rolling her eyes the same way Mariana always did when I tried to pitch coding to her. "It's just not my thing," my sister would always say. I hated that so much. How in the world could she know that, without ever trying it once?

In a bid to stay upbeat, I had Raul click to a list of nonprofits. "All of these," I said, pointing to the display screen, "are groups that can help your child with the basics. Their websites offer *free* online tutorials and *free* mentor groups and all kinds of—"

A small, full-figured woman in a forest-green satin blouse was raising her hand, a polite but firm smile on her face. Her little girl, in a pink tutu and high, pink-scrunchied pigtails, twirled in circles next to her chair.

I gestured to the mom. "Yes?" I said, relieved that someone was engaged enough to ask a question.

"How much does it really cost?" she asked in Spanish.

I sighed. Screw the website presentation. I wasn't going to get through to these women by making a bunch of fantastic claims. Without a doubt, every woman in that room worked harder than I had ever worked in my life, and they were probably still struggling. They had likely been preyed upon by scammers in the past, lured into "free opportunities" that promised paths to success and riches but only ended up costing their families in the end.

"The quick answer is the courses and materials I'm talking to you about today are one hundred percent free, no cost, zero," I said. "I will come back to that, okay?"

The woman nodded. I gave her a dorky thumbs-up and shut my laptop.

"*Ahora, les quiero contar un poco de mi historia y cómo llegué aquí,*" I said. ("Now, I'd like to share with you all a little bit of my own story of how I got here.")

Looking relieved, the women laid down their pens, nodding eagerly.

"I grew up in Miami. My mom and dad migrated to the States from Peru and Bolivia before I was born. They worked hard and built their own business, a chicken restaurant. My parents came to the United States because they wanted my sister and me to have every opportunity in life, the best education. They worked hard, like you all do, and eventually their restaurant became a success. For a while, when it was doing really well, my mom and dad sometimes talked about selling it and moving back to Peru. My mom would joke that our humble family could live like kings in Peru. 'I could have a Mercedes!' she'd say. 'I could have perfect health insurance! Then I could whiten my teeth!'"

The women laughed at that. Even the interns were paying attention now. Everyone got it. Now that I'd found the right way in, I started to relax. *Thank God for my sixth-grade teacher and her obsession with presentation-giving,* I thought, as I often did in these situations. Her class had been my inoculation against stage fright, making it possible for me to look up and deliver my Anyone Can Code message to thousands of people over the last ten years. And hopefully, if I could just stay connected to these women a little longer, my public speaking skills would make it possible for me to convince them.

"So we stayed in Miami," I said. "Even though we could *not* live like kings there. We stayed, even when my parents lost their restaurant, and then our house."

There was a collective gasp at our misfortune from the sympathetic room. "We stayed," I said, "because my parents wanted us to have every chance at success in life."

The women were nodding along with every word I said. A couple of them looked like they might cry. I considered, for a split second, adding that the reason we could afford to stay was because as the App Kid, I'd made enough money to support us for several years. But I decided against that. I wasn't trying to give anyone false hopes. That wasn't the point of this.

"My mom thought I should be a doctor or a lawyer," I went on. "She sent me to a private Catholic school, because she thought this was the only sure path to success: a good high school, good grades, a good college, a good job. She would say that I owed it to her and my dad to work as hard at school as they did at work. But I didn't. I was a bad student. I didn't even get my high school diploma, in fact."

I'd shocked them. One lady crossed her arms, pinching her lips: the classic Disappointed Mom stance. The questioning woman in the green blouse was covering her mouth with her hands, wide-eyed, as if I'd just confessed to a murder. Her daughter stopped twirling for the first time all evening, suddenly intrigued. Why was her education-obsessed mom getting lectured at by someone who didn't even go to school? I probably had thirty seconds before my audience hustled their children out of the room and as far away as possible from the likes of me.

"It's okay, I promise!" I assured them, holding up my hands. "I was a terrible student because I spent all my time building apps. They didn't teach computer science at my elementary school, so I taught myself by Googling 'how to code.' Whatever I needed to know, I found it on the Internet. It was all out there, for free. Just like it is for your kids. Only we're here to guide them."

People were really listening now, even if a few of them still looked a little suspicious. I needed to pivot the story back to my mom, a heroine they could relate to. "We had one computer in our house when I was little. We were all supposed to share it, but my parents could never get on it to do their accounting because they couldn't tear me away. My mom would come home tired from the restaurant and see me at the computer desk in the living room, learning and practicing, and she'd yell, 'Michael, stop playing! You'll never get anywhere in life if you don't stop playing!'" Laughter filled the room. They really could not get enough of my mom. Imagine the minds we could change if I could bring her to these things!

"But little by little, my mom started to see the promise in what I was doing. Do you know what really convinced her?" I could not resist. "When I got my first check from Apple at age thirteen. It was my share of the money that thousands of people had paid to download my game."

"How much was the check?" someone called out, to more laughter.

I thought of my mother's shocked expression as she'd held out that first $5,000 check to my father, his stern, "What have you done?," and smiled.

"It was a lot, to us," I answered. "Enough to sort of turn my mom's world upside down. She had always been taught that there was only one path to success: the pain-and-suffering path. 'No pain, no gain,' she would say. But for me, programming was the furthest thing from pain and suffering. I worked hard at it because I loved it. And I am only standing here talking to you all today because finally, my mom came to understand that I wasn't just playing, I was building a tool kit that would help me succeed for the rest of my life. I want to share that tool kit with your kids. I want them to have the American dream that *you* were promised."

I stopped there. I was getting a little choked up even though I didn't want to consciously admit it to myself, looking out at their hopeful-again faces, and I wanted to stay positive, though I felt conflicted. Even with this tool I was holding out to them with so much—too much?—promise, it wasn't going to be easy for their kids. They were brown skinned, and they were poor, which meant that in fact, what my mom had said was partly true. Even if every one of these kids started to study programming tomorrow, success would not come easily for them. There would still be pain and suffering for them. Especially the Dreamers—I guessed there were at least one or two in the room—whose right to live in the only country they'd ever known wasn't even guaranteed anymore. Growing up with less security, less money, less insurance, and often less safety, they would have to work ten times harder at everything they did in life just to be seen, let alone to succeed. But what could I do, if not share with these moms my story, point them to the only tool I knew of that could help them break through a system that was stacked against them?

Afterward, as the interns passed out printouts listing all the same URLs the women had so carefully taken down in their notebooks, I stood near the exit, sneaking looks at the torrent of messages my manager at Facebook had been sending the entire time I talked. He had questions about the presentation slides I'd started for Instagram Stories and WhatsApp Status, and was pretty excited about it. I'd deal in a minute. Right now, I wanted to make myself available for any last questions. Most of the women were in a hurry to get home and make dinner. They bundled up and rushed past me with big smiles and thanks, prodding their sleepy kids to look up and say goodbye.

The questioning woman and her tutu-sporting daughter were the last to leave. The mom held out her arm for her daughter to use as a barre as she twirled and did graceful dancerly hops and leaps.

"We're excited!" said the mom, holding up her printout. "Thank you for the information! This is Kylie. She loves technology. She's going to love this."

"Really, you guys are so welcome," I said. "Kylie, do you like to code as much as you like to dance?"

"No!" shouted Kylie, at the top of a jump.

"Kylie, you do!" said her mom, blushing a little. "She does! She is always on the tablet thing! She would be on it right now, but we had to leave it with her brother."

"I draw on it," said Kylie. "And I made six movies of my animals."

"Her stuffed animals," added her mom.

"Six movies!" I said, impressed.

Her mom nodded. "I think this will be easy for her. I'll be sure to make her practice. What's the best one for that?" She handed me her printout, and I scanned it quickly.

"How old is she?"

"I'm six," said Kylie.

"Okay, you might be ready for Code Monster, with your mom's help," I said.

"Monster!" Kylie giggled. "My daddy says I'm a monster!"

"He's just kidding, though," the mom said, laughing a little nervously. "She's an angel."

"I'm not," said Kylie. "I'm more like a monster."

"Good for you," I said, loving this girl. "Kylie, if you're fierce like a monster, you'll be great at coding!"

"Okay," said Kylie, bouncing on her toes, glancing at the door. "Mommy, I'm hungry."

As Kylie tugged her arm, the mom looked at me with huge eyes. "Do you really think so?"

"Oh yeah," I said. "She'll pick it up quickly, if she likes it.

If she tries a few times and doesn't, let it go and try again in a year."

The mom pulled out her notebook and quickly wrote down what I'd just said.

A few seconds after they'd left, I followed them outside, where Kylie was talking on her mom's phone, relaying a message from her mom in English.

The mom turned to me, smiling.

I shoved my hands in my jacket pockets, trying to find the right way to say what I was thinking. The best I could do was, "If coding isn't her thing, that's okay, too. She has you, so . . . I'm not worried about her at all."

Chapter 18

A "Surprise" Family Visit

"Sure you don't want something while you wait?" The server was lingering by my table at Chef Chu's, a family-owned Chinese restaurant in the South Bay that I ate at regularly. I'd heard that Mark Zuckerberg went there religiously, and I'd chosen it for dinner with my parents and sister, hoping to get back in their good graces.

"That's okay," I said, looking up from a text from my sister that said, "6 mins away!" "They'll be here really soon." I forced myself to put my phone down and smile at her. "Thanks, though," I added.

"Sure thing," said the server. She looked about my age, with black hair twisted into a pointy bun on the top of her head. She was being especially nice, considering I'd been hogging a prime table without ordering for more than fifteen minutes.

Now she glanced down at the hard-case roller bag by my chair. "Looks like you came straight from the airport."

"Yeah." I smiled again, reaching for my phone. I'd flown home from VidCon early to spend time with my family, who'd gone ahead with their "surprise" visit and had been sightseeing in the city for three days while I was in L.A. My mom had been chronicling all the city sights they'd seen without me. So that no one would know her bad son wasn't bothering to host them on their visit, she would caption each photo as if I were there, with something like: "*Segundo día en California, con Mari-*

ana, con Michael, felices juntos!" My mom cared so much about
what people thought that she'd gone so far as to post an old
picture of Mariana and me posing against an anonymous blue
sky, pretending it was new.

"Let me guess," said the server, tilting her head. "You work
for Microsoft. No, Google!"

"Close," I told the server. "Facebook."

"Aha," she said. "Some of my friends work there. Too bad
I'm not on there."

I laughed nervously, and then went back to looking at my
phone. The waitress wandered away. If my mom had been there,
she probably would have pressured me into flirting with her.

Having spent my life being invisible to 99 percent of the
opposite sex, I had no idea how to flirt—even with the girls I
matched with on Tinder. I'd been on four Tinder dates so far:
two brunches, two lunches. Each time, we'd talked for hours,
but at some point I'd realized that I was bored, the spark wasn't
there, and we'd gone our separate ways. I was beginning to
think maybe I just wasn't cut out for romance. Maybe I was
born to be a lone wolf. I didn't want to be distracted from my
work by relationships. That would explain why I had always
hated it so much when Mariana's friends tried to flirt with me.

I was interrupted from this mental spiral by the sound of my
mom's voice from across the room, chattering in Spanish as the
host led my family to my table.

I jumped to my feet and threw my arms around them all at
once. They were all wearing windbreakers, and my mom and
sister's hair was perfectly set despite their walk over the Golden
Gate Bridge earlier. My mom squeezed my arm tight, pinching
me with her long nails.

"Oh my gosh, Michael," she gushed, pulling away and poking my triceps. "Wow, you have, like, a muscle!"

"Yeah." I pried her fingers away, embarrassed but also proud.
"I'm nowhere near where I want to be."

"You're *skinny!*" shrieked my sister.

"*Te ves bien,* Cocolocho; you look great, son!!" boomed my dad, shaking his head in disbelief as he put his arm around my shoulders. "How did you do it?"

As we took our seats around the table, I started to tell them about my workouts, how I'd finally gotten to the point where I hated my body so much that I'd walked into the gym one day and just kept going back every day after that. I was getting to the part about doing my first pull-up when my sister interrupted.

"If I had a free gym membership and free food from buffets, I'd lose weight, too!"

"You know, Mariana, if you put in more effort, you could lose weight, too," added my mom, *tsk*-ing and shaking her head.

"No," I said. "It's not about effort, Mami, it's about access to resources. I see it firsthand at Facebook: the people who make the highest salaries—programmers, managers, directors, VPs—are mostly strong and healthy. The cleaners, cooks, and bus drivers, on the other hand, seem nowhere near as fit."

"How was your work trip, Michael?" my dad interrupted.

"Let's hope it was good!" said my mom. Subtext: *I hope it was worth leaving your family to fend for themselves after they came all this way to see you. I guess you must not really love us.*

I pretended to take her comment at face value. "It really was! VidCon is crazy! It's the largest gaming convention in the world. Production companies from all over the world send reps, and all these kids come dressed like their favorite YouTube characters. I met so many people. It was really good that I went."

As I spoke, my phone was blowing up with a flurry of messages from the lead engineer on Lifestage, who was apparently still at the office, working on a list of changes I'd sent from the airport that morning. "Um, excuse me a sec," I said to my family. As I scrolled through the string of messages, the waiter returned to the table and began going over the menu.

When the server had left us to make our decisions, my mom hissed, "Michael, you shouldn't have picked this place. We spent all our money on those expensive Alcatraz tickets. We can't afford this."

"Mom, don't worry, it's my treat. No chicken will ever be as good as yours, but I promise you this is the most delicious Chinese food you will ever have. Get it. Get whatever you want!"

Just then, the server appeared with a plate of crab and cheese puffs. "This is on the house," she said. "I'll be right back to take your order!"

The instant the server turned around, my mom was all over me.

"Michael, do you think she's pretty? Are you dating anyone, Michael?"

I admitted that I was on Tinder, then tried to change the subject. As if.

"What about that girl Amy?!" my mom asked.

Amy was my new roommate, a Chinese-American woman who was just two years older than me and worked at LinkedIn. A few weeks ago, I'd come to the realization that I hated living with Selena almost as much as I hated living in San Francisco. Selena needed to live with a real adult, and I needed to live with someone in a similar life stage. So I'd moved into a super-luxury apartment in a high-rise in the suburbs near Facebook with Amy, who was looking for something similar.

"Amy is not my girlfriend," I told my mom. "You know that."

"Mami told all her friends in Miami that Amy is your girl-friend!" my sister blurted out.

"What?" I exclaimed. "Why would you do that?"

"*Michael, escúchame . . . Por qué te amarga tanto?* It's no big deal. People were curious, so I told them you were seeing her, but if you don't like it, I can tell them I was wrong."

In shock, I glanced at my sister. I wanted to know if anyone else at the table thought my mother's comments were insane.

There is no stopping my mom when she gets like that, and we ended up spending the rest of the dinner swiping through girls I'd matched with on Tinder.

"Michael, you haven't messaged a single one of these girls!" said Mariana, frowning at my phone in her hand.

It was true. I hadn't messaged any of the girls I'd matched with lately. I'd stop at swiping right on the ones with interesting bios. (I wasn't interested in their pictures as much as what kind of work they did and whether they sounded smart.) For now, that was as far as I felt like taking it.

"Michael, you have to message them if you want them to talk to you!" said Mariana, pointing at my keyboard.

"Not right now." I put my phone away, red-faced.

By the time I'd put my family into a car, promising to meet them at Facebook's headquarters in the morning, my head was throbbing. In the backseat of my Uber, I opened the window and gulped in the cold air, pressing the sides of my head together to keep it from exploding. The Korean marching music my eighty-year-old driver was blasting didn't help. On any other night, I would've asked him about the music, about his background and life and probably what he'd eaten for dinner, too. But not tonight. Not now.

My phone buzzed in my pocket, and for the first time that night, I ignored it. *Not now. Not now.* No matter who it was—my family or my work—I didn't want to talk to anyone. I probably didn't have a good solution for my Lifestage engineers, whatever problem they were messaging me about. Zuckerberg had responded to the Stories strategy doc I had sent him a few days back, but I figured it was best not to even open it up at that moment. And I didn't have another drop of energy left for my family, who'd spent the whole night trying to analyze me. At least they'd enjoyed themselves. For all my mom's protesting, she'd ended up admitting that the chicken was, indeed, delicious—not easy for a woman who'd served her own chicken for years. My dad was glad he'd gotten to sightsee in San Francisco. And Mariana had definitely enjoyed giving me feedback about my nonexistent love life. So, yes, all in all, the night hadn't gone as badly as I'd expected. Even if I had to laugh off all the talk about why I didn't have a girlfriend.

Chapter 19

This Humbling Lifestage

IN THE SUMMER OF 2016, a year after my family's visit, my team and I were finally putting the finishing touches on Lifestage. It still wasn't right. We'd created and scrapped countless iterations, but each time we thought we were close, either Zuckerberg would offer suggestions on a design element, or a focus group would tear down what we showed them, or I would wake up at two a.m. in a cold sweat, realizing that I had overdesigned the product and nobody would actually use or understand the thing.

> *Don't spend time beating on a wall,*
> *hoping to transform it into a door.*
> —Coco Chanel

I wasn't a fan of quote graphics, I find them super cringe, but that one spoke to me when it popped up on my feed— which had probably happened thanks to all the times I'd been nice and liked my mom's meme posts. It really did feel as if we were mistaking a wall for a door. A door to what? For my team, I was beginning to realize, it led to a finished product and their next opportunity. For me, so much more was on the line. Lifestage was my baby. Every day, various product managers pitched ideas that took Facebook further and I'd once showed

Zuck a screenshot of what Facebook had looked like in 2004: "I want to build that again," I said, "but with the technology we have now." I wanted to create something that celebrated the brand's origins while also appealing to a new generation. That was my original plan, anyway.

Zuckerberg's patience (like my self-confidence) was wearing thin, and we were all desperate to launch. The executives at Facebook thought it was important to time the release with the beginning of the school year. For me, the ticking clock was counting down to my twentieth birthday, a month away. I was convinced that Lifestage's appeal depended on its being built by a teenager, for teenagers. If I launched it at twenty, the optics would be all wrong, giving the app the flavor of a college guy continuing to attend high school parties. We had lots of discussions about how we'd keep adults off the app and about who would ultimately have access to the posted content. While my team worked on those concerns, my priority was shifting from "How do I make Lifestage the best it can be?" to "How do I make it good enough to launch before the start of the school year, while I'm still nineteen?"

One July evening one month before my birthday, I sat with my blurry-eyed team in a little bare-walled room, watching through one-way glass as a focus group of seven teenagers interacted with my still-buggy app. I was thinking about how the glass was unnecessary, since we working stiffs on the other side were completely outside of their awareness bubble anyway. I knew we weren't real to them. And since they were all strangers, they weren't even real to one another. When you're a teenager, the people who matter most are those who affect your life in a direct and meaningful way.

Anyway, I'd called for the focus group because I was having a failure of imagination. At Facebook, I'd stopped relying solely on my ability to conjure up the imaginary test characters

I'd always used to guide my app creations forward. So, even though I knew that it was basically impossible to get honest feedback from teenagers being paid for their reactions in an unnatural environment, I held a tiny sliver of hope that just maybe one of these kids would open their mouth and offer the golden piece of insight that tied all the loose ends together. As they munched on the mountain of snacks we'd provided and swiped around on phones and iPads loaded with Lifestage, I held my breath, studying them the way a scientist studies lab animals. A red-haired girl with enormous black glasses squinted at her screen, scrunching up her nose. "Is that a pile of poop?" she asked the researcher.

The researcher laughed. "Correct! And what do you think of it?"

"Kinda lame?" offered a redheaded boy in a Chance the Rapper "3" cap.

"It's a little immature," said the youngest kid in the group, a chubby guy with braces who reminded me of myself in my Club Penguin days.

I closed my eyes. Changing the icons now would mean delaying the launch until after the school year started.

I stood up. "That's enough," I said. "I don't need to hear any more. We're launching. No more changes."

Two weeks later, with seven days to go before my birthday, I was in an Uber with three bags of takeout sushi from Fuki Sushi in Palo Alto, the fanciest place in Silicon Valley—my last-ditch effort to keep the guys with me till the bitter end. I took a selfie with my sushi tower and sent it to them, typing, "On my way!" then slumped down in my seat. There were still several bugs to work out, and the guys were surly, hungry, and hardly speaking anymore.

By the time I rushed into the office with my offering at

eleven p.m., one of my team members had gone home, and my lead engineer was putting on his jacket. "Sorry, Michael, I'm done. Can't see straight anymore." He grabbed a box of tempura from my arms and walked out. The two engineers left grabbed their food without a word and continued coding while I frantically paced back and forth, looking for ways to help get us to the finish line faster.

At two a.m., it was me and one guy, who kept nodding off, his head swaying over his keyboard.

"Hey, man." I tapped the engineer's shoulder and he jerked awake, knocking his mouse to the floor.

"*Fuuuuck,*" he croaked, wiping drool from the corner of his mouth.

"Look," I said, reaching to pick up his mouse. "You can go. I can finish. Can you just remind me how to submit the final build via Facebook's internal tools to Apple?"

It had been so long since I'd done any coding myself that I'd forgotten how Facebook's internal process worked. My engineer gave me a quick walk-through and headed out the door without another word. Damn. I really was a shitty product manager. But now wasn't the time for dwelling on it. It was two-thirty a.m. I was the only person left at the headquarters, the only person left to get the app into Apple's hands in time. The guys had demolished the sushi before I could have any. Now I was so hungry I couldn't think straight. What was it my engineer had said was the crucial next-to-last step before you submitted? I'd completely forgotten. After lamely clicking around on Facebook's internal engineering support page for twenty minutes, I realized, *Aha, the London Facebook office is just getting in!*

I opened up Messenger and typed to every engineer I could find in the London office directory:

Anyone out there?
I'm trying to submit my app and I have no idea what I
    am clicking on.
Need a walk-through!

At 4:35 a.m., with some major chat handholding by a random London engineer from another team, I was finally ready
to hit submit. Deliriously tired, I touched the button and
leaned back in my chair, waiting for the auto-confirmation
from Apple. But something was wrong. Lifestage was still in
my out-box. I typed to London:

Didn't go through!
??????????!

After an eternity, he responded:

Hold tight. Servers might be down. Try again in a bit.

I needed to throw something. I needed to scream. I needed
to run to the bathroom and punch a metal door just to feel
something worse than the total hopeless frustration I was feeling right now. But that would have taken energy, and I didn't
have any left.

OK, thanks, man.

Eyelids fluttering, I pinched my arm to stay awake. "Don't
you dare!" I yelled at myself. But my eyes just wouldn't stay . . .

I jolted awake. An hour had passed! The sun was coming up!
I had only two and a half hours till the cutoff time. I spun my
chair three times, then started going through all of the steps

again. By seven-thirty, with a half hour to spare, I hit the submit button again. As I waited for the confirmation, people began trickling into the office, bright-eyed, holding smoothies and lattes and bran muffins and yogurts, just like on any other morning.

When it looked as if the submission had gone through, I shuffled, *Walking Dead*–like, to a meeting room and crawled onto a narrow bench. "Just for, like, five seconds," I muttered to myself, closing my eyes.

Outside the meeting room, the day went on as usual. Hours passed as I lay curled on that skinny bench, no longer walking dead, just dead.

"Michael, yo, wake up." My manager was shaking me. "Are you okay?"

"I submitted, I submitted," I slurred into the crook of my arm, lifting my head. "Is it okay? Did something break?"

My manager was staring at me with an alarmed expression. "You submitted the app? I doubt anything broke. It probably went through okay. You should head home and sleep."

"What time is it?" I rubbed my eyes.

"One-thirty."

The Lifestage PR meeting! I was on my feet, running through the halls, dodging my coworkers with their heads in their phones. I was grabbing my computer from my desk and racing back along the hall, smoothing my hair and tucking in my shirt as I went. I was skidding to a stop outside of the room where the communications team had been waiting for me for ten minutes.

"Hi, Michael," said the marketing manager. They were double-checking to make sure everything in terms of upcoming press was solid and on track as planned. For Lifestage to succeed, we needed to promote the heck out of it, and for once, the comms team seemed happy to let me chat it up with the media.

The marketing manager was smiling, which could only

mean that they were laughing at me on the inside. Was it obvious that I'd stayed up all night and slept all day on a tiny bench and not showered since . . . since . . . when *did* I last shower? I tried to look normal and calm. I really needed this to go smoothly.

"Are you okay, Michael? You seem a little tired," said the marketing manager.

"Yeah, I'm great!" I was trying to talk without showing my teeth, in case my braces were gunky. "I've just been here since the day before, um, what day was yesterday?"

A newly hired marketing shadow—an entry-level marketing manager—pulled out her phone. "Should I reschedule us?"

"Yes," said the marketing manager. "There's no urgency here. Once the app is approved, we'll take a week to test it, then roll it out."

"No!" I said. It sounded more like a bark, my throat was so dry. Someone handed me a bottle of water, and every pair of eyes in the room watched me guzzle it. Then I put the bottle down and switched to autopilot, the trick I'd learned on my high school trips to Peru and Bolivia. It had always served me well when I'd have to speak to rooms full of hundreds while jet-lagged, having just stepped off a plane. Autopilot Michael didn't let lack of sleep or gunky braces get in his way. He smiled and stood up straight with his shoulders back. Autopilot Michael explained to the marketing manager and the entire room why it was essential to roll out the press on Lifestage even before Apple approved the app. Because it would 100 percent absolutely be approved. And because once it was, there would be only one single day—for me to talk to reporters as a nineteen-year-old.

When Autopilot Michael was finished explaining all of this, he thanked the comms team for accommodating this schedule (even though they hadn't given any indication that they would do so) and walked out of the room.

Fifteen minutes later, I stumbled off a shuttle outside of my apartment, went up to my beautiful high-ceilinged bedroom with a view of Silicon Valley's Redwood City suburbs and the In-N-Out across the street on Veterans Boulevard, and collapsed, fully dressed, onto the bed, relief flowing through me. I'd done it. I'd submitted the app.

Chapter 20

Serendipity

SIX MONTHS LATER, I was riding the shuttle to work, slumped down in my plush seat, listening to the Cuban singer Celia Cruz on my big earmuff headphones, the ones I wore when I wanted to shut the world out. I was writing up a memo to Zuckerberg.

Once again, he'd been right, his instincts sharper than mine. The Lifestage experiment, now seven months since its original release, did not turn into the next Facebook. The comms team and I had agreed on a "wait and see" approach to the experimental app launch, letting it find success (or not) organically so we could gather the most useful data out of its release and usage. So we did only a handful of interviews for the launch— not nearly enough to counter some of the negative articles. The one from Business Insider was still seared in my brain: "After trying the app I was left puzzled by why anyone would want to use it. Other social networks (particularly Snapchat) already do what Lifestage does along with so much more."

On the bright side, we all knew that the chances were slim that Lifestage would be the next Facebook. That's how the tech world works. You have to take risks.

Together, we'd decided to roll the product back over a six-month period. Meanwhile, my manager had made it clear: we should take what we'd learned from Lifestage and apply it to other projects and products within the company. I had to be

okay with the idea that every now and then, I'd have a failure. Not every project I worked on would change the world,
but that didn't stop me feeling like a failure. Luckily, Stories
ended up succeeding beyond even my own expectations. In
eight months, our launch of Instagram Stories surpassed Snapchat's number of users. By 2018, Instagram Stories had more
than twice as many users as Snapchat. Today, over half a *billion*
people use Instagram Stories every single day.

IG Stories launched before Snapchat went public, but by
the time it did, in March 2017, Snapchat had lost 56 percent
of its value. It was widely reported in tech media that this was
a direct result of Instagram Stories. A lot of Facebookers felt
pretty cocky about that. But I thought we should be grateful
for what Snapchat had taught us—which was that we weren't
the source of all creativity and innovation, nor did we have
to be. Instead of letting pride cloud my vision, I remember
reminding myself to respect Snapchat for what they'd built and
the lessons they'd given us. The lesson I took away from it all
was that it never hurts to enter a new project with the expectation that others probably know something you don't, and the
goal of finding out exactly what that is.

I was now continuing to work on WhatsApp Status and Instagram Stories, and I'd also started helping out with the navi-
gational user interface of the main Facebook app. I buckled
down and did the work from ten a.m. to six p.m. every day,
then went home each evening to work on my own apps, which
I was still building on the side. By that point, I'd built thirty-
four and launched thirty-one, many similar to 4 Snaps. One was
called Show & Tell, a video-format, turn-based online charades
game. Another, Gameshow, worked like Instagram, except its
users posted photos to hint at a specific word.

Anyway, I'd been feeling homesick for Miami, which was
why I was listening to Celia Cruz that day on the shuttle. Her

music always reminded me of home, and I was fully wallowing in "Ríe y Llora" when Kevin, the senior developer who'd been supportive of me since my intern days and would occasionally practice speaking Mandarin with me, bounded onto my bus. Kevin always made an effort to check in with me whenever we crossed paths, which I usually appreciated. It was nice to talk to someone who wasn't on my team once in a while, and it was a lot of fun slowly learning a third language in my free time. But at this moment I was not feeling receptive at all, and I sank lower in my seat, tugging my hoodie down over my eyes and willing him to pass by me and my toxic energy cloud.

So much for that. "Hey, Michael!" Kevin plunked into the aisle seat and gave me a subtle high five. "What up, wunderkind?"

I pulled aside one headphone and looked at him, confused. Was he making fun of me? Had everyone in the company been following Lifestage's epic sizzle?

"Ha ha," I said nervously.

Kevin looked confused. "Is something wrong?"

I shook my head, inching my headphone closer to my ear. "Just thinking."

Kevin nodded but kept eye contact—like he'd gotten the hint but was deciding not to take it. "I'm so glad I saw you. I've been meaning to congratulate you since forever!"

"About . . . ?"

"You were so great with the Teen Talks stuff. People have been asking when the next one is coming up. I also heard there's like five hundred people working on teen engagement with you now. When you started, how many? Three? Pretty incredible!"

As the bus passed the giant blue thumbs-up sign at the campus entrance and turned up Hacker Way, Kevin bounced to his feet—worlds more eager than me to leave the hermetically sealed bus and start the day. Swinging his gym bag over his shoulder, he added, "Seriously, Michael. Your perspective has been *so* valuable here. You've helped us understand what *everyone* wants. I hear so many product managers using your terminologies now. *Nostalgic bias, conglomerate apps, systems versus spaces.* You've redefined workflows at Facebook. I hope you know that."

As I walked down rainy Main Street, past the Times Square–scale digital billboard that currently displayed the message "Happy Taco Tuesday!," something opened up in my head. Lifestage had failed to make a splash, and my communication style still rubbed a lot of people the wrong way, but no one could say I hadn't altered the company's road map. Was my job here done? Maybe what I needed wasn't a different project but a different place, where I could challenge my perspective a bit more, and where my twenty-year-old way of looking at the world was needed. Where, though?

My watch was vibrating with a reminder about a ten o'clock meeting. Ducking into a lounge area tricked out with log-cabin walls and bobblehead figurines, I dropped into an orange butterfly chair and scrolled backward through my messages, looking for the agenda. *Nothing, nothing, nothing, shit, nothing.* I was about to give up and go in blind when another unread message, from weeks ago, jumped out at me.

From: Jacob
Michael, I have a team working on virtual reality at Google. We could use your perspective. Interested in joining? If so, reach out!

I stared at the blue text bubble. *We could use your perspective.* Hmm.

I'd met Jacob only once, about a year prior as he was interviewing for a director position at Facebook; the hiring manager had apparently wanted the token teen guy's opinion on Jacob and asked me to have a quick meeting with him. We'd really hit it off and ended up talking for so long that he was a half hour late for his next interview. I got a talking-to for keeping him, but I think he was offered the job. Apparently he'd gone to Google instead.

I hadn't even seen Jacob's message till this minute. Which was weird, because I was always on Messenger. Had I purposefully overlooked it? Even in my lowest moments at Facebook, I'd never seriously considered leaving before. Not voluntarily, anyway. Facebook was *all* I knew.

We could use your perspective. It was so weird that I'd stumbled on this note only minutes after Kevin had talked about my "valuable" perspective. Too weird to ignore, right? Some would say it seemed like a sign, but I couldn't be any less superstitious if I tried.

No one is more superstitious than my mom. Every New Year's Eve when I was growing up we had to: wear yellow; run a lap around our neighborhood block carrying empty luggage; and at 11:59, chomp twelve grapes in a row as fast as possible. A failure to do all of these things would, my mom said, result in a disastrous New Year. I did as I was told, but I never bought into it. I did not inherit one ounce of my mom's superstitious nature.

On the other hand, I'm a fan of serendipity. There's nothing better than discovering just what you need—maybe something even better—at just the right life moment. Some people think serendipity is the same as luck or coincidence, but it's better, because you can actually bring it to yourself, proactively. If you meet as many new people, listen to as many ideas, and explore as many new opportunities as possible in life, serendipity will find you.

As I raced to my meeting, I quickly typed back to Jacob: "Still interested in talking about that position?"

Things happened fast. Three days later, I sat outside the Starbucks near Facebook, adjusting my earbuds for a call from a

Google recruiter. This was a "screener" interview. If the forty-five-minute call went well, there would be seven more interviews a week later—*all on the same day.* If I bombed the screener, I assumed, I'd be out of the running. *Too bad you suck on the phone,* the mean voice in my head said, just as the call lit up my screen.

The recruiter dove right in, asking me about hypothetical products and problems and how I would improve metrics on certain apps. I answered with as much authority as I could and pointed out how my app-building experience would translate into benefits for Google. I told my interviewer about the role I'd played in Facebook's teen engagement strategy. I described how, as a twelve-year-old, I'd strategized my apps all the way to the top of the App Store charts. I offered some original (*I* thought) ideas for improving Google's social media presence.

I was sure I was proving the mean voice wrong, really killing it, until the recruiter abruptly thanked me and said she'd be in touch. I hung up, a little stunned, and gathered up my things. The call couldn't possibly have been forty-five minutes; it felt so short! I had so much more to say.

In spite of the recruiter's quick sign-off, I couldn't help getting my hopes up about moving to Google. How could I not? Google was the reason I'd gotten to where I was. If I wanted the job, I needed to be proactive, go outside the usual channels, keep planting seeds.

While I waited to hear back from the recruiter, I reached out to Jacob and asked if he would connect me with three members of the VR team at Google. Over the next week, I took two of those connections out to lunch, and then—though I'd still heard zero news—I went ahead and set up lunches with *their* connections.

Next, I needed to establish why I'd be an asset to the VR team I was applying to work with. I knew very little about virtual reality (computer-generated 3D simulations that people "enter" and interact with using special equipment) or augmented reality (technology that superimposes computer-generated images on a user's view of the real world), so the most valuable thing I could offer for now was my unique perspective on what these technologies could mean for my generation.

Until (not "unless," I told myself) I got to the next level of interviews at Google, I couldn't share that perspective in person. But I could do it in writing. I opened up Facebook and began typing out some predictions about how Gen Z would use AR and VR in the future. The note was short and to the point, calling BS on a common claim that these emerging technologies would be antidotes to humanity's smartphone addiction. Unlike many of my older colleagues in tech, I didn't think VR would have us all running around embracing our "childhood selves" by playing with virtual sticks in virtual nature. I called this notion "nostalgic bias" and warned designers that by building VR worlds as rehashes of the pre-technological world, they would be disregarding the very generation they were building those worlds for—my generation, who never played with sticks in the first place. Duh, we played with phones. Why would we want to get rid of them in VR? And I didn't believe that AR glasses would inspire my generation to throw away our smartphones. I said that Generation Z was the first generation never to have lived without smartphones, and we didn't want to, ever. On the contrary, typical Gen Zers would probably embrace VR and AR as excuses to surround themselves with a hundred tiny screens, all at once. We wanted more Internet, less real world.

When I'd said everything I could think of to say, I blasted the article to every Google contact I'd met through my networking meetings. Now I could sleep at night, knowing I'd done everything I could from where I stood to get the job.

The article got an immediate response from the VR guys at Google, who seemed to find it interesting, if alarming. This was good. Even though I wasn't a teenager anymore, I was still a good eight years younger than the youngest person on the

Google VR team, and hopefully I'd just made a decent case for why that could be an asset. I was feeling positive.

And then it came: an email from a different Google recruiter. With my heart clutching in my chest, I clicked . . . Wait, what? It was a rejection letter. It said there was "not presently a position" for me at the company. I was "a strong culture fit," but they "wanted to see more in terms of product and strategic insight." Maybe next time, yada yada, thanks, bye.

No, no, no. This. Couldn't. Be.

Figuring there was nothing left to lose, I fired back a politely snippy response:

It's quite interesting. Didn't expect one 30-minute phone call to be the cut at Google, especially given the position and team under consideration.

Well, I look forward to chatting again sometime soon.

Thanks again!

Michael

A few days went by. I gave up hope. It was over, at least for now. Then, as I was boarding a flight to Bogotá, Colombia (cashing in some PTO days to give a lecture and get over my disappointment), a message from the Google recruiter popped onto my screen. She was so sorry. She hadn't realized my interview had been shorter than the allotted forty-five minutes. She would like to correct this error in protocol. Did I want to schedule a redo?

Before I'd even fastened my seat belt, we'd scheduled a new screener; not wanting to wait, I'd taken their first available date, which was the last day of my trip. There would be just enough time to do the interview from my hotel room before my flight.

Chapter 21

Blond Ambition

THE MORNING AFTER I returned from Colombia, I was getting ready for work. I was pulling apart my bag to find my favorite shirt when it hit me: I'd forgotten about the rescheduled Google interview.

Idiot, said the mean voice. *There goes your last chance.* It couldn't be, though. Nobody had called me. I grabbed my phone, checking to see if the interviewer had called. It appeared they hadn't. Had I said I'd call them? I couldn't remember. Shit. I pulled on my shirt and ran out the door. I would write an apology. What would I say? I was still racking my brain for the right words an hour later when the recruiter sent *me* an apology. The interviewer had forgotten to call! I hit reply and typed: "No worries, I actually forgot too!"

My thumb hovering over the send icon, I stared at what I'd written, frowning. Most successful people I'd met in Silicon Valley spoke less than I did, holding their cards close to their chests. I started again: "Let me know what we can do about it, thanks."

Adam Levine had bleached his hair white-blond. I was binge-watching *The Voice* on demand, trying not to check my phone for a reply from the recruiter.

"That's weird," I said to my roommate, Amy.

"What's weird?" she responded.

"Adam's hair. It's too young for him," I said. "Isn't he, like, forty or something?"

Amy glanced from her laptop to the TV screen, where Levine was on his knees, begging a young country-pop singer to be on his team. "It's not that bad on him," said Amy. "But it would be better on you."

Saturday came, and still no response. I went to CVS and picked out two boxes of hair dye with a platinum-blond male model sulking on the box. I was onto myself, aware that I was doing this impulsive thing just to distract myself from my uncomfortable nervousness about the job. But that didn't stop me. Before I could change my mind, I raced back to my apartment, shut myself in my bathroom, and got to work. If I messed up, how bad could it be? I would look young and dumb; so what? This was good! Better to do it when I'm young than when I'm forty-something, like Adam Levine.

I slathered the first box on my hair and stared at the mirror in anticipation. Slowly at first, then faster, my hair under the white paste faded to a lighter brown, then an orangey yellow. It was working! Next stop, platinum! But there was no next stop. It didn't get lighter. I opened the second box, slathered on some more, and waited. Still, my hair didn't get any lighter—just oranger and oranger. Panicking, I jumped in the shower. Amy had left behind half a bottle of purple shampoo that claimed to make highlights "sassy, not brassy." I dumped some of that on my head and rinsed and repeated till the bottle was empty.

When I toweled off and looked in the mirror, I absolutely did not look like the guy on the box. Instead, a crazy, neon-headed clown stared back at me.

I needed professional help.

Me: [*Entering a hair salon, wearing a knit ski cap*] Hi, I have
     an appointment.
Salon receptionist: You're the kid who turned his head
     orange?
Me: Afraid so.
Salon receptionist: I can tell from the hat. Right this way.
     [*Leads me to a chair*] This is Bethany, your stylist. She'll
     sort you out.
Bethany: Hey, Michael, can you take off the hat?
Me: [*Frozen in terror*] I can't.
Bethany: It's okay, hon, I've seen it all. [*Plucks off my hat,
     gasps*]
Me: [*Pouncing on an incoming call from Google while
     defensively covering my head with my hand*] Hello?
Google recruiter: Michael Sayman?
Bethany: Wow. Okay. Wow. This will take some time.
Me: [*Shouting over hair dryer noise*] This is him . . . he . . .
     me!
Google recruiter: Hi, Michael. Is this a bad time?
Me: [*Hunching over in chair to avoid Bethany's impatient glare
     in mirror*] This is a great time!
Google recruiter: I've made some calls, and we can skip
     the phone screening, go straight to the on-site. If
     you're still interested, that is?

My hair was white. Not blond. Not even platinum. White as
snow. I looked like a completely different person. I *felt* like a
completely different person—or possibly a tall elf. It was not
a look I'd have intentionally gone for two days before an all-
day corporate interview. But I thought it was definitely a good
look for the new Tinder selfies I was taking on my bedroom
balcony at sunset.
     It had been a month or so since I went on Tinder. Now,

minutes after posting the new photos, I had a half-dozen new matches. *Interesting,* I thought. *That's more than usual. Oh look, this one even winked at me.* They were all cute. One was even half Peruvian, with shiny dark hair and a sunburst smile. What guy wouldn't want to date her? Me, apparently. Left, left, left, left, left, left . . . I swiped them all away without even pausing to read their profiles.

Meanwhile, my sister was blowing up my Snapchat.

Michael, what the???
You look like Adam Levine!
When did you do it?
Why????????
All my friends are asking me if you are gay and I'm
   defending u!
Because you're not . . .
Right?

I'd forgotten that in Miami, bleaching your hair was not considered a hip thing like in California. It was considered a gay thing. I typed back:

Yeah, right!
Just having some fun.
Totally not.

The next morning I woke up with a weird thought in my head. *What if I am?* I pushed it away and went to work.

A few days later, after eating some takeout with Amy, I went to my room, threw myself across my unmade bed, and opened Tinder again. Just for kicks, I went to the settings and turned on "Searching For: Males." I left "Searching For: Females" on, too, because of course I did. I just wanted to see what other guys' profiles looked like. As a comparison. It was always good to study the competition, right? And just because these were guys looking to be matched with guys, it didn't mean they weren't looking at girls, too, just like I was. Right?

The "competition" was actually looking good.

Let me just swipe right on a few of them, I thought. *Just for the hell of it.* I swiped right on the ones that I wished I looked like, the ultimate competition. I didn't consider the possibility that I might be attracted to these guys. I was just jealous of them, like in high school, when I'd see an unusually attractive guy and think, *If only I looked like* him, *my life would be so much better.* For some reason, looking at these guys was giving me a weird feeling I'd never had in high school—a feeling I'd never gotten looking at profiles of beautiful girls, either. And yet when it came to looking at guys' profiles, I was much less interested in their bios than I was in the girls'.

Also unlike the women, the men I swiped right on responded almost instantaneously. High on the positive feedback, I kept swiping, and within a few hours, I'd matched with hundreds of guys. It was exhilarating. Addictive. I didn't talk to any of them, of course. That would have been misleading, since I only wanted to *date* girls.

Over the next few days, I continued matching with more and more guys, and eventually, I found myself talking to some of them. Then at some point, I realized that I was actually flirting. And it was fun. "Hey, I love your hair, too. How's your day going?" But every time a guy would suggest meeting up, I'd panic and ghost him. *I am not supposed to be doing this,* I'd think. And then, *But why, again?* And then, *Would it really hurt to go on a date?* And then, *Are you crazy, Michael?* My mind would flash to all those old family dinner-table conversations—my mom gushing about her future grandkids or recounting how her father would rather have died than have a gay son . . .

I couldn't be gay.

All the same, I began to seriously panic about the possibility that I might be. The specter of it hung over me like a threat.

Calm down, I'd tell myself. *It's not a big deal if you are. It's not a fatal disease.* But being gay, it seemed to me, would be a massive inconvenience. How would I ever have a family?

But then again, there was this guy, "Brad, 24," who'd been messaging me, wanting to meet. He looked kinda cute in his pictures. I couldn't stop pulling up his profile to stare at it. Did I owe it to myself to look into this gay thing a little bit?

By "look into it," I meant Google it, at first, of course. Google had never failed me. So now I Googled, "Can gay people legally adopt?" and "What states allow gay marriage?" and "What does an egg donor do?" This is not stuff they tell you about in Catholic school, so it was a happy surprise to find out that apparently there had been progress since my mom got her information.

Chapter 22

The Day of Seven Interviews

WHEN MY BIG INTERVIEW date at Google came, I made a brief appearance at Facebook, then Ubered ten miles south to the Googleplex in Mountain View, as I had taken the day off work for the interviews.

Damn, was I nervous. But at least, thanks to the multiple coffee dates I'd already been on with members of Google's VR team, I didn't have the added stress of feeling as if I were landing in a foreign country. Four or five of those meetings had been at Google, so I was already familiar with the colorful, retro-futuristic campus and knew exactly where to go when I stepped out of my Uber at the gates of the City of Google.

After checking in with security and getting my clip-on visitor's pass, I made my way through a sea of Google bikes and Google buses to wait in a bright, industrial-sized waiting room decorated with murals of robots and spaceships painted in the style of an illustrated children's book. Taking a seat in a hot-pink armchair, I went over Andrew's advice that the most valuable asset is self-awareness. "Nobody is perfect," he had told me that morning on the phone. "Nobody is a total genius; we're all stupid about a bunch of things and that's okay. You just have to own what you know and own what you don't."

Soon, a thirtysomething guy in a plaid lumberjack shirt and ironed chinos led me through a maze of hallways, explaining what I was in for: "The way this works is you'll cycle through

seven interviews with various groups of Google employees—
not necessarily people you'll be working with, though. We like
to have wide-ranging feedback. All our employees take part in
interviewing."

I followed him, nodding and smiling, into a micro-kitchen
hung with splashy art prints. "Here, take a water," said my host.
"You're in for a long haul here, you'll need it."

The metro-lumberjack led me to a small meeting room with
a giant TV screen displaying the Google Hangouts logo and
said, "They should be popping up on the chat in a bit." Then
it was just me and a camera in my face, waiting. Were they
already watching me? I pretended to look out the window
thoughtfully. The TV flickered to life and I was facing a young
Asian-American guy sitting in some other room. The sudden-
ness of his appearance made me giggle, which was embarrassing. Especially because it was immediately clear this guy wasn't
in the mood to mess around. He got straight to it, telling me
about his work as an engineer for Gmail and YouTube, which
are both Google companies, of course. Then he asked me what
was the most important thing I'd learned at Facebook, and I
trusted Andrew's advice and told the truth: "I learned that I
was a bad manager," I said.

The engineer raised his eyebrows. He looked surprised, but
not unpleasantly so. "Oh? Why do you think that was?"

"I was probably too young," I said. His eyes flickered down
to my résumé, probably looking for my college credentials. I
was about to correct course and explain that while I was still
obviously young, I'd matured and now had more experience,
but Andrew's words, *Own what you know and own what you
don't,* echoed in my head. I took a different course. "There
were actually lots of reasons," I said. And for the next fifteen
minutes I outlined them. I knew that this was not in the interview rulebook. It was most probably not advisable to spend
an entire interview talking about one's weaknesses. But in the
end, it seemed to work in my favor. The engineer shared that

he, too, had failed at managing and was exponentially happier now that he'd found the right role at Google. Then he signed off, the screen went black, and someone was knocking at the actual door behind me.

I spent the next half hour walking around campus with a bubbly product manager with four years' experience, discussing our respective approaches to handling various design and engineering problems that teams often face. "What's been your biggest product-related challenge at Facebook?" asked the PM. *Oh no,* I thought, *I have the perfect story for this one, but it will mean spending another interview talking about my failures.* After a moment's hesitation, I told her that Facebook was an old company trying to act young, so I'd launched Teen Talks to address how we thought about and approached the teen market at a deeper level.

"Hmmm," said the bouncy product manager when we were done with our half hour. "That was pretty gutsy." I'd never thought about it that way, but maybe calling Facebook out for being out of touch had been sort of gutsy.

After the walking interview, I ate tacos with a designer who wanted to know about my history before Facebook. By this point I was pretty much over my nervousness and ended up delivering a twenty-minute monologue about how I'd never been the best student, so I'd learned to focus all of my energies on the unique things that I *was* best at. I said that there were a million students in the country competing to be the best at the same things—from Presidential Physical Fitness Tests to the SATs—and that I'd long ago decided instead to be the best at my own thing.

Between gulps from my fifth bottle of water, in a conference room with bright purple chairs, a man in his fifties—a Bernie Sanders type with wild white hair—asked me the weirdest question: "What will be the solution to the VR problem twenty years from now?"

"Which problem is that?" I asked, leaning forward in my chair.

"Obviously," said the man, "the problem will be the world itself. How would you design it better?"

I leaned back in my chair, took another sip of water, and recalled the Facebook article I'd posted a couple weeks earlier, about what I called nostalgic bias. Now I was off and running. "Some people may not agree with me," I said, "but it's my belief that the problem with the virtual world interface of 2040 will be that the middle-aged designers of today who envisioned it created a broken-down, watered-down version of reality. Maybe eventually it'll get as good as the real world, but for now, the real world is infinitely better. These designers were nostalgic for a world they grew up in, where all of our devices didn't exist. But you can't turn back the clock. What does the iPhone generation, who grew up connecting with others by flipping from screen to screen, want from the virtual world, where they can look around, three hundred sixty degrees?"

Bernie leaned forward in his chair.

"Instead of a backyard to play in, they want three hundred sixty degrees of iPhone screens, videos playing all over." I was waving my hands around now, excited. "More screens, more tabs, more bite-sized data, more asynchronous communication!"

"Holy mother of God," said Bernie, falling back in his chair. "I've never heard an answer like that. That sounds like . . . hell." He left me a few minutes later, shoulders hunched. By his body language, I thought for sure I'd blown it with that one. I'd made it all the way to the fifth interview, only to send my interviewer into an existential depression. It was over; I was surely done. I waited for someone to come and escort me out, but that didn't happen.

Instead, a female engineer took Bernie's seat and struck up a conversation about video-compression algorithms (about which I knew nothing). Within minutes, I began to falter. I was trying to keep up, using borrowed engineer language I didn't really understand, but the video engineer's forehead was scrunching up, as she tried to follow my unsound logic. Damn it. I had been so close. And now I was being unmasked as a fraud. My lack of a real comp sci education was indeed coming back to bite me. But then . . . *Own what you know and what you don't know,* said the Ghost of Andrew, whispering in my ear.

I cleared my throat and said to the video engineer, "I would like to do some research and get back to you with some better ideas, if that's okay?"

Apparently it was.

The next thing I knew, I was sitting next to a marketing manager in a blue dress in the shade of a tree on a bright yellow bench, in the midst of my . . . *seventh Google interview*!

What was it about? I was quite delirious by this point. Was it possible I was dreaming? I do vaguely remember offering— hoarsely—some half-hearted ideas about how I would solve a dispute between team members with divergent work ethics. Or it could have been about game theory, for all I know.

While I didn't have a job offer at the end of the day, I felt I'd done everything I could to put my best foot forward. I was drained and dazed and starving, but I felt confident that I'd been true to myself, and I was proud of that.

Chapter 23

Offer of a Lifetime

Soon after the Day of Seven Interviews at Google, the recruiter called to extend an informal offer of employment. For the longest time, I'd been afraid I was hired by Facebook only because I was young and people thought it made a good story, or, okay, maybe they liked my app—but I wasn't really qualified for the job. Google's vote of confidence allowed me to believe that maybe I *was* worth something. I'd climbed and climbed, gotten exhausted, felt like I was going to fall, and just before I did, I took a risk and took that last big leap, onto the next rocket ship. When I opened my eyes, I realized I'd landed on a new peak, higher than I'd ever been before. If I'd been playing a video game, I would have reached a whole new level.

It would take several months of back-and-forth calls to hash out exactly what I'd be doing at the company and what they'd pay me for it. In the meantime, I still had to show up every day and do my best at Facebook. I also continued posting daily notes to the company-wide Facebook page. I was still obsessed with how we should be doing more to engage teens.

One day, after I had posted a note about how much the video features at Facebook could learn from the creator loop on YouTube, my cell lit up on the table. It was the Google recruiter.

She was calling about my salary. Here was another messy situation I'd gotten myself into. When she'd first extended the informal offer from Google, the recruiter had asked me to get back to her with the salary I wanted. Andrew had warned me not to answer—to let them give *me* a number, then negotiate up. That way I wouldn't risk lowballing myself, asking for much less than they might have been willing to pay. I'd tried to take this advice, but the recruiter had called back and pushed me for an answer at a moment when I'd been particularly distracted— riding a bicycle at full speed across the crowded Facebook campus to get to an appointment. So I'd caved, blurting out a figure that was a minuscule step up from my Facebook salary.

Almost immediately, I'd gotten a sickening feeling that, yep, I'd lowballed myself horribly. (When would I learn that it never paid to ignore Andrew's advice?)

"Did you get the salary details I emailed the other day?" the recruiter was asking now. "Is everything okay?"

I answered with an authority I'd never heard from myself before: "I've reconsidered," I said.

Several beats of silence. A rustling of papers. More silence.

"But I went by the numbers you gave me," the recruiter finally said, clearly flustered.

"I know," I said, thinking, *Do not apologize, do not apologize, do not apologize.* "It's just that I've done some diligence, and I now think the offer is too low." *"Diligence"? Where'd I get that word? Who was this guy speaking through me? I liked him.*

"I see," she said. "Okay, well, if you can just—I want you to be excited about joining Google, we really want you here. So what is the number that would move you?"

"I'll let you know," I said. Badass Michael was about to hang up when people-pleaser Michael butted in and chirped, "Thanks so much! Talk to you soon! Bye!" Oh well, it was still a good start.

The call had made me late for my workout with Jasmine. I was always late for Jasmine, even though my hour with her was the best part of my day. We'd become good friends since she'd guided me to my pull-up triumph, and these days, we spent as much time gossiping as working out.

"What's your excuse today, Mikey?" she asked as I ran up, panting, to join her on the soccer field. Jasmine's latest torture method was making me push a heavy sledlike machine called the Prowler up and down the field. I grabbed one and began slogging.

"As always, sorry," I said as several buff, grunting guys pushing Prowlers flew by us. "I got a call from the Google recruiter."

Jasmine frowned, watching the bro team and their bulging muscles storm their way up the field. "I'm sure gonna miss you," she said.

"It's not a done deal yet. We're still discussing the salary."

"Still think you lowballed yourself?" said Jasmine, then, "No, don't stop! You can do it!"

"Definitely," I huffed.

"Hmm," said Jasmine, skipping in slow motion beside me as I push-crawled my way forward like an ancient dung beetle. "Hey, I wonder what would happen if you asked for a crazy amount of money?" She was bouncing up and down now—Jasmine was always in motion. "Ha, what if you asked them for, like, twice as much, just to see what would happen?"

I stopped in my tracks, still gripping the Prowler, head down, sweat trickling from my nose onto the toes of my trainers, and thought about that. I swiveled my head to look up at Jasmine. "You know what? You're right! Wait, no, why stop there? What if I ask for *more* than double my current salary?" I was one of the only people out there who had both youth and years of experience creating apps. Over the past eight years, I'd made thirty-four of them, after all. Some had had good runs, and some had failed out of the gate. But what mattered was that I'd never stopped creating and would not stop until I struck gold—actually, not even then. I'd never stop making. I made that pretty obvious to anyone who talked to me for more than five minutes. But above all, I knew the value of being the go-to young adult in Silicon Valley. "I'm gonna ask for half a million!" I blurted.

Jasmine stopped bouncing. "Oh, Mikey, I was sort of kidding. I don't know if that would honestly work! Maybe you should ask for a slight increase?"

I always had trouble picking up on sarcastic jokes. I straightened up. "Nope, I'm doing it."

Jasmine's face lit up. "Well, okay then!"

Two minutes later, we'd abandoned the Prowler in the middle of the field, and I was striding back toward my gym bag. I unzipped it and dug around for my phone.

"Um, Michael, do you think maybe you should take a minute, plan what you're going to—"

I waved Jasmine away, already holding the phone to my ear. The call was going through.

"Michael!" said the recruiter. "That was sooner than I expected! Have you thought about a figure?"

I took a deep breath and said: "I've given it a lot of thought, and I believe a fair salary would be—"and I proceeded to ask Google to pay me what amounted to two million dollars over a four-year vesting period.

The recruiter let out a little gasp and then went silent. I bit my lip, waiting.

"I'll have to get back to you on that," she said.

Looking back as I write this now, half of me still can't believe I had the nerve to negotiate as hard as I did that day. But the other half of me believes it just fine. I might not have realized it at the time, but I'd learned a very valuable skill from being followed around by news crews throughout my childhood: the key to projecting confidence when you don't have it is to throw away your negative thoughts—just toss 'em. *Now* you're in the driver's seat, negotiation mode. It's all about seeming positive, focused on your strengths and accomplishments. No matter how stressed or worried you are, just remember that you can throw that stress and worry away and pick it up after your interview or negotiation.

Today, I tell anyone who asks me for advice: don't be shy about negotiating for whatever you can get. Your biggest opportunity to claim a good salary is the first time you get hired. Sometimes an employer will make vague promises about giving you more over time, but don't count on that. Know what you're worth *today,* and fight for it.

For the next two weeks I waited, bracing for the recruiter to come back with a list of reasons why Google could no way, no how justify the crazy sum I'd thrown at them. I figured that in a best-case scenario, they would counter with a slightly higher amount from their original offer. Worst case: I'd offended them, and they would retract the offer.

And maybe that wouldn't be such a bad thing, I told myself. This job was still fun, sometimes. For example, there was Snapchatting with Mark Zuckerberg. How many people could say they did that? Zuckerberg's snaps always cracked me up, and I enjoyed explaining to him how a typical teenager might use the product versus how he'd used it. There were less cool things than giving one of the most powerful men in the world Snapchat and feedback on product strategy of the multibillion dollar company.

Scared to death of change, I was grasping for any reason at all to stay at Facebook, the only job I'd ever known. I was even beginning to wonder if I'd subconsciously tried to sabotage the Google opportunity by asking for an impossibly high salary. Which would be so F'ed up. Wasn't there a certain convenience to staying within my comfort zone?

By the time the Google recruiter called me back days later, I was 97 percent decided that I would turn down the counteroffer and stay put.

"Michael," said the recruiter on the phone, "I have some very good news. I have approval to give you *almost* exactly what you wanted." She then rattled off a mind-boggling series of figures.

She paused, waiting for me to respond. But this time my silence wasn't a power move; I was in too much shock to get a sound out. When I finally found my voice, it said the most incredible thing: "Thank you. Can I think about it for a little bit?"

"How long is *a little bit*?" said the recruiter with a steely tone that I'd never heard her use before. Understandably. After two months of back-and-forth, the woman had gone to bat for me, more than doubling the salary I'd originally asked for. How had she justified it to her higher-ups? I wondered. Was I really worth this much? I never dreamed of it. I was going off what people told me I was worth, but it was hard to grasp being worth this much. I should be proud of myself for getting them up to this number. And yet, I was hesitating.

"Um, three days?" I said.

"Okay, talk soon," she said.

I spent my allotted three days looking for reasons to run the other way from the offer of a lifetime.

What if it was just a giant cosmic trick? What if I wasn't really qualified and everyone around me was just telling me that I was? If only I hadn't pushed for millions! I could've lived well and *slept well* on less than half what they determined was my market value to them.

Google clearly had high expectations. They were offering me millions of dollars to do a job they felt I was qualified for, but I still had trouble rationalizing it. What if my unconventional opinions about the future of VR, which had so excited them, turned out to be all wrong? What if I was totally unqualified for this job?

As I was having these conversations with myself, the recruiter called back once again. It had only been two days, and I needed more time to think. I let it go to voicemail. She called back. I picked up.

"Michael, I made some more calls and was able to get you an additional signing bonus of seventy thousand dollars."

Was I hearing her right? Was she seriously offering me *more* money?

"There's just one thing . . ."

I cleared my throat. "What's that?"

"I'm really sorry about this, but the VR team no longer has head count to bring on a new hire. So we'll have to find a different spot for you. I'm sure it won't be a problem."

Chapter 24

I Kissed a Boy

I'd decided to give "Brad, 24" from Tinder a chance. How did guys dress on dates with other guys? It wasn't the kind of question I could ask Andrew, for once, so I just stuck to my favorite girl-date outfit: a long-sleeved white T-shirt, dark burgundy pants, and a black leather jacket. Brad had picked a restaurant in the North Beach area of San Francisco. *Please don't let him be taller or shorter than me,* I thought on the walk from the train. I thought that if he was shorter, he would be the "female," and if he was taller, I would be the "female." I hadn't grown up knowing any gay couples, or any openly gay people at all, so this was my ignorant guess at how it all worked.

The restaurant turned out to be an old-school Italian place, all red-checkered tablecloths and gold-speckled mirrors, dark wood and brass railings. I spotted Brad right away, hunched over his phone at a table by the window. I went cold. In the few seconds before he looked up, I had the flash of an impulse to turn around and walk out the door. Too late. Brad had seen me. He was smiling. He looked nice enough. I forced a smile and sat down opposite him. We exchanged some fill-in-the-blanks small talk, just like on hetero dates—how long we'd each traveled to get here, how happy we were it was finally sunny, what looked good on the menu, etc. Brad's hazel eyes were really something, though; they glimmered every time he smiled in a certain flirty way. I tried to focus on his hazel eyes, not on how everything else about this person was different from what I'd expected. I still couldn't tell how tall he was, but he didn't look like his Tinder pictures; he wasn't as cute. In the week that we'd been messaging back and forth on Tinder, I'd been picturing someone more thrilling, a little mysterious. But Brad was more earnest than exciting in person.

As we talked, I devoted all my mental energy to analyzing Brad's every gesture and word. Why did he put his fork down and tilt his head like that when I said I hadn't gone to college? Did he pity me or something? When he said he "enjoyed" his job in marketing, did that mean he found it fun and stimulating or that he hated it but didn't want to complain? He didn't seem in any hurry to make his mark on the world. This depressed me a little. I hoped there was some drive inside this guy but kind of doubted it. I had yet to meet someone in my age bracket who didn't still think of going to work as "adulting."

I ordered a pizza margherita and a glass of red wine—willing our gray-mustached waiter not to card me, which he didn't. I hadn't gotten around to getting a fake ID and rarely drank, so I felt the effects of the alcohol pretty quickly. By my second drink, I'd stopped swiveling my head around like an owl to see who might be staring at us (no one was, duh, this was San Francisco). I felt myself letting down my guard, hand over hand, like lowering a drawbridge across a moat; the wine had made me too swimmy and lazy to hold it up much longer. I was telling Brad a story about my family when he cut me off midsentence:

"You have the cutest smile. I love that you have braces."

I clamped my mouth shut, feeling a blush creep up my neck. I'd never been complimented on my smile or any aspect of my appearance by a guy before. It was disorienting; I felt like I was in one of those old Disney Channel movies where a boy wakes up in a girl's body and gets to experience life through her eyes. I was pretty sure that "You have the cutest smile" was something guys said to butter up girls, even if I'd never said anything so flirtatious myself. How interesting that gay guys used the same cheesy lines as straight ones, I thought.

"Uh, you do too," I finally said, taking a big chug of wine. Truth was, I hadn't even noticed his smile, because every time it came, I was focusing on his hazel eyes. I wasn't about to compliment him on *that,* though. It would be too sincere, and I wasn't ready for sincerity.

Brad shook his head with possibly fake humility. He was obviously used to this back-and-forth and seemed to be enjoying it, though in a slightly impatient way. He moved his chair closer to mine and leaned in till his face was inches from mine and I could smell the garlic on his breath. "You obviously work out," he said.

"Ha, a little!" I scooted my chair away from his.

"Sorry." Brad straightened in his chair. "I hope I'm not making you uncomfortable?"

"Oh, no, not at all!" I said. He was, of course, but not because of his transparent moves. Brad didn't exactly turn me off, even if he wasn't what I'd hoped for. But I wasn't ready for this to go any faster. It was just all so new and weird. I briefly thought about telling him that he was my first guy-date ever, but then I thought, *Nope, still not ready for sincerity.* Maybe I could try a little harder, though, to see if there was something to this . . . thing?

So, I ordered a third glass of wine and tried to find the commonalities between us. We both liked our pulled pork sandwiches! We both liked the wine! I'd never worked so hard to find common ground on a date before. With the women I'd gone out with, it had been the opposite: whenever my date had seemed excited about something we had in common, I'd feel indifferent, with no desire to pursue the conversation further.

After dinner, we walked to a theater to see *Despicable Me 3,* the only movie playing at the right time that didn't have subtitles or women in corsets on the poster. As it turned out, Brad was a little taller than me, but contrary to my ignorant fear that it would make me the "female," I wasn't bothered by it at all. At the cinema, I made sure to get popcorn, as a handholding-avoidance tactic, but Brad grabbed my hand anyway a couple of times. It felt weird, holding another guy's hand. I was playing at something I still didn't understand. When he began tracing the lines on my palm, I pulled away. Too intimate. Not ready.

Later, when we'd ditched the movie and were walking along a pier at Fisherman's Wharf, listening to the yowling sea lions, Brad took my arm and pulled me to a shadowy stretch near the railing.

"Want to see something?" he said. A flash of his grin in the dark.

My pulse drummed. *Please no,* I thought. *Please don't let him pull it out.*

"Stand here, next to me," said Brad, turning me to face the water, then turning that way himself, so our shoulders were touching. "Now close your eyes and stretch your arms up."

I did, feeling our arms brush as he did the same.

"Now lower them," said Brad.

As we lowered our hands to our sides, my right palm fell into his left. Now we were holding hands. It was kind of a sneaky trick, and while it felt extremely corny, it was kind of cute—if I had to be honest. We looked out over the choppy gray bay rocking the boats in the harbor. I did my owlish neck swivel to see if anyone was watching us, but the pier was empty, thank God.

I never knew before what people meant when they said they felt butterflies in their stomach. I thought it was just an expression, like "It's raining cats and dogs." I never knew that this was something you could really feel, like dozens of creatures were flying around inside of you. I wasn't sure if it was good or bad, but it was happening. I guessed it meant I was excited, on top of being scared. On dates with girls, I guess I'd just been scared.

Brad led me to a bench facing the water. The butterflies were getting annoying now. He leaned over and kissed me, very gently. *Oh,* I heard myself think as the kiss went on. Not, *Wow!* Just, *Oh.* As if I'd asked a question and gotten an answer that made sense. My mind was not blown—while it was happening, at least—but I felt weird. As Brad pulled away, I realized that the butterflies had gone quiet, suspended in midair, waiting for me to decide how I felt.

I felt exhausted, and also ready to go home. I needed to be alone to process what had just happened. "I should get going," I said to Brad.

He looked disappointed but gave a little shrug. "Cool."

We walked back down the pier in silence, and Brad didn't try to take my hand again. I felt a little bad about all the mixed signals I'd been sending, but I didn't want to make it worse by apologizing. My initial exhaustion was morphing into a muted panic. What had I done? I'd tricked myself, that's what. Told myself the date would be platonic, for research purposes. But I'd never really wanted it to be, I realized now. Maybe I'd wanted something very different all along?

We stood awkwardly under a streetlamp, waiting for my Uber. "Thanks, that was fun," I mumbled, suddenly shy again, not quite meeting Brad's eyes.

"Yeah, I enjoyed meeting you," he answered. There it was again: *enjoyed.* My car had come, thank God. He stepped to the curb to open the door for me, and I got in, turning to wave as we pulled away. But Brad was already walking in the other direction, hands shoved so deep in the pockets of his tight jeans that his arms were straight as fence posts, his shoulders pushed up to his ears.

I spent the ride back to Redwood City having an internal dialogue with myself. Thankfully, the mean voice stayed out of it. From talking to friends at Facebook about how they dealt with challenges and disappointments, I was starting to learn how to circumvent the negative self-talk that I'd indulged in for most of my life. The best tip I'd gotten for diverting a negative spiral? Ask yourself questions! Here's what that sounded like in my head now:

This can't happen again.

No, of course not.

But why not?

Wait, do you even want to go on a second date with Brad?

Brad was nice. His eyes were nice. He enjoys marketing. He enjoyed our date. He was patient. He didn't push.

But no, I don't think I want to see him again.

Maybe a different guy, though?

I pulled out my phone, tapped the Tinder app, then felt sleazy. I tapped over to Facebook Messenger. Immediately, a new message from my mom to our four-member family group chat pinged on my screen. "How's it going, *hijitos*?"

The question was directed at both my sister and me, but had she sensed that I had something important to tell her? Was she inviting me to open up? Weren't moms supposed to have a sixth sense for this coming-of-age stuff?

I texted back into the group chat, where my mom, dad, and sister were included. "Hey Mami! Nothing much, I just went on a date with a guy. It was pretty cool."

This was not going to be a big deal. My family was fine, deep down, with gay people, no matter what they'd been saying all these years.

No response came from my mom for a good few minutes. Then: "*ok hijito, ten cuidado,*" which meant, "Okay, son, be careful."

She signed out, leaving me sitting there with my heart right out in the open.

Huh.

—

The next morning, I tried Mariana. She didn't respond to the group chat message, and I was dying to talk to someone about my date, but figured I should ease into it:

Me: Did you get all the classes you wanted for next year?
Mariana: Yeah, but all on different days and times.
Me: Very ironically, I went out with a dude last night. [*Hysterically laughing emoji*]
Mariana: and different teach . . .
wait what
like a date?
with a guy?
so you are gay
?
my friends were right
lmao and i defended you
Me: I don't think I'm gay [*hysterically laughing emoji*]
Idk I like girls a lot
But I was like lemme just try it [*hysterically laughing emoji*]
Like I can't imagine ever marrying a guy
But it was fun to try [*hysterically laughing emoji*]
Idk it's all just weird now hahahaha
Mariana: did you kiss the guy?
how did you end up going out?
Me: I guess we like super matched or something. idk how that works but it like showed up for me and I was like ok let's try [*hysterically laughing emoji*]
I only had girls on the app
I really like girls
Mariana: are you sure you want to do that, tho?
Me: Cuz why not?
Good to try everything [*hysterically laughing emoji*]

Mariana: This is going to sound fucked up
but I don't want people to hurt you if they find out you
    are gay
Me: Anyway, I'm almost done building the first test of
    my new game!
Mariana: I just don't want you to get shit from people so
    like I think you should be careful.
Me: I'm not gonna write a Facebook post dude
It was nothing special.
Mariana: OK.

And that was the last I heard from my sister for a whole week, during which I carried our exchange with me like a brick. *Are you sure you want to do that?* The words rang over and over in my mind until I started to ask myself the same thing. I would backtrack, I decided. I would try with women again. There was still hope for me. I hadn't gone too far.

Ignoring Brad's repeated messages asking for another date, I went on Tinder and, with a heavy heart, changed my settings back to "Searching For: Girls."

Chapter 25

Twenty-one

Two MONTHS LATER, EVERYONE my sister had ever met, and everyone *they* had ever met, and a bunch of people *those* people had just met in the hotel lobby—were all at my party. It was my twenty-first birthday and I was standing in the center of the living room, holding a dripping ice bucket and pouring champagne into outstretched glasses belonging to total strangers. I was wearing my TV smile and welcoming everyone with gusto. My neighbor from when I was ten showed up with some friends but didn't recognize me until I said, "Pedro, it's me, Michael!" We tried to catch up, but the music was too loud for conversation, and Pedro and his friend wandered onto the patio. The same thing happened with some kids I knew from high school. It didn't matter. The important thing was that the contract with Google was signed; I'd made it. And for the moment, at least, I wasn't alone to enjoy it.

We were at the Fontainebleau, the most popular resort in Miami. The celebrations were under way and they were already beyond excessive. The room cost $8,000 a night.

Technically, I was supposed to be working for Facebook until September 1, but they'd let me finish out my time with them from Miami, where I was "working remotely" and using up all of my saved vacation days. They were so accommodating about everything—a little *too* accommodating, from my ego's perspective. When I gave notice, my manager didn't physically jump for joy, but I think his words were, "Okay, great! Yeah, that makes sense!" We both knew my heart hadn't been with my work at Facebook since the day I started looking at opportunities at Google.

There was an awkward moment when my sister and her friends picked me up at the apartment I was renting. I complimented one of her friends, Samantha, on her latest manicure. "Your nails match those flowers exactly," I said, pointing to the birds of paradise lining the driveway. "Go like this, I want to take a picture."

But Samantha yanked her hand back. "Haha! That's so gay."

We rode in silence. I felt stung but stupid for being so sensitive. Samantha, like all the kids I knew in Miami, was never one to be politically correct. That was just how they talked; it wasn't personal. But the word *gay* now hung in the air between me and our friends. Earlier, Mariana had warned me not to talk to our friends about "gay stuff." Mariana had said that she and my mom had discussed it and thought it was better if people in Miami just didn't know I was exploring my sexuality options. "You know how Latinos talk," she'd said. "You tell one person here, and the next day it's all over Peru, and, you know, it'll just be a big mess."

I'd agreed to keep my explorations to myself, and I had no intention of getting into it now, but Samantha's throwaway comment had made me realize that I really needed to talk with my sister.

Let's get back to the party, though. Someone turned on a giant flat-screen. The Mayweather fight was happening, and everyone wanted to see it.

"Can we buy it, Michael?"

"Of course!"

I told yet another stranger the story about how Mayweather's crew trashed this very room the night before we came. The fight was intense and bloody and filled the party with a weird charged energy that I couldn't decide if I liked or not.

The elevator kept depositing more new people, too many people, into the suite, and I was drinking more and more to stave off the panic attack that had been trying to come on for some time now. When I'd had enough alcohol, I ran into the master bedroom and locked myself in and started to cry. Birthdays have always filled me with anxiety, and the alcohol was only making it worse.

"Michael? Open up!"

I let Mariana in and went back to the bed to continue sobbing. She stood next to me and gently rested her hand on my shuddering shoulder. "What should I do, Michael?" I couldn't answer her, because I was crying too hard, and I didn't have an answer anyway. "Okay, I don't know what's wrong with you right now, but I am just going to make sure that the suite doesn't fall apart out there, okay?" I nodded, wiping my face, and continued sobbing some more, but less intensely now. My heart had started to slow down; the alcohol-induced emotional wreck I had turned into seemed to be passing.

As Mariana tried to leave, one of her friends stormed past her, slamming the door. Now it was the three of us. The friend was crying even louder than me. Mariana should really become a wedding planner or something else that requires total calm in the face of other people's emotional breakdowns. Her hand was on the friend's shoulder. "Oh no," she said calmly, "what happened?" The friend had just caught her boyfriend making out with another girl. And then the boyfriend came running in to find her, and they started screaming at each other. Mariana disappeared, and I realized that I'd stopped crying. I was watching this couple fight like it was the finale of *Jersey Shore*. The girl threw a remote control at her boyfriend's head, but of course she was too drunk and it missed. "I want him out!" the girl screamed. I looked around the room, which had now filled up with bystanders, to see who she was talking to. "Michael, I'm serious, get him out!" Oh, she was talking to me.

I followed the boyfriend out of the master bedroom but then forgot what I was supposed to do when the elevator door opened and a string-bean-skinny kid with pink dreadlocks walked into my party with a case of malt liquor. It seemed like a good time to kick *everybody* out, so I started the process.

By six a.m., it was finally just me, Mariana, and a few of her friends. We ordered a shit ton of room service—chicken nuggets and French fries and pizzas and everything else that screamed "teenager food" on the menu—and sat around the living room, eating in silence, red plastic cups and empty bottles at our feet.

"Hey, what's that?" Mariana pointed to a pinch of white powdery stuff on the glass coffee table.

We all put down our plates and circled around, peering at it.

"Something not-good," said Mariana's friend Victoria.

"Don't touch it, nobody touch it!" I said.

For the next ten minutes, we speculated on what type of brain-damaging substance we were looking at and whether or not it could be valuable enough for its owner to come back for. Thankfully, it didn't seem to cross anyone's mind to try it. I was Googling "What is the consistency of cocaine" when my sister leaned over the pile like it was a birthday cake and blew the white powder all over the room.

There was a period of shocked silence as the four of us took in what she'd done: the pinch of white powder disappeared into the carpet, a lampshade, the curtains, the shiny leaf of a banana plant. "Mariana," I finally said, "why'd you do that?"

My sister just flipped her long black hair and, in her very Mariana, very eighteen-year-old way, shrugged. It was the best moment of the whole night.

—

The next night, we did it all over again, except I didn't cry. The hotel had a three-night minimum stay, so at the insistence of Mariana and her friends, we had a second party, just as raucous. I was too exhausted and overcome by déjà vu to feel my emotions. It felt like I was already in the future, and the guy with diamond-studded teeth who was peeing in the banana tree in the hallway of my hotel room was already in the past. Along with those bridal shower girls in cardboard tiaras who were sloshing their pink drinks all over the white sofa for which I was responsible. I said nothing to the rude party crashers. Weirdly, I was almost grateful to them. They showed me that none of this shit was the answer to my loneliness, and it never would be.

It was the day after, an hour past checkout time. Mariana and her friends had gone. I was signing my $26,000 hotel bill at the front desk when my mom appeared by my side in a sun hat and paisley beach muumuu. She and my dad were using the pools—the Fontainebleau has eleven of them; I'd seen none—under my reservation. "Don't *gooooo*! Come hang out with me and Papi!" begged my mom, hugging me to her. "They've got music and they've got breakfast! They said it was complimentary for those in the Presidential Suites!"

At first, I'd worried about what my parents would think of this ostentatious celebration. There were two options, I figured: either my mom and dad would be uncomfortable and annoyed, thinking I was rubbing my money in their faces, or they would be ecstatic, taking my splurge as confirmation that I was loaded enough to support them from this day on.

It was definitely the latter. I decided not to be a cynic about this. My parents have always been comfortable embracing the good life, even if it is beyond their means.

What I really wanted to do was go home to my apartment and sleep away the ten days until I was due to start at Google.

I worried that if I spent too much time with my parents, they would start in about the money they wanted for a down payment on a better house, or for a desperately needed renovation to the town house, or to help my sister with her college book expenses, and I would feel cornered but too tired to argue and leave another twenty grand poorer. But my mom was giving me her puppy-dog eyes. I followed her to the cabanas and changed into my swimsuit to join her and my dad in the hot tub they'd taken ownership of for the day.

"*Hijo!* How was the party?" called my dad over the roiling jets he'd turned up to the max. In the bubbling water he held a Bloody Mary in one hand, a bitten stem of celery in the other. I lowered myself into the water across from him and my mom and told them almost everything—leaving out my panic attack and the white powder on the coffee table, but including the plant-urinal guy. My parents hung on every word, appreciating my stories, as they always do. Eventually, I stopped worrying about them bringing up more serious stuff. I should never have worried about it in the first place, really. Why was I so hard on them all the time for just wanting to be happy?

"Hey, Michael!" said my mom.

"Yeah, Mom?"

"Stop thinking!" She splashed me and I splashed her back. I realized that this was all I'd really wanted the whole weekend. I just wanted to laugh.

Chapter 26

The Noogler

"GO AHEAD," SAID OUR leader encouragingly, "get Goo-gley!" Along with a couple dozen other new employees gathered in the brightly painted room, I sat at a low kindergartner-style table, knees up to my ears, cutting out construction-paper shapes with miniature scissors. It was our first day of orientation, and we all wore "Hello, My Name Is" name tags. I was having a blast making cut-out stars and comets, but the others at my table—all appearing to be about twice my age and dressed in corporate-friendly blazers, skirts, and button-downs—did not seem to share my enthusiasm.

"*Oof,*" muttered the woman sitting to my left. She'd taken off her pumps to fit her legs under the table but still looked pinched and uncomfortable in her gray wool pantsuit.

Technically, not all of us were "Nooglers," as they called first-week Google employees. Google was one of several companies owned by Alphabet, our parent corporation. Back in 2015, Google was pursuing so many projects—self-driving cars, longevity research, urban innovation, and so on—that the founders, Sergey Brin and Larry Page, decided to spin off each non-Internet division into its own company. They created Alphabet to hold them all, including Google, the biggest. I could not believe I worked at Google now! Everything I'd ever learned—how to code, program, design—I'd taught myself through Google. It was like if Dorothy had gotten to Oz and the Wizard had offered her a job. I'd been following the yellow brick road to this moment for half my life. And the best part was, I could say, "Just Google it," again. The comms team at Facebook frowned upon using "Google" as a verb when speaking to the press. They preferred "search the web."

When the orientation leader was satisfied that her new recruits had sufficiently expressed themselves with scissors, she clapped her hands and said in a singsongy teacher way that I hoped was just her being in character, "Now it's time for an exercise in critical thinking and group work!"

Uh-oh, I thought, putting down my scissors. Group work: not my strength.

"Each table," the teacher continued, "is going to concep-tualize a game and build it with the materials we've laid out for you. Make up your own rules, write them down, and then we'll share. The team that creates the clearest, most effective user experience wins!"

A bearded dad-type across the table began carefully rolling up his plaid sleeves. Like everyone at the table but me, he wore a wedding ring. "Let's dig in, team!" he said. "Ideas?"

I'd told Andrew that I would try my best to be a team player at Google, and there was no time like the present. I picked up a stack of paper Dixie cups. "A tossing game?" I suggested.

"Sure," said another team player, "why not?"

We came up with a game where people took turns throwing a paper ball into a cup. If they made it, they could ask another player a question about themselves. If they missed, they'd share something. Sounded simple to us. No one else thought so. When it was time to "launch" our creation, the other tables couldn't read our crayon-scrawled directions and just seemed generally confused by Paper Toss, the Game, as we'd named it. As our competition listed off their complaints, I was amused to note some head shaking and puffing by my tablemates, who seemed to be taking our loss very personally. "*Pffft,*" went Pinched Gray Suit. "My four-year-old could've followed those instructions."

I was going to take something away from today, even if it was only the orientation leader's reminder: "If you don't like testing your product, most likely your customers won't like testing it, either." The New Michael was all about growth, and if that meant embracing the lessons of adult kindergarten, I was up for it. I would embrace it all, even wearing the rainbow-colored beanie with a little propeller on the top that the orientation leader gave to each Noogler at the end of the session. The hats were supposed to be worn for our entire first week. Unlike some of my more high-minded table compatriots, I wore mine proudly as we were led outside for a group photo in front of the Noogler statue, a giant green Android wearing its own beanie. When more senior Googlers whizzed by on rainbow bikes, yelling, "Welcome!" I waved back, beaming.

At four p.m., our leader clapped her hands again and in the elementary school voice announced, "Any minute now, everybody, your managers will be here to pick you up, take you to your buildings, and introduce you to your teams!"

After the opening in VR had fallen through, the recruiter and I had decided I would be a good fit with the Google Assistant team. The Assistant was the artificially intelligent helper that Google had launched a year earlier, in May 2016. Just like Siri, you could ask the Assistant to do things for you—find song lyrics, check flight information, call your mom, etc.— and sometimes, sometimes not, you'd get what you asked for. The goal was to keep improving it until it became humankind's go-to method for searching the Internet, writing emails, and carrying out all the other day-to-day jobs that keep our lives going.

My new manager—I'll call her Violet—was one of the lead product directors for the Google Assistant. I'd never met her in person before, but now I assumed she was the woman with light brown skin and long dark hair power-walking toward me with her hand extended.

"Michael, nice to see you! Come with me!" After a quick handshake, she continued on. I tried to keep up without breaking into a run. Now that I'd been separated from the other Nooglers, I felt like an idiot in my propeller hat, the frat pledge with underpants on his head; I was dying to take it off but didn't want to appear unpatriotic or something. I was beginning to get a sense of Google's scale. Around half of Alphabet's seventy-five thousand worldwide employees worked at the Googleplex. The place made Facebook's fourteen-thousand-person Menlo Park campus seem quaint.

"I'm so glad you're here," said Violet, who was somewhere in thirties-land. "We really need a millennial perspective."

"Actually—" I started, then stopped myself.

The old Michael had almost explained that, while I was born at the tail end of the millennial generation, I related much more to Gen Zers, kids born from 1997 onward. But I was New Michael now. I was aware that Old Michael's habit of pushing back on every little thing had not been super effective at Facebook. New Michael was learning from his mistakes.

". . . I'm so glad to be here too!" I finished.

As we talked, I was excited to be looking into a Latina face. I'd see many people I assumed were Latino that day, but I wasn't sure if they were working full-time or on contract, or if they were even Latino, as we have a wide range of skin tones. One thing I did notice about her right off the bat—she looked fierce and badass. Everyone who passed gave her a quiet smile and nod. She commanded respect, instantly—and I knew she would expect me to ramp up very, very fast.

The Assistant team was housed in three brick buildings that connected via two interior bridges. Violet led me inside, pointing out the perks of the open floor plan: the lobby with pool tables and foosball machines; a row of private massage rooms for soothing stressed shoulders; "nap pods" that looked like giant white Pac-Men with people's feet and legs sticking out of their mouths; a fully stocked micro-kitchen, which did not seem micro at all, but more like the brightly lit set of a cooking show; and best of all, only ten feet from my new desk on the second floor, a silver spiraling slide that led down to the lobby and gaming room. "To encourage that sense of youthful adventure!" said Violet.

"I love it!" I said.

"Good. *Someone* should use it," she said, glancing at her smart watch. "It's almost five, so most of your team is gone, but let's meet who's still here, shall we?"

"Great!" I said. As usual when I was nervous, I could only seem to speak in affirmative declarations. I looked around the football-stadium-sized floor, the rows and rows of now-empty desks, the micro-kitchens, massage chairs, plants, minibars, and couches. "How many are working on the Assistant, again?" I asked Violet.

"Over one thousand," she answered, as if this weren't a completely ridiculous figure.

What the hell do they all do? I wanted to shout, but instead I said, "Amazing!" and followed Violet around, shaking hands and immediately forgetting everyone's names. Each time someone asked, "What will you be working on?" I'd say something like, "Still refining that!" or "I'll let you know!" I needed to figure that out. Violet was giving me some time to propose my own scope of work. I was being given a significant amount of trust.

By my fourth day on the job, I was beginning to regret that trust. I'd been working and reworking my project scope to present to Violet, and I had a headache from all the straining and second-guessing.

When it came right down to it, I was terrified, feeling like a child. The slide next to my desk (I used it every chance I got) and the boxes of Legos in every lounge area (I was resisting) didn't help. Nor did the puzzles and toys scattered throughout the office, or even the giant ball pit in one of the buildings. It was very confusing, this mix of inner-childing and adulting.

Scared and insecure as I was, I would not go to the dark, self-hating place. I would stay open. I was New Michael.

After a few more days of talking to my colleagues and taking notes, I figured out what I wanted to do. I thought it would be cool to teach the Assistant to read between the lines of its user's speech. Since most people weren't used to barking commands at a real-life assistant, I figured they might be more comfortable using the Google Assistant if it could take hints, or even figure out what the user needed before the user did. For example, the Assistant was good at executing commands like, "Remind me to get a haircut tomorrow at two p.m." But that's how someone would talk to a computer, not to a person. If you were talking to your flesh-and-blood assistant, you might complain about how bad your hair was looking, and they would understand that you were really asking for help. In short, I wanted to teach the Assistant that if a user said, "How do I bleach my own hair?" it should respond, "Perhaps I should book you a salon appointment?"

Violet gave me the green light, and I assembled a team, which consisted of reaching out to a few engineers, asking what projects they were working on and whether they wanted to help us build out the Assistant. (It was a safe bet to assume that any engineers working at Google were going to be good.) Our team was just one of the two hundred or so devoted to the Assistant. The Google Way was apparently to have many teams working independently, with the strongest projects rising to the top.

Pretty much right away, I discovered I had no idea how to function within this system. I didn't know what questions to ask or whom I had to talk to in order to get anything done. I didn't know how to best communicate with people, to look them up internally, set up calendar invites, or book meeting rooms. Google's internal tools were foreign to me. I was used to the ones Facebook used. I didn't know which meetings I was supposed to go to or which calendars to schedule my own meetings on. With my past failures as hindsight, I might have been equipped to take on one project with one team, but nothing had prepared me for the challenge of negotiating and blending within a network of two hundred teams.

This was a job for someone who'd had a big three-ring binder with organizer tabs in high school, not someone who'd stuffed his papers directly into his backpack and forgotten about them. I'd only just begun, and already I was afraid that I might suck at this job.

Chapter 27
_____

That Christmas Feeling

IT WAS THE SUNDAY after Thanksgiving, and my Target shopping cart was three-quarters full of Christmas shit. I threw in a wooden SANTA STOPS HERE sign and stared at my loot: two boxes of blinking garland lights, a snowman cookie jar, "Feliz Navidad" hand towels, a snowman plush toy, a Christmas tree snow globe, and a pack of limited-edition apple and cinnamon Holiday Air Wicks, to make the apartment smell like home. Normally, the sight of all that stuff would've made me overwhelmingly happy. But for some reason, it didn't lift the blue feeling I'd had all weekend.

I'd thought it was just burnout from a week of working all day at Google, then pulling all-nighters to make improvements to my new app, Lies, which was garnering media attention but not retaining users. Work stress was usually something I could alleviate pretty well with a little rest and relaxation, and I'd been getting plenty of that this weekend. Instead of spending the holiday with my family like I always did, I'd stayed in California for a "Friendsgiving" with three of my colleagues, then killed the rest of the weekend playing video games and watching TV. Now I was doing my favorite thing ever, shopping for ugly holiday decorations.

So what was my problem? I had no regrets about skipping Thanksgiving (and the inevitable family drama that went with it). But maybe all the same, I did miss my family.

I'd been thinking a lot about my post-birthday-blowout afternoon with my parents at the Fontainebleau pool. It had been the happiest time we'd spent together in years. I wanted it to be that way again. Maybe I'd take the four of us to Disney World, our happy place, for Christmas. Or maybe . . . I picked up the snow globe and gave it a shake. Duh, of course! Christmas in New York! A cold-weather Christmas, with ice-skating and real trees and maybe even—to top the fantasy of all fantasies—some snow. That's what we needed. Especially my mom.

My mom loved Christmas so much. That was where I got it from. It was her favorite holiday, or at least it had been before the recession, when the restaurant was doing well and she could shower us with presents and everyone would get matching pajamas. She still talked about Christmas 2004, when my dad had just put a brand-new dark red Ford Excursion on the credit card and we drove it from Florida all the way up to New York City. Mariana and I were seven and eight. I didn't remember much about the trip, but I felt like I did because of all the times I'd heard my parents talk about it. To this day, they would still reminisce about the hotel we stayed at, the Marriott Marquis in Times Square. "Remember the circular restaurant, and how the yellow taxicabs way down below looked like bugs?" my mom would say. My dad always used to answer, "One day, we'll go back." But I hadn't heard him say that in years.

It was perfect. I'd take us all to New York. I took out my phone to FaceTime my family with the invitation.

A month later, there we were, together again, in the lobby of the Marriott Marquis. I'd timed our flights to arrive at JFK at the same time, and we'd taxied into the city together, squished into a yellow cab in our new puffy coats.

"Look at that tree!" My mom peered up at what appeared to

be a giant sequoia planted in the lobby, dripping with super-sized decorations.

"Michael, can you ask someone to take our picture all together?" My mom was looking around, holding out her phone. In Miami, she was always calling strangers over in Spanish to take our picture in restaurants or museums or anyplace nice enough to post on Facebook. But she was much shyer in places where the expectation was to speak English if you were in public.

"Or we could just do a selfie," I said, pulling my family in close and holding the camera over our heads. My dad was too tall to fit in the frame, but I quickly snapped one with his head cut off and said, "Let's check in!" before my mom could start organizing a portrait session.

"Just one room?" said the desk receptionist, looking from my dad to my mom to me to Mariana. I nodded. We'd always shared a room when we traveled. Were Mariana and I too old for that now, from a non-Latino perspective? Whether we were or not, I didn't care. This was already going to be an expensive trip, and the possibility that things might not work out at Google was growing by the day, as was the plan I was hatching to go out on my own as a solo game developer. I'd been talking to a couple of investors about it, but I wasn't going to tell my parents that. I knew it would terrify them.

I did love my job. But it didn't always align with my operational style. I tended to have divergent thinking: either I was giving my all to Google, or I was giving my all to my own apps. There were moments when the two worlds intersected, but mostly I felt like a garden hobbyist who couldn't wait to leave work so he could get his hands in the soil.

"Just the one room," I said.

The receptionist nodded. "We currently have you in a north-facing room, but you do have the option to upgrade to a Times Square room." She twirled her screen to face me, pointing to a picture of a glamorous room with a towering view of glittering skyscrapers, billboards, and thousands of cars trailing up Broadway. That room was almost $700 more.

I looked at my parents, who were taking in the same view from the lounge. My mom was pointing out all the landmarks she remembered from our 2004 trip with giddy excitement. It was so good to see her Christmas spirit back. "Yeah, I'll take that," I said.

Mariana gasped. "Papi!" she called across the lobby. "Do you know what Michael just did?"

"Mariana, shut up!" I whispered, collecting our room keys and heading toward the giant circular elevator bank in the center of the room.

"What did he just do?" said my dad.

"Michael, tell them!" Mariana's eyes were glinting with the secret.

I shrugged, like it was nothing, which it was, compared to what I'd spent on the Fontainebleau. "I got us a view of Times Square."

"No, no!" cried my dad, clutching his chest. We were in the elevator now, shooting up to the thirty-third floor.

"Michael, you didn't have to!" said my mom, slapping my arm.

But then we opened the door to our room, and everyone gasped at the same time and rushed in. The view was even better from up here. It was starting to get dark outside, and the sky was cotton-candy pink. The billboards were all futuristic now; a couple of them looked like holographs with 3D effects.

My mom was making little murmuring sounds, like she was praying.

"Ah, I *love* it! We're in Times Square!" said Mariana. She pulled out her phone and opened Snapchat, then took a bunch of selfies to post. "Can you imagine if it snowed? A white Christmas? Oh my gosh." She pulled out her phone to check the weather again. When we'd come for Christmas in 2004, the only thing missing had been snow. I hadn't seen snow since I was three.

My dad sat down on the bed, looking out at it all with tears in his eyes.

"Everything okay, Papi?" I sat next to him, looking out.

"I thought I was going to die without being able to do it again," he said, wiping his eyes. Then he smiled and clapped me on the back. "Thanks, Cocolocho."

I felt proud, bad for my dad, and shitty, all at the same time. It was so easy to make my parents happy. And I had—at least for now—the means to do it. Why didn't I do it more often? Why did I always have to second-guess every generous impulse I had? I'd worried that by taking them on this trip, I'd be setting up the expectation for me to start paying for their whole lives again. When they saw how much I was spending, someone was bound to bring up how much money I had now, which would make me defensive, and then Mariana would call me selfish for not doing more, and I would regret ever having done anything—or else feel so guilty that I'd end up opening my bank account to them again. I shuddered. My family and I, we had to learn to communicate better. Not just about financial stuff, but about the me-possibly-being-gay stuff, which had gone unaddressed since I'd tried to share it with them, months ago. My parents' nonreaction to my announcement that I'd dated a guy had been weighing on me. My plan was to bring it up over a cozy restaurant dinner—tell them lightly that since the Tinder date I'd mentioned, I'd also dated another guy for a while. I'd say that it hadn't been serious, but all the same, I'd come to the conclusion that my interest in guys wasn't just a passing thing.

I didn't end up saying this at dinner that night in the hotel restaurant. We were having too much fun, and I didn't want to see my dad's smile go away.

And I didn't find the right moment the next day, as we walked around the city, bundled up in our coats and knit caps decorated with snowflakes and pom-poms, embracing our tourist status with pride. I knew my family wasn't interested in seeing the "authentic" New York. They wanted *Aladdin* on Broadway and Tiffany on Fifth Avenue and I Heart New York souvenirs—all the things we'd seen and done on our 2004 trip—and I wanted to fulfill every wish.

On Christmas Eve, we took selfies at the Boathouse in Central Park; walked arm in arm down the High Line, blocking everyone's way; popped into a store that sold only cookie dough; and ended up at the 9/11 Memorial Plaza, where all the trees were winter-bare and the bronze walls of the twin memorial pools were freezing cold, even through the three layers my mom made everyone wear. We were all in a row, propped on our forearms and looking down over the edge, even though you weren't supposed to, listening to my dad's detailed history of what had led to the terrorist attacks of 1993 and 2001—and the wars the United States had been waging in the Middle East ever since then. It was getting dark, and we were all shivering, but no one complained about the cold or interrupted once. I was in kindergarten in 2001, and I had only the most basic understanding of the 9/11 story, so I was listening closely to my dad's impressively detailed lesson. It was one of those rare moments when he was actually playing the role I'd always wanted him to—teacher, authority figure, capital-D Dad.

After the lecture, my sister took my dad's arm and they walked over to stare into the second empty footprint. My mom and I stayed where we were, listening to the falling water for a minute, and then she turned to me, her eyes big and serious. "There's something I wanted to tell you," she said, reaching up to tighten my scarf like I was five again.

"Okay," I said, bracing myself. What would it be this time? Had they defaulted on the car payments? That was probably it . . .

"The night before we left, the Peraltas had a Christmas party . . ." She was gripping my sleeve. Her nails, painted white with red snowflakes, puckered the fabric to the point that I thought she might puncture it.

I nodded. Where was this going? Did she break something of the Peraltas'? Mrs. Peralta had that collection of porcelain figurines . . . Had she had a little too much punch and knocked one over? I wanted to stop her right there and tell her that whatever it was, I would pay for it. She didn't have to be scared.

"Well, everyone was talking and we were having a very good time," continued my mom. "And then, you know how people at home can sometimes say things that are . . . insensitive? Like, make fun of people?"

I nodded, starting to see where this might be going. In Miami, it was pretty common to hear people casually spout clichés about African-American people, or Asian-American people, or lame jokes about LGBT people. It was something that had always bothered me, growing up, and I tried to push back where I could. It was eye-opening to see how these topics were addressed in California, where there seemed to be zero tolerance for those kinds of comments.

My mom continued, "Well, somebody at the party, they made a joke about . . ." She looked down at her pink snow boots for a few seconds, then back up at me. ". . . about gays. And you know, always before, I would just laugh it off. But not this time. I was mad, Michael. I said, 'No! You can't make those kinds of jokes. They're not funny!' I think everyone was surprised I got so mad, but I didn't care. I don't care so much what people think anymore."

Wow. Not what I'd expected. But nice. I gave my mom a hug. "Thanks, Mami."

I felt kind of bad, standing in one of the saddest places in the world and feeling so happy.

That night, we did the most Christmasy thing we could think of and headed to Rockefeller Center to see the giant tree. In

Miami, real Christmas trees were extremely rare, a huge luxury, and my mom couldn't get enough of them. Even after the recession, she'd always gone to huge lengths to get us an actual, once-living tree. So it was worth it to brave the crowds to see the Rockefeller tree, the pinnacle of Christmas tourism. Mariana and I even endured the hour-long line to go out on the tiny little ice-skating rink for about five minutes, just long enough for my mom to take a thousand pictures of us stumbling around with crazy grins on our faces.

At midnight, freezing and hungry, we were headed to the Hard Rock Cafe, another pinnacle of tourism, when it started to rain. "Just like in 2004!" said my dad for the hundredth time that week.

And then I noticed that the rain was falling slower than it fell in Miami.

"Is the rain falling slower?" I said to everyone. "Or am I just really tired?"

We stopped in the middle of the sidewalk and looked up at the falling drops.

"No, you're right. They are falling slower," said Mariana.

And then the four of us at once let out a huge cheer. "It's snowing!" we yelled over and over again, jumping up and down. "It's snowing!"

Never mind that it was bullshit snow, more of an icy rain that melted as soon as it hit the sidewalks. It was snow to us.

Chapter 28

Unblocked

"WHAT'S SO FUNNY?"

I looked up from my screen to see Jacob, the VR director who'd gotten me my first interview at Google, standing over my beanbag chair.

"Oh, hey, man—nothing!" I jumped to my feet, closing my laptop on the e-card a designer friend from Facebook had sent me. She'd taken that famous painting, *The Scream* by Edvard Munch, and written over it in festive gold font: "Happy 2018! We're All Gonna Die!"

It had been three months since I'd spoken to Jacob—practically since I'd started at the company. A few days ago, I'd sent him a message via chat to let him know that I didn't feel very excited about my job and was thinking of leaving. He'd told me he was also making a change—leaving the VR team for a new division at Google called Area 120, where there might be a place for me, too.

I gave Jacob a bro hug.

"Got time to grab a coffee?" he asked. I had to smile—everyone *always* suggested coffee. I hated the stuff. Usually I just said yes, then ordered water. This time I suggested, "How about a bite?"

An hour later, at Heritage, one of my favorite restaurants at Google, Jacob shook my hand and left me sitting in front of my empty plate. I was a little bit in shock. What we'd just discussed—it was almost too big to process. I did a little trick I'd employed since middle school, rapidly jiggling my knee and taking in a long, slow "smell the tea" breath through my nose, then blowing out a "cool the soup" breath through my mouth. Better. Now I needed to organize my thoughts. I closed my eyes and started to draw something like a bubble chart in my mind, separating the key data points from my conversation with Jacob into individual circles to keep everything from jumbling up and overwhelming me. I pictured each of the bubbles in shades of yellow (happy data) or gray (negative data).

In circle one: Area 120; sunny yellow. Apparently, Area 120 was an incubator, where people got to work on their own shit, all day long. How cool was that? It was inspired by Google's "20 percent time" tradition of allowing employees to spend a fifth of their working hours on personal projects that might help the company in the long run. At Area 120, Googlers spent 100 percent of their time on 20 percent projects. Hence the name Area 120.

In circle two: Jacob; yellow. He was about to transfer from VR to Area 120 to work on something very futuristic and top secret.

In circle three: what Jacob knew/the rumor; murky gray. What exactly had he said? It was something like, "There's a rumor you're talking to investors about leaving to start your own app company." Yeah, he'd definitely said "rumor," which meant other people had heard this, too. Had Violet? It wouldn't have surprised me. She seemed to be sort of scarily all-knowing. I'd told her I wanted to stay at the Assistant. I'd promised to try. This part definitely felt murky.

In circle four: the possibility of leaving Google to start my own company; amber yellow. The rumor was true. Just before my family trip to New York, I'd been contacted by a couple of venture capital investors—partners in their own firm. They knew of my many apps and were impressed with Lies, in particular. They didn't care that it was bombing, and I didn't, either. I'd spent only a couple of weekends building it, and I never updated it. In fact, that was why the investors liked me so much: I was fast and prolific. Jacob had once mentioned that I was the fastest mobile app engineer he'd ever worked with. If my personal track record proved anything, it was that I didn't let failure stop me or even slow me down. I just kept experimenting and building and failing some more. One day, the odds were sure to be with me.

In circle five: the VC guys themselves; dark gray. They'd been super aggressive about wanting to back me to leave Google and go out on my own. They didn't care about the content of the apps I made; they just wanted a piece of whatever they were. Which meant they'd have a piece of me for a very long time, if not forever. Did I want to be beholden to the opinions of a couple of money guys? If it could end with me being financially stable for life, possibly. So I'd taken a couple of meetings with them but was putting them off, not feeling quite right about it.

In circle six: Google Assistant; cement gray.

In circle seven: the offer Jacob had just made me; screaming electric yellow. Okay, it wasn't an offer. Not technically. But it sounded like Jacob was taking his cue from someone high up at Area 120. I'd memorized exactly how he'd put it: "You've been floated as someone they want to support." When I'd asked what that meant, Jacob had had the answer ready: I'd get to keep my same salary and benefits, and build all the apps and games I wanted. If an app succeeded, I'd be compensated for that, on top of my salary. Area 120 would own anything I'd created while I worked for them. Fine with me! Games never lasted forever, anyway. I'd have taken the salary, benefits, security, and freedom Jacob was describing over ownership of any of my previous apps in a heartbeat.

That was better. I understood everything clearly now. I stood up and walked outside feeling weirdly light.

—

Three weeks after my conversation with Jacob, there was still some paperwork to finish, but it was basically settled: I'd said goodbye to the Assistant and a relieved Violet, and moved over to Area 120, where my whole job was just to do what I loved: invent and build games. The only difference was now I got to do it in the daytime, when my brain was fresh and working at full capacity, instead of after hours in my bedroom. If I envisioned the next Snapchat, Area 120 would own it, but I would at least get to keep a piece of the valuation, plus what I thought of as a "success bonus," if the app did really well.

It took me no time at all to find my groove at Area 120. Right away I began the process of sketching out an idea for a social media app I'd been thinking about for a while. The idea for this one was simple: players would guess things about each other, then find out whether or not they were right, building a friendship via a game. I had a desk, but I couldn't remember where the assistant who'd shown me around said it was. Too embarrassed to admit this, I'd been coming in and plunking down on the same red couch every day to do my thing.

The Area 120 offices looked even more like a day care center than the Noogler orientation room had. Every wall was crowded with colorful art, and there were Legos everywhere. There had been Legos scattered around at the Assistant building, but they weren't a *theme* or anything. At Area 120, we loved Legos on a whole different level. There were giant bowls of both the Duplo and the classic kinds on desks, on Ping-Pong tables, and in the VR rooms, along with little toy cars, Jenga sets, and puzzles—though I never saw anyone playing with them.

The place was so full of toys that on my first-day tour, I'd asked if people brought their kids to work with them.

"Um, these aren't for kids. We like to encourage folks to take breaks and have a little me-time to explore their creativity,"

I was told by my tour guide. "We want our founders to be able to relax and be themselves. Think of them as creativity-unblocking tools." Interesting.

My creativity was already unblocked. My creativity was flowing from so many jets, it was like the Fountains of Bellagio in Las Vegas. But it wasn't because of the toys. It was because I'd been listening really closely, these past few months, to my intuition. It had told me not to give up on my apps, to make them my priority above all else. And then I'd had to listen extra carefully when the venture capitalists came around and kept upping their offer to fund my gaming app start-up. It had been a tough call, turning down that opportunity. But instead of leaping at it with my eyes closed, like I normally would have, I'd sat with it a while, tuning into how I felt whenever I talked to the VCs and imagined partnering with them. As excited as I'd been to work on social gaming apps, the feeling I got about the VC situation had stayed gray. When the Area 120 opportunity came up, I'd run the numbers, comparing the potential financial upsides of creating under the incubator's umbrella versus founding my own start-up with the investors. Financially, both options were pretty sweet, but the solo option offered more potential upside—my friends kept reminding me that I could become a billionaire. But I didn't care about becoming a billionaire. On the other hand, Area 120 would give me stability and the opportunity to be guided by people I really admired. As I'd weighed the options, I'd just kept checking in with my mental bubble chart, tuning into the colors I saw in each bubble. Area 120 shined the brightest, no doubt.

So here I was, settled into my bright red couch, making little designs for my new social media app, while other Area 120 founders buzzed around like quiet bees. At a nearby conference table, Laura Holmes, the founder of a smartphone app called Grasshopper, was meeting with her team. Holmes had created the app to teach curious beginners to program through games and quizzes. Like the learning platforms Khan Academy and (today's) Mimo, this was exactly the kind of thing we needed in the world. It made me downright happy to hear Holmes talking about "expanding the digital ecosystem" and "helping bring underrepresented groups into technology."

She was obviously a good manager, pausing to encourage her team members with constructive feedback while walking them through a long list of assignments. Listening to their animated discussion, I felt a twinge of the familiar "odd man out" feeling I'd had through most of my life—especially at Facebook, when I could be surrounded by my own team members but still feel completely alone. At least I had my test characters, the imaginary kids who used to help me with my apps in high school. At Facebook, I'd been so stressed out that I'd lost my motivation to conjure them, which was probably why Lifestage had turned out so totally non-intuitive and wrong. But as soon as I'd started working on my own games for fun again, they'd started to come back to me. Now, as I waited for my imaginary Drama Club president to pick her favorite button, I failed to notice someone standing directly in front of me.

"So sorry to interrupt, Michael . . ." It was Jon, the soft-spoken managing director of Area 120, trailed by several engineers, all looking at their phones. "Would you have a minute to talk about your team?" asked Jon.

"My team?" I said. "More than happy to!" I knew it was expected of me to hire one. To build things, you needed support. That was just how it worked. While I'd been contentedly going about my work solo, my manager had been expecting me to act like a manager and compile my dream team. I had something else in mind.

"How many designers and engineers are you thinking of hiring?"

None! I thought. But no one at Area 120 had ever done that before. In fact, it was the opposite of how everyone else at Area

120 worked. But with more people comes more political process, and more process leads to slower execution time, and slower execution time results in fewer product launches, and fewer product launches mean a decreased chance of launching a winner. I learned this from my mistakes at Facebook.

I had my answer for Jon. We walked together into the hallway, the other guys off to the side, comparing calendar openings—my most hated activity.

I was just going to say it. "I don't want to hire anybody. I want to start alone."

Jon stopped walking, clicked off his phone, and put it in his back pocket. We were standing near a micro-kitchen, where the Google barista was in residence for the day, making custom brews for a line of workers. The gleaming cappuccino machine screamed and sputtered like an ancient freight train. "I know it's unusual," I yelled over the noise. "But in the best possible world, to get the best possible results, I think I'd rather do it all on my own, until we land on a promising prototype where we can scale the project up into a fully staffed team."

The calendar people were looking at me with their mouths open.

Jon squinted, as if he were trying to picture me fulfilling his expectations solo. This simply wasn't done. The way it worked in Silicon Valley was the people in charge of the money gave lots of it to the people with the good ideas, in order to turn those *ideas* into *things* as quickly as possible. And the people with the ideas took the money and rolled with it, because, supposedly, more resources meant less work for them.

And now here was an idea guy who didn't want the money to build his own team. What was my game? Jon was probably wondering.

I explained further. "I don't need to be alone forever," I said. "But if I could just code and design my own prototypes and do the initial testing on my own, that would be . . . fastest. After that, we can hire the team to expand and grow the products."

The calendar people and I were all looking at Jon, who was rubbing his short beard, head tilted to the side, eyes closed. That coffee machine was so damned loud. I balled my fists up to force myself to shut up and wait this excruciating moment out. Finally, Jon opened his eyes again, looking refreshed. He was waiting for a lull in the cappuccino steaming, I realized, because he was not the kind of person who ever yelled to be heard. When it went quiet, he finally spoke. "You're the founder," he said, referring to the start-up I was running within Google. "So I suppose we should let you follow your instincts, shouldn't we?"

Chapter 29

Blue Eyes and Purple Flowers

I WAS NOT GOING to have sex with someone I didn't love. I did not like the idea of hooking up with a Tinder date I'd never see again. How it generally worked instead was: I would match with someone on the app; we would go out for drinks or food; maybe we'd kiss; they would immediately push for sex; I would say, "We're not going to have sex"; the date would end; and I'd never hear from them again.

Mariana thought the problem was with my Tinder bio, which was trying to be funny and failing epically because, I'd been told, you had to know me for a few months to understand my brand of funny. The bio didn't mention anything about my career. I wanted to be likable for who I was, not for having a good job, not for my money. But Mariana told me that she would only match with guys who seemed stable and successful, with a "high quality of life," as she put it. She thought my profile was probably turning off more serious guys who wanted a partner with ambitions beyond having fun. I followed her advice and updated my bio to say I worked at Google as a software developer. But I refused to take out that my three favorite things were Disney World, going on cruises, and Panda Express.

Since Area 120 didn't care where I did my work, I'd been going to Miami pretty often to visit my sister (though not always my parents), and also to stay in touch with what the average American teenager was doing on their phone. My biggest fear was that if I never left the Silicon Valley bubble, I'd accidentally start making apps that appealed only to millennials and, God forbid, Gen X–ers. Though my sister's friends were basically my age—Mariana and I were fourteen months apart—they all had younger siblings and friends, and I loved talking with them about my games and hearing their brutally honest feedback. Plus, I laughed more in Miami.

On one of these visits, I was bored and decided to swipe around a little on Tinder. I didn't want a Miami date, I just wanted to make some new San Francisco connections, so I put my location pin in San Francisco and began looking. Right away, "William" super-liked me. As soon as I swiped right, a message popped up:

> William: Hey, your bio is super impressive—except for the Panda Express thing.
> Me: Don't worry, I recently banned it from my diet, just left it there out of nostalgia.
> William: Where are you?
> Me: I live in California, but I am visiting my sister in Miami. Maybe we can meet when I'm back?

This guy was really cute and sounded smart in his bio (a grad student), and there were no pictures of him in his underwear—a good sign that he wasn't the have-sex-and-leave type. Quite the opposite: there were pictures of him in a garden, with his sisters! William seemed wholesome, the kind of person you could see introducing to your parents, when your parents were ready. I was getting excited, until:

> William: Oh no, I don't live in CA! Just here to chaperone my little sister on a school engineering competition.

We were both away from home to visit our little sisters. Now I liked him even more—and he wasn't even a possibility?

Me: Where do you live?
William: Florida. This is so funny.

It was funny. But I was kind of sad. I'd finally matched with this amazing guy, and now I was about to fly back to California, and he was going to fly back to Florida, and we wouldn't get to meet. But we could talk, at least. And for the next few days, we FaceTimed our faces off. I learned that William was also not a sex-on-the-first-date guy. He was studying biology and was really into plants. I could appreciate a nice rosebush, but I'd never understood the appeal of gardening, and I'd inherited my mom's affection for fake plants. I had them all over my apartment. I loved them because no matter how dry and dusty they got, they never died. Still, I liked listening to William talk about plants, which he did a lot. He talked about watering them, putting them in greenhouses, changing the light levels for them, giving them special food . . . William was as into his plants as I was into my games. I'd never dated a guy who cared so much about what he did.

I couldn't stand it. I had to give it a shot. "What airport are you flying into?" I asked.

The next week I flew back to Florida, this time landing at the Orlando airport, where William had left his car in long-term parking and flown from because it was cheaper than going out of his local airport. He was a grad student who worked in a lab, I reminded myself, so of course it made sense that he would drive two hours to a cheaper airport. We'd planned to meet there, and then I'd take him to Epcot at Disney World for our first date. He had never been to Epcot before, and this was the perfect time because their big spring flower festival, which I normally would've gone out of my way to avoid, was happening. I liked this guy so much I couldn't wait to go to a plant show. I'd never been so excited about anyone.

William was waiting for me in the pickup area in a silver 2008 Ford Focus. As I approached, he was being yelled at through his open window by an airport security woman who wanted to clear the curbside spot he'd been hogging for fifteen minutes because I was late. The woman went right up to his window, waving her hands around and getting louder and louder, while William, I noted with a twinge of excitement, stayed coolly indifferent. "It'll just be another minute, sorry," he kept saying. I broke into a run. "I'm here!" I yelled, jumping into the passenger seat with my Facebook-branded backpack.

"Hi!" I said, grinning at him with a face full of metal. In only two weeks I was going to get my braces off, after more than a decade. It felt like my confidence was about to be unchained, too. But not yet.

"Hi!" said William, grinning back. He had bright blue eyes that made my stomach do flip-flops, and . . . Was that a plant between his legs? "Oh yeah, I wanted to give you this!" he said, handing it to me. I didn't know anything about plants, but this one was covered in hundreds of tiny purple flowers and contained in a blue pot, which was wrapped in transparent plastic to keep the soil from falling out in the airplane.

"Wow, thanks." I ignored the muddy water that was leaking onto my pants and did my best impression of a person admiring a plant. "Did you get this at the airport?"

"Ha ha, no!" William seemed really shocked that I thought he would buy a plant at the airport. "I flew with it. I saw it at Home Depot, and it was your favorite color, so . . ."

I looked at the purple flowers with a new appreciation. He'd asked about my favorite color three days ago, near the beginning of our first Tinder conversation. "I love it," I said.

—

I had planned out the entire day while I was on the airplane. But because there were giant topiary statues of Disney characters and flowers everywhere you looked, William was as much the tour guide as I was. He would run from plant to plant, explaining where each one was from and what was special about it. Did I know that bamboo could grow thirty-five inches in a day? I did not! Had I ever heard that vanilla extract came from the pod of an orchid? It was news to me! William's excitement was so cute that at one point, I got over my self-consciousness and grabbed his hand. We walked around like that for a little bit, but it wasn't worth it. It wasn't that people *stared,* or gave us disapproving looks, but every single person we passed would take a tiny glance at our clasped hands as it registered for them, *Oh, that's a gay couple.* And all of those glances, they added up to one continuous, exhausting gaze. So we went back to just letting our fingers brush, which was easy because it turned out we were the exact same height, five foot seven. I loved that William and I stood exactly eye to eye.

Once William had identified every bromeliad and bonsai in the park, I took him on one of my favorite rides, Soarin' Around the World. It's a simulator ride, where you hang-glide through the Swiss Alps and swoop around the Sydney Harbor and weave through elephants on Mount Kilimanjaro. I'd been on Soarin' a hundred times in my life, and it had never occurred to me that it or any ride could be romantic. But flying above the world with William was the most romantic thing I'd ever done in my life. At the end, after the simulated fireworks display, there was a moment of pitch-darkness, and suddenly we were kissing. Then just as suddenly, the lights were on and a teenager in an Epcot vest was banging the side of our little car. "Okay, everybody, move along!" he said as we fumbled, red-faced, with our seat belts.

To recover from that awkwardness, we rushed to the World Showcase "Italy" pavilion for some limoncello, then on to "Japan" for some sake, then to "France" for a glass of Bordeaux.

Woozy and sun-baked, I thought of how, when I used to come to Disney with my family, we would find a patch of grass and lie down on a blanket my mom brought and nap until the lines thinned out. Sometimes it would take an hour or so, but we were never in a hurry. Now I grabbed the cuff of William's sleeve, pulled him over to a little green hill, and fell onto my back. "Let's take a siesta," I said, my eyes falling closed.

"Oh, okay." William sounded confused. But there wasn't time to explain. I was out cold.

When I snapped awake, the sun had fallen behind a topiary Pluto, casting us in shadow, and William was sitting next to me watching a dad chase his little kid around on the grass.

"Oh, shit! Did I fall asleep?" I sat up, looking around.

"Yes, you *did,*" said William, looking very amused.

"Oh no. Did I snore?" I covered my face with my hands.

"You did. Look, I took pictures of you." He pulled out his phone to show me the most hideous picture I'd ever seen. I lay with my head twisted to the side, mouth gaping open, arms splayed out at crazy angles. My nose was bright red from the sun and alcohol. I looked as if I'd just fallen out of a hang glider to my death.

"Oh God, how awful!" I put my head back in my hands, wanting to disappear. "I'm so sorry! I'm so embarrassed. I ruined our date!"

"Ha ha, what? No you didn't!" said William. He was rubbing my back, making tiny comforting circles. "I didn't mean to embarrass you. I only took that because I thought you looked really . . . cute."

Slowly I lifted my head. Was he teasing me? He had to be. But judging by his serious expression, maybe not. He stood up and held out his hand.

Chapter 30
_____

Diving Blind

AFTER EPCOT, WILLIAM HAD driven me back to his cozy little apartment, where he'd moved from the Northeast two years ago to go to grad school. I'd taken a small chance and booked my ticket back to San Francisco for the day *after* our date. If it had gone terribly, I could have stayed in an airport hotel. But it had gone the opposite of terribly, in spite of my narcoleptic episode on the grass. So I'd stayed the night with William. Nothing racy or anything. Since we'd already discussed how neither of us wanted to move fast, sexually, that pressure was off, and we just lay in bed and talked and watched Netflix and fell asleep early. As I was getting dressed to leave the next day, William said, "You know, I've got a couple of empty drawers, if you want to leave some stuff behind." The whole flight home, I couldn't stop thinking about that. I couldn't stop thinking about his blue eyes. So when he called and said, "You should come back and stay a bit, and then we can figure out what to do," I thought, *If he wants me to be with him, well, why not?*

Three weeks later, my new roommate, Matthew, was helping me pack. Amy had moved up to the city. While I tossed my living room stuff—a couple of emoji pillows I couldn't bear to part with, a Happy Hanukkah garland, old Bernie campaign T-shirts, and the fold-up fake Christmas tree that was still up in April—into the nearest open box, Matthew had taken on the kitchen. He sat cross-legged on the marble countertop in a Toronto Marlboros hoodie, peering into a mostly barren cabinet.

"Where are your plates?"

"Don't have any," I said. I'd never gotten around to getting dinnerware; I just ate directly from the takeout container, if I was at home.

"No way," said Matthew. He climbed down from the chair and carried his box into the living room. "I guess that's everything. Should I tape it up?"

I looked into the box. It contained two unopened packs of dish towels and a blender. There was still room for my Nintendo Switch. "Nah, just put it over there," I said. "Thanks, man. You sure you don't mind keeping the couch?"

Our couch was a black modular IKEA thing with a big rip down the center where its white guts spilled out. We'd logged a lot of Super Mario Odyssey there, but otherwise, I'd spent most of my time at home in my room, coding in bed. Matthew said he'd keep the couch. "I'll let my new roommate replace it if they want," he said. Since I was moving out so suddenly, we hadn't found my replacement yet, but I'd reassured him that I'd cover the rent till then. Luxury apartments like the one I had been living in were in high demand in Silicon Valley, so I wasn't too worried about it.

I was having one of those dive-into-the-pool-blindfolded life moments, but I felt pretty good about my odds. Maybe it wasn't even that crazy—I was just moving my stuff into a room in my friend Fred's apartment in San Mateo while I tested the waters in Florida, with William. For now, I'd fly back and forth between California and Florida every couple weeks. I rarely went into the Area 120 office, anyway—I worked much better from my bed—so nothing would really change from their perspective.

Even before William, I'd been thinking about moving

back to Florida. The truth was, I missed being around other Latinos—the Spanish, the Latin jokes, the loudness. But also, I missed Florida's theme parks and its diversity of lifestyles, career paths, viewpoints. I even missed the contrast of talking to Trump supporters, as half of my Miami friends were. In most Silicon Valley circles, someone who'd voted for Trump was simply not welcome. So everyone just talked about how happy or sad we were in unison. And almost everyone I knew worked in programming, advertising, or marketing at Facebook, Google, Apple, Yahoo!, or Microsoft.

If I had the economic freedom to be able to support living part-time in Florida, why not? If things didn't work out with William, I wouldn't be homeless, I'd just stay in California. There was only upside.

Now I was standing outside FedEx, next to a stack of four boxes that contained most of the warm-weather clothes I hadn't donated to Goodwill. I'd just realized I didn't have William's address, so I pulled out my phone and snapped a picture of my box tower and attached it to a message.

> Me: Where am I sending these?
> William: ?
> Me: What's your address?
> William: . . .
> William: . . .
> William: . . .

That was weird. Did he have to look up his zip code or something?

I paced around the boxes a couple of times. I had a meeting with Jon, the managing director of Area 120, to get to. I'd asked to give him a progress update on the latest social media game project I was working on, but mostly I just wanted to make sure he remembered what I looked like before I left for Florida. I wanted to be a real person to him.

Now the typing dots weren't even there anymore. Shit! I dialed William's number.

Just as it was going to voicemail, a text popped up with his address. No "Can't wait to see you." No favoriting my picture. It was fine. He was probably in class or something. I mailed my boxes and hopped on a Google bus to show my face at work, trying not to worry about the fact that William hadn't liked the box picture. Should I call him and make sure everything was okay? I didn't want to sound needy. My strategy was to keep it light and easy—like I was just coming for an open-ended visit, which, technically, I was. He didn't need to know I'd moved out of my apartment. It seemed like too soon for a Big Life Conversation. Not that I was worried about how he felt about me. The whole thing had been his idea, hadn't it? So there was nothing to worry about on that end. I just didn't want him to feel any unnecessary pressure. We'd spent only three days together in person, after all.

Chapter 31

Adulting

THANK GOD, I WAS just being stupid. There was never anything to worry about. A couple of weeks later, things were pretty blissed out with William and me. It was so much fun living together. I loved how, unlike me, he was relentlessly positive; I loved driving down to Orlando with him to walk around Disney World and Universal Studios with drinks in our hands, going on endless rides; I loved that we had the same taste in clothes. Even if I had a stack of clean T-shirts in my drawer, I'd reach for one of his instead, because it was his. I feel so cringy writing this, but I was crazy about William.

I'd been in Florida for two weeks, and we were still keeping it pretty light, not getting into the "What next?" conversation yet. We hadn't been in a single serious argument yet, either. This was mostly because William could see only the good in things. If the two of us were a glass, William would have been the full half. No matter how pessimistic I was feeling about a clunky line of code I'd rewritten fifty times, or a climate-change horror I was doing nothing about, or myself in general, William would always have a brighter perspective to offer me. The only thing he seemed to struggle to feel positively about was my phone relationship with my mom. My mom and I talked at least once a week, but even after all the fun we'd had in New York, our conversations still often turned into yelling matches. Meanwhile, William and his mom didn't feel the need to be up in each other's business to nearly the same degree. When they did talk, it was friendly and to the point.

I'd been secretly hoping that William's friends would bring out his wilder side. I'd imagined that they'd be less like my Silicon Valley friends and more like my people in Miami, who laughed loudly and teased and interrupted all the time. I was dying to be disagreed with again, even shocked by an opinion, once in a while. Whatever problem I was having, whatever creative challenge I was sorting through, the best thing for it was always hanging out with my sister and her friends—the people I grew up with, who made me laugh, no matter how stressed out I was.

Angela and Liam, the couple sitting across the table from William and me at a noisy Mexican restaurant filled with college kids, were not delivering on this front. I'd just met them five minutes ago, but I was quickly figuring out that we had nothing in common—in a not-colorful way.

"Cardi B dropped a new song today," I said, thinking I'd just wielded the ultimate icebreaker. "Did you guys hear it?"

The three of them, William, Angela, and Liam, looked at me blankly over their $4 margaritas. Oh, right, I thought, we weren't in Miami. Cardi B was not a deity here. "So what kind of music do you guys listen to?" I asked.

"I don't really listen to music," said Liam, refolding his napkin. "I'm more of a podcast guy."

"I guess I like country?" said Angela.

William, who also did not share my appreciation for rap, gave me an apologetic shrug.

"So you're a software engineer?" asked Liam.

"Yeah, sort of!" I said. "I make games."

"Like, Call of Duty–type games?" said Angela, tilting her head.

"Oh, no, I make apps for iOS. The iPhone," I said, my pulse ticking up a notch. I'd been trying to rein in the tech talk with William, who was interested in my stories about Google culture but got a faraway look in his eyes whenever I tried to explain what I actually *did* at work. "Right now, I have this huge idea for fixing social media. I want to build a social network that has no AI content-ranking algorithms. AI will *only* be used to help you figure out who you want to send your post to." I took a sip of water, about to tell them the best part—my network would be decentralized; nobody would own it.

But I was suddenly aware that Liam and Angela were looking at me not with interest, but more like bafflement—or was it just plain boredom? I might as well have been describing a new toothpaste formula I'd invented, for all they cared. Actually, they probably would've cared *more* about that, being scientifically minded. After a few seconds of awkward silence, Angela said, "Very cool," and the three of them launched into a heady debate about herbicides for killing weeds. I gestured to the server for another round of margaritas, preempting the group's objections with "On me!" Their MO, I'd discovered, was to hit happy hour at the very beginning, order one round, and spend the next hour refilling on the free nachos. If I wanted to eat or drink more, I'd have to pay for it, which was fine by me, of course. The cost of living in North Florida was probably 70 percent lower than in the South Bay; I would have happily treated William and his friends to dinner five nights a week if William hadn't asked me to stop paying for things. It made him uncomfortable, no matter how many times I explained that it wasn't a big deal. But tonight, too bad, because *I* was uncomfortable, and I wanted another drink.

William reached over and squeezed my shoulder sympathetically.

"You guys are so damned cute," said Angela, cutting Liam off. "How long ago did you meet again?"

"Oh, about a month ago," said William, who had to know it hadn't been that long. Didn't he know it had been exactly sixteen days?

"Wow," said Liam. "Who knew William was so spontaneous!"

"I'm not," he said, taking my hand. "But Michael is enough for both of us. He just shipped a bunch of boxes to my place one day, and I was like, Oh shoot, I didn't know you were moving in!"

Everyone but me was laughing.

"I thought we agreed to move in," I said, forcing a smile.

"What?" William shook his head.

"William!" I definitely wasn't smiling now. "Are you saying I moved in without your permission?"

He looked as surprised as I was. I could see him registering the fact that we had completely different interpretations of how I'd come to be sitting here, and possibly about everything else in the world, too.

"I knew you were bringing some clothes over, but I didn't think you were getting rid of your apartment," William finally said.

"This has been so fun!" Angela said, pushing her chair back with an earsplitting scrape.

"That went well," said William minutes later, in the car. "Don't you think?"

For a second, I thought he was being appropriately sarcastic, but then I remembered he was William. The restaurant hadn't blown up, no one had choked on a tortilla chip, so it had gone well. I continued staring out my window.

"Michael?"

"I thought that was awful."

"Are you serious? It looked like you were having fun! You had a smile on your face the entire time."

Because that's what I do, I wanted to say, but I'd decided not to speak to him.

We pulled up in front of William's cute apartment, with its little oasis of flowers and miniature palm trees in the front yard. William turned off the car and opened his door, but I didn't move. I wasn't trying to be dramatic; I *couldn't* move until something, anything, made sense again. I started thinking about when I was a kid and my mom and I would sit together in the car after a money fight, neither one of us able to snap out of our frustrated, teary silence. I felt no less lost and confused and disappointed than that fourteen-year-old version of myself.

"Michael, please, please, say something." William looked so worried. Mad as I was, I owed it to him to try to explain.

"You made me sound like some stalker," I said. "Like I just showed up with my boxes. You were the one who said I should come. You said, 'Come, and we'll figure out the rest later.'"

William ran his hand through his hair and sighed. "I meant come for a visit," he said. "Then you sent that picture of all the stuff you were mailing, and I realized I'd been . . . unclear."

"Guess it's all cleared up now," I said bitterly.

"But then I thought about it," William went on, "and I realized, what's the worst that could happen? You had mobility, you could leave if it didn't work out."

A giant moth was stuck in the porch light, beating its shadow wings frantically against the glass. It had gotten in, but it couldn't get out. That wasn't me, I told myself. William was right. I could get out of this any time I wanted. I still felt like that moth, though: claustrophobic. Back at the restaurant, I would've given my iPhone to be able to snap my fingers and be back in Menlo Park, numbing out on video games till the sting of what I'd just learned stopped hurting so much—to at least have had the *option* of ghosting William forever. But all my favorite clothes were in his bottom two drawers and I'd left my laptop open on his kitchen table. So here I was—still here.

"Just come in, already," said William. He'd gotten out and was holding open my door for me, like a chivalrous prom date.

Maybe it was okay to be stuck, for now, in whatever this was. Maybe my stuck-ness was the only thing giving us a chance. With my games, I'd realized that if I gave people the freedom to do anything they wanted, with no rules, they got bored. They walked away. But if I gave them constraints, they seemed to find pleasure in working within them. The more challenges I built, the better the game became.

Chapter 32

"*Soy Gay*"

MICHAEL SAYMAN, GOOGLE'S SUCCESSFUL HISPANIC
ENGINEER, SAYS HIS TRUTH: "I'M GAY"

By Lena Hansen, August 24, 2018

The successful Google engineer Michael Sayman, of Peruvian and Bolivian roots, turns 22 today. And to celebrate this special date, Sayman contacted *People en Español* to tell the world his truth: the young man who became a millionaire creating apps and who also worked for Facebook is gay—and he does not want to hide it.

"I really believe that this will be able to help other Latinos who go through the same situation," the young man revealed. "I'm afraid that despite my accomplishments of being the youngest engineer contracted by Facebook at age 17 and Google's youngest product manager at 21, there is still a voice in my mind that tells me: 'No one will take you seriously anymore if you are gay.' I think it's time to prove to others that it's okay and that you can be successful without being afraid of who you are."

Even though he has supported his family since he was a teenager—helping them out of an economic crisis when his parents lost their jobs and their home—Sayman admits that he fears how his loved ones will react to his sexual orientation.

This secret, which he kept for years for fear of rejection, is one that he no longer wants to keep quiet. "I'm gay, and coming from a Hispanic background, I decided to stay in the closet [for years] because I was always afraid to share that about myself, especially because thousands of young people in Latin America send me messages saying I'm a role model for them."

For his birthday today, instead of accepting gifts, Sayman will ask his friends and family to donate money to the nonprofit organization the Trevor Project, which helps people in the LGBT community in crisis situations and at risk of suicide.

I'D OUTDONE MYSELF THIS year. Convincing *People en Español* to publish my coming-out article on my actual twenty-second birthday was definitely my best birthday milestone yet. It was better than being featured on CNN International right before my fourteenth birthday; better than traveling to South America right before my sixteenth birthday to speak in front of thousands at various universities; better than getting my internship offer from Facebook right after my seventeenth birthday or getting hired at Facebook the day after my eighteenth birthday; definitely better than launching Lifestage the day before my twentieth; and even better than signing my Google contract at the Fontainebleau on my twenty-first. It was better than all of those milestones because it was the most honest thing I'd ever done.

My coming out had taken months of strategy and planning. This wasn't just about publishing and sharing the article; it was about project-managing the whole operation down to the last detail to minimize the potential fallout. Every domino had to be lined up perfectly, in this order:

Two months before my birthday: Book birthday cruise with William and Angela and Liam, who were now my favorite of William's friends; I loved them.

One month before: Contact *People en Español* to gauge their interest in covering my coming out.

Three weeks before: Have William take a hundred pictures of me. Pick the only good one and start filtering and retouching it for social media.

Two weeks before: Do interview with *People* writer Lena Hansen. Provide Lena with retouched photo.

One week before: Spiral into dark place, worrying that everyone who knows me in Latin America—specifically my extended family and the majority of my thirty-five thousand Facebook followers—will be disappointed in me.

Morning of: Change status to "In a Relationship."

Wait for it.

I really didn't know what I was waiting for, but I knew I didn't want to give my aunts and uncles and cousins in Bolivia and Peru the opportunity to pretend they hadn't seen my coming-out post and act like nothing had happened, the way my parents had when I first told them. The whole reason I'd insisted that the article come out on my birthday was so I could link to it and let it explain my post about William on the one day of the year when there was absolutely no chance of my relatives missing it. In my family, and for many Latin Americans, it is considered very rude not to call or write to your family members on their birthdays. Everyone would be doing that on my Facebook page, where you literally could not miss the news.

Also crucial to the orchestration of my coming out was the timing of the cruise. I'd found one that sailed two days after my birthday, which gave me enough time to do some interviews with newspapers and radio stations in Bolivia and Peru that had picked up the story but not too much time to obsess over the social media feedback. I'd purposely not paid the ship's add-on Wi-Fi fee, so I wouldn't have it in my room and be able to obsessively check the comments on social media.

Which was of course what I was doing as Liam, Angela, William, and I boarded the Royal Caribbean ship for our weeklong excursion to Jamaica, Mexico, and Honduras.

"Michael, you promised," said William.

"I know, I know, I'm sorry!" I clicked out of Facebook and put the phone in my back pocket, lifting up my hands to show him I was no longer carrying it. "I'm done now."

"So how has it been?" asked Angela. She was looking as put-together as ever, wearing a wide-brimmed straw hat and big sunglasses and a flowing dress.

"Oh my gosh," I said. "If I'd only known they would take it this well, I would've come out in high school."

The reactions to my coming out had been universally accepting and kind. California people gave the thumbs-up, if they bothered to react. This was a nonevent to them. But almost all of my uncles in Peru sent me supportive private messages or left nice comments on my post. The youngest of my mom's four brothers, my *tío* Miguel, wrote in a mixture of Spanish and English, "Michael, feliz cumpleaños! I want you to know that I admire your strength and congratulate you on your grand valor." From my friends in Miami, there were lots of hearts and X's and happy emojis and a couple of "I kind of guessed it but wasn't sure, and I'm glad to know!" texts. My sister's childhood friend Ana, who'd always made a big joke about having a crush on me, wrote: "That's awesome, and I'm happy for you, but you know I'm still gonna marry you, right?"

Whether some of them were privately thinking, *Oh man, that sucks,* I didn't care. What I cared about was not having to hide who I was and showing other Latin American young people that they didn't have to, either. Times had changed since the mid-2000s. I wondered if I would've understood myself earlier if the culture had been predominantly open and accepting when I was in high school, more like it is now—where there's not an automatic assumption that everyone is straight and you can go out and figure out what you are for yourself. I definitely would've had more fun in high school. And maybe I'd have liked myself a little more today.

That's what cruises were for—making up for all the not-fun times in life. I was so excited to be taking William on his first cruise. We were on one of Royal Caribbean's massive ships, which was more like a city. It had multiple stories; dozens of restaurants, bars, and nightclubs; all kinds of swimming pools; an ice-skating rink; a golf course; a boardwalk with a carousel and other rides; a shopping mall; and its own "Central Park" garden. It was so big that you couldn't feel it move. Basically, it was like being in a Las Vegas hotel—until you stood at the edge and looked out at nothing but clear blue water for miles and miles.

Now that I was officially "out" to everyone in the world who knew me, I was expecting that it would feel more natural, on the cruise, to be openly affectionate with William. For the first two days, though, I felt weirdly nervous about it, especially around Latinos, because of the whole machismo thing.

"I think we're the only gay people on the ship," I told William on our second evening as we followed Liam and Angela into a Latin-themed nightclub.

"Don't be ridiculous," he said. "There's like five thousand people on this boat. Statistically, there are a couple hundred others, at least."

A live band was playing onstage in front of a light-up mosaic dance floor, where a handful of couples were attempting to salsa.

"You'll have to show us some moves, Michael," said Liam. For the occasion, he'd shed his standard uniform of a T-shirt and athletic shorts for a black button-down shirt and black jeans. I wished I'd worn all black instead of the white shirt and light jeans that made me glow like a firefly in the dim room.

"First," I said, "I need to drink until I can't see past here."

I extended my hand to show where my vision would have to start blurring in order for me to start dancing.

Half an hour and three Long Island iced teas later, the four of us had formed a circle on the light-up floor, with me attempting to demonstrate my salsa dancing skills. I'd never actually learned how to dance salsa, but no one seemed to notice. We were having so much fun as a group, everyone laughing and trying to one-up each other's moves, so I didn't know why William wanted so badly to pull me away and dance alone with me. I was doing my best not to make eye contact with him, to keep dancing toward the group. I needed to keep this circle intact! Now William was doing some kind of dirty-dancing move, and I was starting to feel eyes on us. Didn't he get that I just wanted to be like everyone else in the club? Didn't he remember that I was twenty-two to his twenty-five and still, in spite of how I *wanted* to be, painfully aware of what people thought?

"Why won't you dance with me?" he shouted in my ear over the loud music.

Now I felt so self-conscious that I couldn't dance at all. "No, no," I yelled back. "Let's all just dance in a group!"

"Fine!" said William. After a half hour or so, we decided to leave. He grabbed my hand and started pulling me through the crowds toward the exit. I followed obediently, not daring to pull my hand away, even when a group of Latino couples turned their heads to watch us pass.

As we zigzagged through the cocktail lounge, a hand reached out from nowhere and tapped William's shoulder. It was a guy in his thirties with male-model facial stubble, wearing an expensive suit with a gold pocket square flaring up from his breast pocket.

"I'd like to invite you to my party," he stated.

William and I looked at each other. So this was what happened when gay people held hands in public, I was thinking.

They attracted random invitations from possibly murderous strangers.

"It's an engagement party," said the man. "The Royal Loft suite, ten p.m., tomorrow."

Before we could respond, the guy had vanished, and Liam and Angela had appeared in his place.

"Who *was* that?" said Angela, on her tiptoes, scanning the room.

"That was awesome!" William said. "He just invited us to his engagement party."

"Do you think it's a gay engagement party?" I said.

"Of course it is!" said William.

"Are you going to go?" asked Liam.

William and I looked at each other. It was definitely weird, how he'd appeared out of the blue like that, touching William's shoulder with such confidence, like, *I choose you.* What if "engagement party" was really code for "gay sex party"? I blinked away an image of William and me chained to a bed in leather harnesses.

"I think we should go," said William. "We would have so much fun!"

The next night, tired and Jell-O-limbed from our port day of cave swimming, market hopping, and tequila sampling, William and I stood on the Pocket-Square Man's balcony, which, as William pointed out, wrapped around the tip of the ship. Through a wall of floor-to-ceiling windows were about twenty guests, mostly straight couples and a few families, talking and laughing with our hosts, Pocket-Square Man and his shorter, more muscular fiancé. A young woman played jazz on a grand piano while white-coated waiters carried silver trays of shrimp. I felt ridiculous for my paranoia about it being a sex party. I really needed to get over some of the sordid stereotypes I was carrying around. I needed to be more like William, who had come out only a few months ago himself but was somehow already a fully realized and empowered gay man. Not that he didn't have his insecure moments, but when it came to his sexuality, I found it miraculous that anyone could be so comfortable with who they were.

It really was an incredible suite—not quite the Fontaine-bleau's Le Sable Presidential, but considering that it was inside of a cruise ship, not bad at all. Hey, my parents' twenty-fifth anniversary was coming up. How fun would it be to get this for them? I had the money. Every time I looked at my Charles Schwab report, I didn't know whether to jump up and down or hang my head in guilt. Everyone talked about how America was the land of opportunity, and if you worked hard enough, long enough, you would be rewarded with enough money and privilege to sit back and enjoy your life. But for my parents, that reward would never come. Even if they'd been the saving type, there was so very little to save now, after taxes. They'd never cross the threshold I'd already crossed at the very beginning of my career—where the more money I made, the more tax breaks I got, and the more my money could grow in the stock market without my lifting a finger. Given the inequity between my parents' experience of the American dream and my own, didn't it make sense to shower them with nice things, to make them feel a part of it, too?

Wait, I needed to check myself. That was not how it was going to work anymore. I'd be doing them a much bigger favor putting the forty grand or whatever this place would cost in the bank for their retirement years, which I'd surely be responsible for. And I needed to start thinking about saving for my future, too. Could William and I be engaged one day? I could easily slip into the fantasy of spending the next forty years traveling around the world with him. I could work on my apps from anywhere, so why not?

But then again, I could just as easily picture myself running away from him. Loving someone was easy, it turned out. Trusting was the hard part. I knew I was being overly sensitive, but it had taken me three whole months to get over the revelation that William hadn't realized I was planning to move in. To put a finer point on it, I worried that I liked William more than he liked me—and that fear persisted for months. Trust was so important to me that I'd made a graph on my laptop where I charted my trust-in-William levels over time. There was a faint horizontal line running about 20 percent above the x-axis, which was my baseline for staying in the relationship. If the chart didn't stay above that line for at least 90 percent of the time, the relationship wasn't sustainable. I marked a dip down for the moving-in argument and two other dips from our half year together, including right before we'd left for the cruise. I wasn't planning to tell him about the graph at first. In my paranoid way, I thought that if he knew about it, he might start trying to skew the results. Then I decided, screw it, and showed it to him the day after I made it. We'd had a good laugh about how weird his new boyfriend was.

"Michael! Over here!"

I snapped out of my thought spiral and saw that William was waving at me from the pointed tip of the ship balcony. I made my way over to him with caution, nervous about getting too close to the rail. We were far out to sea now, and the ship had picked up a fair amount of speed, though you couldn't feel the choppiness of the water, just the wind. It was so smooth, it felt like it was breaking the laws of physics. Looking down at the dark, rolling waves, I had a sudden vision of myself falling overboard, disappearing into the black water. I glued myself to the wall behind me, moving as far away from the railing as possible. Hell no. I wasn't getting anywhere near that edge.

"Michael, come over here! Why are you so far away?" William was looking at me curiously over his shoulder.

He approached and extended his arm out for me to grab his hand. "Come over. You're really going to like what you see."

Very slowly, I made my way to the railing and forced myself to look down. After a few minutes of staring at the ocean in terror, I looked up to give William an *I'm ready to go back inside* smile.

"What are you afraid of?" he asked.

Feeling silly, I told him about my vision of falling overboard, adding, "There's no nets or anything. By the time you got help, I'd be dead."

"Don't be ridiculous." William pointed to an orange life preserver strapped to the balcony wall next to an emergency alarm. "I'd grab that, pull the alarm, and immediately find a crew member."

Of course William suggested that. Would I have the presence of mind to act instinctually? Or would I stand there frozen, or worse, black out? I hated that I didn't know. Of the two of us, I was the less brave, the less good, for sure. I didn't deserve him.

Chapter 33

Area 120

IN THE FALL OF 2018, I was flying to California every other
month to work at Area 120. William and I were still "unoffi-
cially" living together, but things were going so well that I was
considering a permanent move to Florida. I was really happy
whenever I was in Florida, but I wasn't exactly loving the logistics of my new life. Spending twenty-four hours a month suspended in the air inside a flying metal tube wasn't my idea of
fun, and it seemed like no matter where I was, I was missing
my friends on the other side.

But when it came to my job, I liked Area 120 quite a lot.
I didn't mind that it was set apart from Google and all of its
perks. Moving from Facebook to the main Google campus had
been seamless in many ways, everything so similar and shiny-
happy and coddling that I sometimes used to forget I'd moved
at all. But Area 120 was lower-key. On this part of the campus,
there were no restaurants or gyms. You had to drive yourself
to work or take a smaller Google bus connection from the
main campus. I think this was all deliberate—they'd built Area
120 with the hopes that we'd be more creative outside of the
Google bubble. It might have helped a little. But there was no
escaping the fact that we lived and worked within the larger
bubble of Silicon Valley, the greatest echo chamber of opinions
and ideas that's probably ever existed. In Silicon Valley, there
was a lot of cheering on of ideas, even when those ideas were

not necessarily ones people outside our bubble would agree with or even care about. I sensed that this was why my manager was so open to me spending so much time outside of California. And why, even when I was working locally, he seemed to have no problem with me rarely coming into the office.

Unlike my "full focus" time in Florida, where my calendar was sparsely booked and I worked from my bedroom all day—testing and building and testing and building in an infinite loop—I spent most of my time at Area 120 running from meeting to meeting. By then, all my colleagues knew who I was and what I'd accomplished with Instagram Stories and at Facebook. All day long, people would come up to me, asking, "Michael, what are we going to build next?" Since I no longer had to write code, I was able to spend more energy making critical decisions such as whether to increase the budget of an app we were developing, or how to foster the growth of a company in which we'd invested. Nobody cared if I spent thirty minutes on my computer all week, as long as I hit my goals.

Of course, I still agonized over every decision. But I stopped rushing into work late looking like a mess and cracking jokes about how I had no idea what I was doing. For the first time in my career, I was getting good reviews from people on my own team, which felt great. The truth is, I still cared a lot about what people thought of me, but I'd developed a new definition of growth and success: if I looked back at myself a year earlier and cringed, I knew I'd grown. If I continued to look back and cringe at myself every year that followed—I would consider myself a success.

On the side, I was still constantly building apps on my own. My true passion. That October, I was deep into building a game called BFF, which revolved around friends asking one another questions, then trying to guess who was lying. It was a friendlier variation of Lies, the app I'd launched on my own six months before—and then immediately abandoned as soon as I realized people weren't connecting with its snarky vibe. (The tagline "The Game That Ends Friendships" had apparently been a mistake.) Despite its failure, I still liked the concept of Lies and was now taking its best features and all the wisdom I'd gained from building it and trying to spin the whole thing into something positive.

For months I'd been perfecting BFF. I had it on my phone, and any time I was in a social setting, I'd take the opportunity to show it around and pay attention to people's reactions and feedback. I was on track to launch in a month.

At the same time, the digital landscape was changing so fast, and had morphed so much since I started coding, that I was beginning to question whether or not there was still a place for BFF on the map. The app world had become much less competitive. People weren't downloading countless apps like they used to. So, I'd been toying with putting BFF on indefinite hold.

One fall afternoon, after a day of meetings at the Google campus, I decided to treat myself to dinner and a movie in my old neighborhood, Redwood City. Across from the theater in Courthouse Square, a Day of the Dead celebration was in full swing. I wandered into the thick of the festival, past food trucks and the smell of sizzling tacos carnitas, children zig-zagging through the crowds in colorful skeleton masks, and hundreds of elaborate altars that people had made to celebrate loved ones who'd passed on. Despite it being a remembrance of the dead, there was no sadness in the air, just lots of wide-open and joyful smiles.

I walked on, past a gray-haired man who was kneeling to put the finishing touches on a sidewalk mural in neon chalk. It was good: a young woman's smiling face, framed by red roses and the dates 1957–2012. Who was she? I wondered. In Miami, I'd have stopped to strike up a conversation with the man, but I wasn't comfortable approaching him; I didn't have the courage. Most of the people at this festival were Latinos who'd lived in Redwood City since long before the influx of people like me—wealthy engineers who'd sent the cost of living in Silicon

Valley through the roof and driven the majority of its original residents out.

There was no getting around the fact that no matter how much Spanish I spoke, no matter how much time I'd spent in Peru, no matter what struggles I'd faced in Miami, I was different. With my fancy iPhone and AirPods, I was a privileged outsider. Yes, I was a Latino. But thanks to my light skin and the opportunities I'd had as a kid—most important, the opportunity to learn English when I was eight or nine years old and develop an American accent—I was still part of the problem.

That knowledge lived under my skin, always nagging at me. I wanted to make an impact in tech, but even more than that I wanted to make a difference in my community.

The next day, I found my manager, Jon, and asked for a moment of his time. We ducked into a conference room across from a giant, ever-evolving wall of Legos. "At Facebook, I did quite a bit of speaking to the Latino community at conferences and school events," I said, "helping them learn about tech and how to find work in Silicon Valley. I want to continue doing that."

Jon nodded. "That sounds reasonable."

I was caught by surprise. As a whole, the tech industry was extremely conservative when it came to public relations. I'd been taught early on to be careful about anything I tweeted or said that could be misconstrued as speaking on behalf of the company. And I still had bad memories from my misadventures with the comms department at Facebook.

"So, it's fine if I do these events and even speak to the press as a representative of Area 120?" I searched his face for a flicker of annoyance but found none.

"I don't see a problem there."

"Wow, thanks," I said. "That's great."

I left the meeting feeling like whistling. This was a decisive win as far as I was concerned. There was a reason there were so few Latinos in tech, comprising well under 10 percent of the workforce at Facebook, Google, and Amazon, despite the fact that we make up about 17 percent of all U.S. workers.

I needed to look no further than my own upbringing to understand why people in my community did not go into tech. In my family, there were two professions to aspire to: doctor or lawyer. In the late nineties, when the PC revolution happened, most American households got a computer. But that didn't happen in Latin America, where computers were prohibitively expensive. It wasn't until the invention of the Smartphone—when computers and phones became cheap enough to afford—that tech started to appear in every household. So while American families had been slowly exposed to computer science over decades, many Latinos in Latin America had not had access to those resources. And once they did, they faced the problem of inadequate broadband access—an ongoing problem that activists have been trying to highlight to Congress for years. And then there is unconscious bias. People tend to hire workers who look like them.

For all of these reasons, education and outreach to bring more diversity into tech is badly needed—and that was where I felt I could help.

In the months following my conversation with Jon, I did a few events in Latin America via videoconference, and some television interviews with Telemundo and Univision about my transition to Google. In these talks, I always made sure to share the fact that I'd had terrible grades in school and came from a family that struggled financially. After each of these presentations, messages would pour in on Facebook and Twitter from kids who'd watched the interview and wanted to thank me for inspiring them. They liked that I didn't pretend to be some supergenius—I was just like them.

Even years after doing an interview, I would still receive messages from people all over the world telling me they'd been inspired by my story and had become successes *themselves* building their own products and apps. "I reached out six years ago when I was a kid and now my entire career revolves around computer science," a recent college grad wrote from India. Or I heard from a young woman in Peru, "I've been doing so well and making a lot of money—and you were my inspiration!"

Six months into my new job at Area 120, I visited a small college in South Florida to speak to students studying computer science and business. The room was filled with a happy, crackling energy. I loved talking to a small group, where I could listen to their questions and take the time to give a thoughtful response, rather than just lecture. As soon as I finished my talk, hands shot up. I called on a kid in the front who looked to be about my age. He stood and a moderator handed him a microphone. "I come from a Peruvian background, like you, and I think I might want to become a product manager," he said eagerly. Sensing that he didn't even know what that was, I spent a lot of time explaining what a product manager actually does, so he could make an informed decision. Another student asked how to network. "Make sure you set up meetings with everyone who works at your new company and ask them to give you the names of people you should meet with," I said. "Become someone that everyone knows." A third stood up and asked about the path to becoming a manager. "Just because the job title has the word 'manager' in it doesn't mean it's the job you want," I cautioned. "Be very careful because to be a good manager, you have to actually enjoy doing the job of a manager."

I felt good about the advice I was offering; these were concrete, real-world tips the students could actually use.

Then a student rose to his feet in the back row. He had dark hair and a medium build and was wearing a hoodie; he would have fit right in at Google. Someone handed him a microphone and he asked the question I was least prepared to answer: "How did it feel to come out as gay so publicly?"

Ever since my *People en Español* story had hit newsstands, there had been articles about my sexuality all over the Internet. I was thrown by the question, because I was conflicted. On one hand, I didn't want to be known as "the gay engineer"; I wanted to be defined by my success, abilities, and skills. I also wanted to blend in and be seen as "normal." But only 5 percent of the population is openly out in the United States; in other countries, that statistic is a lot lower. I'd decided to do the article as a way to face my fear that coming out would kill my career, or cause my book deal to get canceled, or destroy my relationship with my family. And thankfully, none of those things happened. I'm lucky, of course; those kinds of things (and worse) *do* happen to some people who speak their truth— and it's tragic. So, in answering the question, I wasn't sure if I should address how coming out had impacted my life, or simply stress that I didn't think it should matter.

I sputtered for a minute and said, "It was like swimming down into a deep, dark pool and holding my breath for years— then reaching the bottom, and finding that there *was* air to breathe. It took a big weight off my shoulders. I was caught off guard by how calm and relaxed I felt once I came out with it. Because none of the fears my parents had instilled in me actually happened. My mom, especially, worried that none of our family would want to talk to me anymore, or that they would become two-faced, saying one thing to her in person and another behind her back. She passed those fears down to me not because she wanted me to be afraid, but because she wanted me to be safe. But coming out, thankfully, didn't affect my life as negatively as I feared it would, or cause my career to collapse. And my mom and dad are finally seeing that, and coming around to supporting me in the reality that I live in."

The student smiled, looking relieved. "Thank you," he said, taking his seat.

I vowed to myself then and there that I'd always carve out space, no matter how busy or stressed or exhausted I felt, to share my story in its entirety. Whether these face-to-face connections happened through screens, in college auditoriums, or on the sticky floors of elementary school cafeterias, it didn't matter.

Chapter 34

Thankful

"SHOULDN'T WE BE HELPING your mom in the kitchen?" said William. "Nobody's doing anything."

"Mami!" I called out. "William just asked why I'm not helping you cook!"

"Because *I'm* the one who cooks!" my mom yelled back with a laugh.

William looked puzzled, but I didn't know how to explain, without digging myself into a hole, that my mom didn't want us in the kitchen. My mom was too busy to deal with us: simultaneously basting the Thanksgiving turkey, tossing vegetables in a pan, assembling a flan, and checking Facebook updates on her phone. She had a *system*.

A minute later, my mom burst from the kitchen, holding up a white straw basket brimming with camcorder tapes. "Movie break, everybody!" she said in English.

What timing. She had a captive audience, with all of her houseguests gathered in the living room, chatting and watching TV. My sister, who'd brought her new boyfriend, Rick, was turning off the lights and helping my dad connect the camcorder to the receiver; William was petting the dogs I was allergic to; and Tío Kike, visiting from Peru, was attempting to talk to William as I translated.

"William and Rick, you will love these old movies of little Michael and Mariana!" said my mom. Normally, she had

me translate for my non-Spanish-speaking friends, but she'd
been making a big effort to speak in English for William and
Rick.

"Oh, awesome," said William. He'd been almost unbearably
nice and quiet and well mannered since we got here, trying to
put his best foot forward with my mom, who seemed equally
invested in impressing him. She was dressed for company in a
bright blue silk shirt and white jeans. A row of bangles jingled
on her arm as she waved the remote.

"Sit, sit!" she said, pushing William into the prime spot in
front of the TV, where the dogs usually sat.

Once everyone was settled—me and my mom in kitchen
chairs; my dad in a recliner holding his teensy teacup Yorkie,
Sophia, on his lap; William, Rick, Mariana, and Tío Kike
squished together on the couch—the show began. The first
thing that came up was a grainy, shot-from-the-back-of-the-
room elementary school Christmas play. If you peered hard,
you could see Mariana and me standing off to the side of the
stage in our regular clothes, watching the others.

"Wrong tape," said my mom. "Micky, put in the other one
that says *dos mil dos cumpleaños,* on the"—she snapped her fingers three times—"sticker."

The professional tape was of my sixth birthday party, one
that I had no true memory of. Had my mom been going for
a *Great Gatsby* theme? An Oscars after-party theme? It was at
our old house, and there was a massive balloon-festooned tent
in the backyard, with dozens of circular tables set with white
cloths and colorful plates. There were waiters flitting around
in butler outfits, a magician performing tricks, and me, still
a healthy skinny kid, watching openmouthed with my kindergarten friends. Oh, and a full bar and a live band playing old-timey Latin, cumbia, merengue, and salsa songs. The
weirdest part was seeing my parents and their friends fifteen
years younger—my mom was thirty-three and my dad was
forty-two. My mom had never looked more beautiful, flutter-

ing between her guests without a care in the world, it seemed. (No one we knew was worried about the state of the country back then.)

"See, see, William?" said my mom. "I bet Michael only say what he do for us. I bet he never say what great things we do for him, right?"

"Um," said William, looking at me. I shook my head to say, *Don't answer that,* but William was too nice to leave my mom hanging. "I definitely never had parties like this," he said.

"Did *anyone* have parties like this?" I looked back and forth between my parents. "Anyone we knew? Anyone in the neighborhood?"

"Only us!" boomed my dad proudly.

"That's right," my mom added. "We always have the best parties."

"But how did you pay for it?" I said.

"We are doing very well this year," said my mom.

I knew the reason my mom mostly spoke English in the present tense was because she'd never mastered the past tense, but this quirk was seeming symbolically loaded right now, as if she were willing the past to be her new present.

"The restaurant make over one million dollars this year," added my mom proudly.

"*What?*" I yelled, utterly shocked. I insisted she repeat what she'd said in case I hadn't heard her correctly.

"Yes," confirmed my mom. "I say one million dollars! It is a very good—"

"*Ves esto, es por eso que estás en una mala situación hoy!*" ("You know this is why you are in a bad situation today, don't you?!") interrupted Tío Kike, for whom my sister was now translating.

My mom ignored her brother, who was right, of course. This was exactly why they'd lost their house, their self-sufficiency, everything. And they really were in a bad situation now. My parents didn't have real health insurance, and they were about to lose their car. But instead of settling the overdue payment with a recent tax refund they'd received, my mom had spent it on a flight to Peru to pursue a new jewelry-making idea. And my dad was miserable trying to sell subsidized apartments that were still too expensive for the people who needed them most—people who had been flattened by the recession because they didn't have a penny of savings to fall back on, just like him and my mom.

"Awesome camper!" said Rick.

I looked back to the screen, where evidence that we'd taken a family cross-country trip in an RV was being shown. I didn't remember the size and scope of that trip. I remembered renting out a little truck and driving along winding roads for hours, eating homemade meals and making a few pit stops in tiny towns—but nothing at all like this!

"Oh my God, I always wanted to go on one of those!" William said. I shot him a dirty look.

And on went the Sayman Family Pre-Recession Greatest Hits reel. There we were, outside the Louvre. And here was yet another one of our elaborate parties, with dozens of tiki torches and a chef in a big white hat and . . .

I jumped to my feet. "Were those *ponies* in our *backyard*?" I couldn't take it anymore. Couldn't anyone besides me and Tío Kike see how sad all this was? And why was everyone looking at *me* like I was deranged? "I am not the crazy one here!" I huffed, pacing in front of the TV. "You threw our college and your retirement away for . . . ?" I paused to gesture at the screen, which now showed our old backyard transformed into a petting zoo—next to the biggest bouncy castle I'd ever seen outside of a theme park. I had no more words. "*Arrgghhhhhhhhhhhh!*" I yelled.

"*Ay ya . . . Ay ya . . . con lo mismo!*" said my mom. ("Here we go . . . here we go . . . with the same thing again!")

"Whatever, Michael!" snapped my sister.

"Michael!" my dad topped it off. "*No seas tan egoísta!*" ("Don't be so selfish!")

"Stop saying that!" I yelled back, storming up to my old bedroom. "*Stop calling me selfish!*"

I sat on the corner of my old bed, which still had the same gray sheets, sobbing.

Soon my mom came in and sat down next to me on the bed, and as soon as she did, she started sniffing and dabbing her eyes with the backs of her fingers. She'd be speaking only in Spanish now.

"Michael, why don't you think we're great parents? We did all this stuff for you!"

"Yeah, and look where it got you!" I snapped.

She looked taken aback. "Don't mind me. You are a success! I don't understand why you can't just be happy." She paused. "It's okay. You don't have to help us. You do you."

"Mom, I *do* want to help! I've bailed you out again and again. I take us on trips, I—"

I took a deep breath. This was the same fight again. The same level of thinking. I needed to put my emotions aside— *myself* aside—and start again.

It was time for us to really talk. Finally. I told my mom that, yes, she had given us everything we wanted before the recession happened. But she and my dad had skipped an important step. They had gone straight from making lots of money to spending lots of money, without the in-between part of prioritizing college funds for me and my sister, putting money aside for emergencies, and saving for their own retirement. The crazy stuff, the trips and the huge birthdays, should have come *after* that, not before.

To this, my mom said what she always did: "But, Michael, the important thing is to enjoy life! At least we have our health and happiness!"

I stopped her right there. I asked her if she would still be enjoying life if Mariana got sick and they couldn't afford treatment. I told her that without some money, health was difficult to keep. Now, what about happiness? Was she happy not being able to take the smallest trip without my help? Was she happy worrying all day about how to pay the mortgage, without ever being able to relax and take a breather? I said I knew that she didn't want to be hearing all this from me, her son. I said it didn't have to be this way, that I truly believed she and my dad could get back on their feet if they tackled their problems in earnest. I reminded her of her ability to start businesses and succeed far beyond what she'd imagined. She still had her skills as a restaurant owner and manager, even if the restaurant she'd started no longer existed. I realized in that moment the extent to which my mom's low self-esteem had trickled down to me: her own unique talents, her formidable successes, and the lives she had touched all went unnoticed by her. I said, "Are you really happy with your life, Mom?"

When my mom got quiet, you always knew that something deep was going on inside of her, and it was best to give her some time and space to listen to what it was. She straightened her blouse and dried her eyes some more and said, "Maybe you're right, Michael. Maybe I don't have any of the three—health, money, or happiness—to the degree that it matters."

I could feel her starting to cry again, so I softened a bit. "Things will get better, Mami. You might need to make some big changes to your worldview, but that's just progress." She nodded, dried her eyes some more, and went downstairs to check on the turkey.

I sat there for a while, feeling weirdly calm and thinking about everything, especially about my mom. I'd just spent half an hour lecturing her about how she needed to get her life together, and I was glad that I'd finally found the voice to articulate those things. I'd never even admitted those thoughts to myself before. I hadn't even realized how much I identified with my mom's self-esteem issues. Usually the anger and frustration over the way my parents had handled their finances—

and mine—stopped me from going any further. But I was starting to understand the thought patterns that had always kept my mom, and my whole family, from feeling free for longer than a fancy dinner or a trip to Disney World or New York. I was starting to see everything more clearly, as if the window I'd been looking at my family through had been grimy with disappointment and negativity, and I'd just washed it clean.

When it came to my mom, there were so many good things—wonderful things—to see. I didn't want her to feel bad about who she was, not for one second. It would be the biggest tragedy of all—bigger than losing everything that had gone away in the recession—if she lost that spark. Was it even possible to lose something that had been in you since birth? Tío Kike had just been telling William and me about their childhood in Peru, including something I'd never heard before: My mother's mother had gotten pregnant with my mom in her midforties, which was very rare. Her doctor had told her that there was a high chance that my mother would be born with "complications," but my grandmother had chosen to have her anyway. This is why she had been so insistent on giving birth to my mother in Lima, for safety.

When my mom was born healthy, with her firefly spark apparent from day one, her parents were so relieved that they spent the rest of their lives showering her with everything their money—until it finally ran out just before they passed away—could buy. He'd said that my mom, the baby sister to four brothers, had been nicknamed la engreidita de la familia, which basically means "the spoiled one," because by the time she came along, her parents had built a strong financial bedrock, by Peruvian standards.

It was my grandparents' generosity that had funded my mom's first trip to Miami, which then set in motion the course of the rest of her life, and mine. And of course, my mom had brought more than her joyfulness and love of the good life with her to North America. She had brought her family's tradition of hard work and entrepreneurialism. I was still processing the news that El Pollon had made over $1 million the year I turned six. Until an hour ago, I'd thought I was the first millionaire in our family! Maybe I shouldn't have been so surprised. The same mother who threw lavish *Great Gatsby* parties and lived beyond her means had shown me by example how to tap into my creativity and turn it into *work*. And while I didn't remember that *Gatsby* party, or the RV road trip, who knows? Maybe those early experiences were what planted the idea in me that it was okay to want bigger and better things in life, to believe that the American dream applied to me as much as anyone else.

All of that history—all of the traditions and superstitions and memories and characteristics and cultural touchstones from my Peruvian and Bolivian ancestors—was woven into me so deeply that I could never unstitch the tapestry, even if I wanted to. *I'm not who I am in spite of being an immigrant; I'm who I am because of it,* a voice inside me said.

My personality, that of every child of immigrants, was made up of a proprietary blend of inherited and new ingredients. The new ones, of course, were the American ways of thinking and doing things, which I'd had to discover for myself. Maybe I didn't know it at the time, but it was the American impulse to innovate that drove me to make apps, the winners and the losers alike. It was the Silicon Valley credo that work should be fun that gave me the nerve to reject the "no pain, no gain" mentality of my parents and seek work that moved my spirit at every turn. And how lucky I'd been to grow up steeped in the American belief—or fairy tale, depending on how you looked at it—that anyone could reinvent themselves at any time. That was the spirit that had driven me to wake up to who I really was.

Epilogue

It's been more than a decade since I built my first app, and in my early twenties, I'm no longer the literal "app kid." Not long ago, I found myself stepping back onto a stage to give a talk at a conference at Menlo College, in the heart of Silicon Valley. The theme was "This Is America," and I'd chosen to talk about the meaning of success. To say I was nervous would be a pretty big understatement. While I'd given dozens of lectures at Facebook during my Teen Talks era, and a bunch more in Latin America throughout my career, this was different. Those presentations were about social media, gaming, and programming—topics I loved, even lived, to think and talk about. I'd barely had to prepare for them. But today's topic, what success meant to me, was much more loaded. I'd been thinking a lot about my place at Google and in the world. Was I on the right path? I thought these events were for people who'd already figured it out. I'd written this speech to try to get to the bottom of that question.

William and I eventually broke up. He was my first real love, and he showed me unconditional acceptance and what the "life" part of "work-life balance" was supposed to look like. He also inspired me to dig deeper into my family issues. Even before the breakup, I'd started regularly seeing a therapist and was already in deep soul-searching mode about my life, work, and family. It probably seems obvious to anyone reading this book that my parents were squarely in the wrong when they spent all the money I made as a kid. But it really did take years to open my eyes to the fact that my parents were—at best— profoundly imperfect. All the criticism, the name-calling, the manipulations and lies seemed normal to me—a mindset I've had to work hard to undo. Since then, I've come to accept that my parents and I may always see things differently. They might never completely understand me, and I may never completely understand them, but I love them dearly. They might never be the perfect parents, but no one's parents are. I might never understand their point of view, or maybe one day I will. I've learned to do all I can to reserve my judgment of others. Not because I don't want to form any opinions of my own, but because I want to leave the door open to the future possibility that I am wrong. I do not know what my parents' lived experience was like. One day, I hope to understand them better, with the goal of passing down to my future children a broader perspective than the one that was passed down to me. I will never be able to understand everything all at once right away. I can't expect to wrap my head around others' perspectives with mine. Some things will just take time for me to grow into grasping—and so I've adjusted my thinking around that premise. I'm also learning to say, "*Es importante querer cuidarse,*" or, "It's important to want to take care of yourself." Actually, it's more than important—it's necessary and good.

Those realizations gave me the space to start thinking about what I *really* want—and whether I'm headed in the right direction.

Squinting through the stage lights, I nodded at two of my friends from Silicon Valley in the front row holding little GO, MICHAEL! signs. Beyond them was an audience of several hundred young, mostly American college kids—a very different room from the one at the first big talk I did in Bolivia when I was sixteen. For a second, I found myself thought-spiraling back to that room. How eager those kids had been to find out if they, too, could make big money by making apps. Had I inspired any of them to take up a career in programming? I wondered. And then: Would my speaking here today make a difference for *these* kids? This was obviously not the time to worry about it, so I did what I've always done—I put on a smile and dove in.

My speech started with an abbreviated TV version of my life story—about making my first app at twelve, supporting my family as a teenager, being Facebook's youngest software engineer ever, making it onto the *Forbes* 30 Under 30 list when I was twenty-one, and landing a dream job at Google. "That's where that success story ends for now," I added. The audience shifted in their seats, probably wondering where I was going with this.

Where *was* I going with this? Let me try to explain:

Ever since I published my first app at thirteen, people have used the word "successful" to describe me. But even when I was a kid doing all those TV interviews about my success, no one actually asked me what the word meant to me. The assumption, obviously, was that because I was making a ridiculous amount of money for my age, I was a success. So I'd smile widely and accept the compliment because successful people were supposed to be confident and happy, right? People were always congratulating me on finding what I wanted to do with my life at such a young age. But I never had a chance to ask *myself* that question. Think about all the kids who grow up in survival mode, their families living paycheck to paycheck. When you don't know where your next meal is coming from, you're not thinking about whether you should become a doctor, a lawyer, or an engineer. Growing up, I had just one focus: to put food on the table and keep my family above water. So when I look back at my own journey through Silicon Valley, I can see that I never knew what I wanted to be. I tried to convince myself that this was not the case, but inside, I felt like a fraud. The point being that I had a complicated relationship with my own so-called success.

After sharing the most emotionally charged version of all of the above in my speech, I remembered that I had an audience waiting for me to get to the point. I said out loud what the room was definitely thinking: "So what's the takeaway?"

The wisdom I'd come up with—for myself as well as my audience—had two parts. First, you'll never feel successful if you let someone else define what that means for you. And second, there's room in every success story for some doubt and fear and confusion. In fact, maybe success doesn't come in spite of those things but because of them. Maybe if we looked at our fears and doubts as building blocks instead of stumbling blocks, we'd have a much easier time in life.

Since giving my speech, I've been trying to follow my own advice. I'm getting closer to defining success on my own terms, which turn out to be not about making the next big tech product but about working and learning and living a comfortable, happy life. I'm also learning not to beat myself up for still feeling like a scared, confused, doubtful ten-year-old half the time. That insecure ten-year-old got me where I am today.

Oh, I've also been trying to embrace getting older. I used to think that being the youngest programmer on any team was my superpower. Despite what my coworkers told me, I convinced myself that having a direct connection to the teen audience was the most valuable thing I had to offer at Facebook and then, too, at Google and Area 120. Naturally, I dreaded my superpower's expiration date. That's why I put so much pressure on myself to reach a new career milestone with every birthday. But over time, with the help of people wiser and more experienced than me, I've come to understand that I'm good for more than plugging into what teens want. Actually, it turns out

I have a pretty good knack for understanding what *people* want. I no longer want to create things for just one demographic. I want to create things for everyone, with the mindset that all human beings need the same fundamental things: to feel seen, known, and understood.

Absorbing that truth has turned out to be incredibly valuable for me, making me a better programmer and even, believe it or not, a decent manager. These days at Google, I'm working mostly virtually but spending less time alone and more time with my team of ten designers and engineers, developing new features for Google Chrome. It took me forever to figure this out, but one excellent benefit of working with a team if you're instinctually a lone wolf is that you can't spend unhealthy amounts of time in your own head. With more feedback, you're not working in a vacuum, so you're probably going to come up with a product that resonates with more people—a *better* product.

I also spend a lot of time helping other teams reach their project goals. Every week, I'll reconnect with various teams across Android, YouTube, Chrome, and more to strategize on everything from workflow to scheduling to design to how to overcome the mental blocks that stand in the way of their progress. It feels pretty good to be able to help other people overcome the very same hurdles that used to trip me up on a daily basis. Of course, I still need help myself sometimes. Admitting this out loud early and often—and seeking guidance and feedback not only from more experienced people but from *all* of my colleagues—has been revolutionary for me. One thing I've learned to do with my teams is to pull at least one person aside after every meeting and ask, "Hey, is there anything you think I'm doing really badly or could get better at? Anything at all?" Often, the person's first response is, "No, everything's great!" When I get that, I'll just sit there and wait until they inevitably say, "Well, there's one thing I've noticed . . ." And then I thank them genuinely for their honesty, something no high-functioning team can do without.

Having grown out of the survival-mode mentality that I grew up with, I'm trying to take more risks, for better reasons. Instead of just churning out fun, addictive things, I'm one of a growing number of people in tech who want to start helping people use technology more mindfully. My latest projects in the works actually parody the way social networks operate— hopefully they will make users more self-aware about what they're *really* doing every time they pick up their phone and touch their favorite app. By reminding us of all the ways our phones trick our brains into delivering brief hits of unsustainable happiness, I hope to do a little to help humans take back the upper hand in our relationship with technology.

About that relationship: *so much* has changed since I arrived at Facebook as a wide-eyed, metal-mouthed intern in 2014. Back then, "fake news" wasn't a household term and Russia's election meddling was yet to be a story. I believe that Zuckerberg, and many others in the tech industry, underestimated the vulnerabilities that could be exploited on large social networks, as well as the degree of damage that could be caused to the world. In those days, Silicon Valley as a whole was a much more optimistic place. Most of us thought we were the good guys, helping the world get better and better. Despite a handful of sociologists and journalists warning us about the dangers of digital media consumption, very few of us in the tech world were focused on what could go wrong.

In recent years, obviously, the Internet has shown us a hell of a dark side—from the 2016-election-swinging Cambridge Analytica scandal at Facebook to regular security breaches for all kinds of software that compromise millions of people's private information to the rise of hate groups successfully spreading their awful messages online. What probably worries me most about the Internet is how it's changing the news we read. On Facebook, where most Americans get their news these days, we can pick which news "reality" we want to subscribe to. At the micro level, people want these features and are happy when they see things they like and agree with. At the macro level, these features drive an already divided society further apart.

I think some in Silicon Valley are asking, Can we fix the problems we've created by turning back? Can we undo the damage? But I believe we're too far across this valley to turn back. The better question is: What's on the other side of the valley? I believe there can be an upswing, a future where we use technology to end all the pointless suffering in this world. And if anyone can lead us to that higher place, it will be young people. Today's youngest kids are often called the Alpha Generation; teens and early twentysomethings are called Generation Z. But I break it down a little differently. I like to think of everyone under twenty-five today as the Anyone Can Generation, because they've grown up knowing no limits on their creativity. In their Internet-centric model of the world, anyone can be influential or famous. *Anyone* can do *anything*.

Older people who write off these selfie-loving kids as being vain or overly focused on themselves are definitely underestimating them. I believe that members of the Anyone Can Generation will change the world for the better precisely because they've spent their entire lives online. They understand the relationship humans have with our all-consuming Internet better than any of the masterminds working in Silicon Valley right now. Which is why I'm optimistic that in the coming years, as coding becomes a more commonplace skill, the Anyone Can Generation will begin building us all a fairer and more equitable Internet. And I'm sure they'll do it in some pretty creative ways.

Think about it. These are kids who feel confident expressing themselves to the world as kids never have before—putting themselves out there in vlogs, TikTok routines, Instagram Live stories, and a million other ways. I love the fact that Disney and ABC and CNN now have to compete with eighteen-year-old LGBT YouTubers who grew up taking selfies. I love the fact that Latino teenagers—even while under daily assault by our government and its policies—can come home from school and create safe spaces to share their talents and stories. I love that so many people of color have millions of subscribers and the power to make a huge impact. It would've been impossible for nonwhite people to have that kind of media spotlight in the sixties, seventies, eighties, or nineties, when there were so many entrenched walls to climb as they navigated from the outside in.

One of my biggest hopes is that by sharing my story, I've opened some minds to the idea that programming is a path anyone can take. And for all my rambling about the Anyone Can Generation, I don't just mean young people. No matter what your age or education or background, if you have curiosity and determination, you can learn to code. If this resonates for you, teach yourself! What's stopping you? Once you've got that basic ability, it will be your choice whether to create your own products or find yourself a job within a company. Both roads can lead to endless possibilities. If the thought of being an entrepreneur makes your heart pound in a good way, then trust that feeling. Start by building something you wish already existed in the world. If this thing would make your world a better place, I bet others will feel the same way, too. On the other hand, if you crave security and stability, like me, I would advise you to take the job route—and then work to change the tech world from the inside. Once you're securely established, you'll have the luxury of being able to reflect on how to make the biggest impact.

Then, slowly and surely, you can build the tools to do exactly that.

Finally, whatever road you're on in life, whoever you love, may you find *your* definition of success—and have the courage to live it.

Acknowledgments

I am grateful to my agent, Amanda Urban of ICM, for believing in me from the start, and for helping me navigate the unfamiliar waters of the book publishing world. I want to extend my deepest gratitude to Anne Messitte, for first taking a chance on my manuscript, and the amazing crew at Alfred A. Knopf, in particular my brilliant and gifted editors Tom Pold and Cristóbal Pera, and Alexandra Torrealba at Vintage Español. I also want to thank Laurie Sandell for her outstanding editorial guidance; this book wouldn't have happened without her.

Thanks also to Michelle Castillo-Flores for encouraging me to share my story, and to Mark Zuckerberg for taking a chance on me before my prefrontal cortex was fully developed. A huge thank-you to my colleagues at Facebook and Google, who must have wondered at times how they ended up working with a teenager, but were willing to see the value in what I could create. Ari Grant pushed me to greater heights in my career, challenging me in my approach while advocating for my weird way of thinking. Ryan Hoover believed in me long before I believed in myself.

I also want to thank the tens of thousands of kids and parents who came along with me on this journey, reaching out to me on social media and at talks and conferences to share their stories. So many of them went on to become examples in their own communities of the kind of opportunities the Internet can provide.

My Tío Kike, Luis Enrique Galvez, provided a sounding board throughout my life that proved invaluable as I grew. A huge thank-you to all of my friends in Miami for never letting me forget where I came from. I am forever grateful to my parents for always loving me despite the challenges we faced as a family. *Los quiero muchísimo.* And to my sister and best friend, Mariana, I thank her for being there for me, always.

A Note About the Author

Michael Sayman is a Latin American app entrepreneur, product designer, and software engineer, best known for creating chart-topping apps as a teen. With the launch of 4 Snaps, a turn-based photo game, Sayman caught the attention of Mark Zuckerberg, becoming Facebook's "teen in residence" and playing a pivotal role in the creation of Instagram Stories. By eighteen, he was described by CNET en Español as one of "20 most influential Latinos in tech." At twenty-one, Sayman was lured to Google, where he became a product manager and founder in residence, working on a social gaming startup. Today, he splits his time between Miami, Florida, and Silicon Valley, where he continues to innovate in the social media space.

A Note on the Type

This book was set in a version of the well-known Monotype face Bembo. This font was cut for the celebrated Venetian printer Aldus Manutius by Francesco Griffo, and first used in Pietro Cardinal Bembo's *De Aetna* of 1495.

Typeset by Scribe,
Philadelphia, Pennsylvania

Printed and bound by Sheridan Minnesota, a CJK Group Company,
Brainerd, Minnesota

Designed by Michael Collica